Rural Deprivation and Planning

RURAL DEPRIVATION

AND PLANNING

edited by

J. Martin Shaw

©   J. Martin Shaw   1979

ISBN   cloth   0 86094 020 9
         paper   0 86094 019 5

published by Geo Abstracts Ltd.,
              University of East Anglia,
              Norwich NR4 7TJ,
              England.

'Not least among the problems of our villages is the difficulty of
convincing a largely urban nation and its parliamentary representatives
that there is anything urgent to be done. Bad housing in the towns
affronts consciences which are remarkably quiet about the shared cold
water taps, pail lavatories and tin baths still common in many rural
areas. The cost of providing services in the countryside is heavy. To
maintain hundreds of miles of rural roads, transport thousands of
children to secondary school, keep open village primary schools and
police stations, and help support even skeleton bus services, all this
lays a heavy burden on county and district councils who have very
limited rate resources. If we do want to keep villages alive, then a
fairer distribution of central government money is essential'.
(Letter to The Times, 4th September 1978)

'In rural areas children and old people are deprived beyond what I
would have believed possible prior to coming to live in the country
and taking on the responsibility of parish chairman. Many children are
completely isolated and in many villages a child's circle of friends
is extremely limited. But unlike me 40 years ago, my children have
little mobility and no access to the facilities accepted as normal
by the city child. In the end social deprivation is about lack of
opportunity'.
(Letter to The Guardian, 14th March 1978)

'Mobility is a privilege which can mitigate some of the worst effects
of the withdrawal or centralisation of these essential services.
Children are, however, the most vulnerable to poor local transport
facilities. Surely it is the mobility of the modern teacher that should
be exploited, with the teacher driving to the pupils rather than
bussing the pupils to the teacher in some new urban school? Vast
subsidies are not necessary to ensure the survival of village life.
Private enterprise and self-help would, if unrestricted by red tape,
remedy some of the problems without cost to the ratepayers. But it is
not just a matter of cost. The value of rural life must also be
considered against the crude cost of location. This is not happening
at present'.
(Letter to the Daily Telegraph, 28th August 1978)

'It is pointless to clash over the problems of keeping small schools
open. It is futile to berate the diocesan authorities for the reduction
of the clergy and the threatened closure of churches. It is impossible
for small shopkeepers to keep open when they can buy goods more cheaply
from a supermarket shelf, and when the Post Office withdraws its
franchise from the village P.O. stores. It is useless to petition the
breweries to keep the village pubs open (now many must drive to get a
drink). The bus company cannot provide buses if there are not enough
people to ride on them.
Sir: My point is that the small villages are not just dying: they are
being killed. This process has been going on for a long time. There
are many people who would be willing to live in villages, but
unfortunately quite a proportion of the few who still get the
opportunity also have homes in London, Birmingham and elsewhere. Surely
it is not too late to restrict this process before the village
community and its facilities have disappeared completely'.
(Letter to the Eastern Daily Press, 10th March 1978).

CONTENTS

ACKNOWLEDGEMENTS

My thanks are due to the individual authors
for contributing to this volume. Although
the views expressed are those of the
individuals concerned (and not their
employing authorities) the editorial
responsibility is mine. I gratefully
acknowledge the assistance of the Royal
Town Planning Institute, under whose auspices
a major conference on Rural Deprivation
was held in 1977, at which many of the ideas
in this book were aired. I am indebted to
the publishers for their guidance, and to
Miss Betty Pearl for typing the drafts.

J. Martin Shaw
October 1978

LIST OF CONTRIBUTORS

COLIN BELL Professor of Sociology, University of New South Wales

DAVID CLARK Lecturer, Department of Geography, Lanchester Polytechnic

TOM HELLER General Practitioner, Sheffield

ANDREW LARKIN Housing Aid Officer, Shelter

MALCOLM MOSELEY Lecturer, School of Environmental Sciences, University of East Anglia

HOWARD NEWBY Senior Lecturer, Department of Sociology, University of Essex

JOHN PACKMAN Planner (Rural), County Planning Department, Norfolk County Council

BETTY RICHARDSON Countryside Officer, Community Council of Shropshire

DAVID ROSE Lecturer, Department of Sociology, University of Essex

PETER SAUNDERS Lecturer, Department of Sociology, University of Sussex

MARTIN SHAW County Planning Officer, Norfolk County Council

DICK STOCKFORD Principal Research Officer, Social Services Department, Norfolk County Council

CERI THOMAS Research Officer, Low Pay Unit

KATHRYN UNWIN Lecturer, Department of Urban and Regional Planning, Lanchester Polytechnic

NIKKI VENTRIS Research Associate, School of Environmental Sciences, University of East Anglia

ROGER WATKINS Deputy Director, Centre for Information and Advice on Educational Disadvantage, Manchester

STEPHEN WINYARD Lecturer, Department of Social Policy and Administration, University of Leeds

LIST OF FIGURES

1

EDITORIAL INTRODUCTION

Martin Shaw

The 1970s have witnessed a growing interest in rural matters. This is reflected in an increasing volume of literature, a welter of academic analysis and studies, frequent political statements and extensive public debate on the existing state of and future prospects for rural Britain. How far this vogue results from the inevitable cycles of fashion among social scientists, planners and politicians is not yet clear, but the last decade has seen an increasing recognition of the social and economic importance of the rural areas which is both welcome and justified. However, this general awareness has not been matched by a systematic appraisal of the nature and extent of the social difficulties experienced in many rural areas, nor has there been adequate documentation of the need for positive action, and of alternative ways of tackling the problems of rural disadvantage. It is to these questions that this book is addressed.

An examination of the post-war literature both on rural problems and on countryside planning reveals a clear sequence of works dealing with particular aspects of rural Britain, with few attempts at an overview of rural issues until the present decade. In terms of volume both the analytical and the prescriptive literature demonstrate the general neglect of rural issues by comparison with the growing body of knowledge on the nature of social and physical change in cities and the effort applied to find solutions to the problems of urban deprivation.

A rigorous assessment of the social well-being of rural Britain has been bedevilled by the romanticism which tends to be associated with most descriptions of the English countryside. This traditional view of rural society prevailed well into the post-war period, due partly to the preoccupation in the rural literature with agricultural land resources and the appearance of the countryside, dating from the Scott Report (1942).[1] With the exception of Bracey's description of *Social Provision in Rural*

Wiltshire (1952)[2] which pointed to some of the problems of living in villages, the major social issues were generally identified with rural depopulation, which in turn was associated with the rural parts of Scotland, Wales, and the northern and western parts of England.[3] In lowland Britain, however, the traditional image of peace and quiet has survived into the last quarter of the twentieth century. Indeed, the last decade has witnessed a new wave of nostalgia for rural life, reflected in a renewed popularity for Hardy's novels as well as in many contemporary novels which, like the oral histories of Ronald Blythe and George Ewart Evans,[5] are harking back to a world we have lost. The social scientists too began searching in the 1960s among the remote villages of upland Britain for settlements which could be described as communities;[6] these offered a marked contrast with the 'Urbs in Rure' of the metropolitan fringe discovered at the same time by Pahl in Hertfordshire.[7]

Although there is, of course, a significant element of truth in the romantic vision of rural Britain, and in the overall outward prosperity of the rural parts of much of Midland, Southern and Eastern England, recent studies have demonstrated that the real world is less simple. Descriptive work has shown that the rural population is in many areas becoming weighted in favour of the retired, the well-off, those who do not work, and those who do not (and cannot find) work within the rural area. The beauty of the English countryside is, in this sense, a disadvantage, and itself contributes to an imbalance in the population of rural settlements, to a shortage of low cost housing, and to the neglect of many rural areas by national agencies; the rural areas rarely attract much government aid, except in the north and west of Britain.

The depth of analysis of rural problems has been relatively weak, at least until the 1970s, and the role of descriptive geographers has often looked as deficient as that of the romantics. Early geographical studies were largely concerned with generalised data assembly, while sociologists have tended to focus on detailed case studies whose results were presented in a form which was unrelated to public policies and planning. Until the 1970s neither geographers nor sociologists have been concerned with the identification of disadvantage and with potential conflicts in rural society, though recent research, in various countries, is attempting to redress this imbalance.[8]

While it may well be true that the history of planning in the twentieth century has not been adequately researched, even a superficial examination of the planning literature reveals a general absence of a 'rural attitude'. This is doubtless in part to be attributed to the traditional view of the countryside noted above in the descriptions of rural problems. There was certainly very little recognition in most post-war planning studies that, in Gordon Cherry's words, 'the rural planning problem is both broader and rather different from earlier town planning concepts'.[9] In particular the early post-war planning objectives were focussed on the physical aspects of land use and development, and especially on the protection of the countryside.

Indeed, this corollary of urban containment was fundamental to the philosophy underlying the 1947 Town and Country Planning Act (and to much subsequent legislation). All of the early post-war planning initiatives were based on an urban viewpoint, and even the planning of recreation, introduced by the National Parks Act 1949, was geared to the needs of city dwellers.

Additions to the literature on planning for the best use of rural land resources as well as on the analysis of land use problems have been significant throughout the post-war years, and the 1970s have seen further major contributions on the changing countryside from an economic and aesthetic viewpoint (Table 1.1). By comparison there

Table 1.1. The post war literature on rural problems and planning - some examples. These examples are selected to demonstrate the relative importance of the literature in relation to various themes. They represent a personal view of some of the most signif-icant contributions but are *not* exhaustive.

Decade	1940s	1950s	1960s	1970s
Theme				
Land Resources	Scott (1942)	Wibberley (1959)	Best and Coppock (1962)	Whitby et al. (1974) New agricultural landscapes (1974) Centre of Agricul-tural Strategy (1976) Food Production in the Countryside (1977)
Rural Depopulation		Saville (1954)	House (1965)	H.M. Treasury (1974)
Sociological Case Studies		Bracey (1952) Williams (1954)	Pahl (1965)	Ambrose (1974) Newby (1978)
Recreation			Dower (1965)	Patmore (1970 Coppock & Duffield (1975)
Accessibility				Suffolk and Devon Case Studies (1971) Moseley et al (1977)
Environmental Planning			Country-side in 1970 (1965)	Green (1971) Thorburn (1971) Cherry (1974) Rural Communities (1977) Gilg (1978)

has been a marked paucity of major contributions to the
planning literature on the social and economic aspects of
rural life until the present decade, though there were
several, largely geographical, works on rural recreation,[10]
and two official case studies of rural public transport at
the end of the 1960s.[11] The costs of rural settlement,
with particular reference to the depopulating areas, were
the subject of a special report by an interdepartmental
team of civil servants in 1974,[12] and the beginning of this
decade saw several attempts at a synoptic approach to rural
planning. The major initiative was taken by the 'Countryside in 1970' Conference, which was followed by near comprehensive summaries of rural environmental planning by
Bracey, Green, Thorburn and Gilg.[13] All of these statements were, however, focussed on physical planning issues
and policies. Cherry's essays on *Rural Planning
Problems*[14] stressed the social and economic dimension of
rural change, though at a general level and from a
statutory planning viewpoint, rather than detailing policy
options to cope with the difficulties of particular social
groups. The political interest in the countryside led to
the setting up of a special study group of civil servants
to take a broad view of rural policies in the mid-1970s,
but the Countryside Review Committee's discussion paper on
Rural Communities[15] was significant in showing little
understanding of rural deprivation. While attempting to
eschew an approach confined, in the words of the Minister
for Planning and Local Government, to 'what are commonly
thought of an countryside policies - landscape, nature
conservation and opportunities for recreation', the
Countryside Review Committee failed to analyse the extent
to which existing rural planning policies are effectively
coping with social problems.

The trickle of sociological case studies of village
life and social change, dated from William's study of
Gosforth (1956) through Pahl's research on change in rural
Hertfordshire (1964), to Ambrose's study in Sussex (1974)
and Newby's research in East Anglia (1978), has now become
a flood.[16] It is the earlier of these sort of studies
which should perhaps be regarded as the forerunners of the
more explicit approach to both the analysis of social
problems and ways of tackling them which has emerged in the
mid-1970s. The deficiencies in the literature on rural
areas have yet to be remedied (with the exception perhaps
of rural transport)[17] and the lack of an adequate rural
dimension to some aspects of public policy is still evident,
but there are signs of a genuine concern for the quality of
rural life. This is reflected in a series of conferences
which have been held on the nature and extent of social
disadvantage (at which some of the contributors to this
book gave papers), in various community development
initiatives, in the interest of local authorities in the
coordination of public planning policy for the rural areas,
and in the extensive coverage given to rural problems by
the media.[18] The empirical evidence advanced in these
contributions has often disturbed the sepia image of rural
tranquility, and has reinforced the case for a wide view
of rural society comparable to that being adopted for the

cities, and for a coordinated approach to social problems
in villages.

It is within this evolving context of knowledge about
social well-being in rural Britain that this book has been
framed, in order to focus attention more clearly on the
nature of rural deprivation, and to project the discussion
of possible solutions in a constructive direction.

In Chapter 2 Rose and his colleagues, who have been
researching into various aspects of rural society and land
ownership in Suffolk, examine the extent to which the
attitudes of members of some local authorities coincide
with the interests of low income groups in a part of East
Anglia. This case study raises serious questions about
the effect of the operation of local housing and planning
policies on some village residents.

Thomas and Winyard consider the question of rural
income levels in Chapter 3. They begin by examining the
strength and weaknesses of the various sources of
statistical information on rural incomes, and go on to
consider the actual pattern of earnings in rural areas.
Since farmworkers still represent probably the largest
purely rural workforce in Britain, this chapter examines in
detail both the wage levels and apparent living standards
of agricultural workers. This is followed by an appraisal
of the level of financial benefits available to particular
income groups in rural areas. Finally, the chapter
considers the overall evidence for the distribution of
rural income in a case study of rural Wales.

In Chapter 4 Packman discusses the problems associated
with the provision of and access to jobs in rural areas.
Nationally, the number of people in the working age group
is likely to rise and only the service sector is expected
to show net growth in employment, most of which is
expected to occur in urban areas. The creation of new
sources of rural employment therefore poses a particular
challenge to private industry and public authorities.
The choice of accessible jobs is particularly limited for
married women, and this is reflected in considerable under-
employment, alongside the more obvious evidence of high unemployment in remote rural areas.

Chapter 5 deals with various forms of rural housing
deprivation. Larkin begins by identifying the main types
of housing need in rural areas in relation to different
types of tenure. Next he discusses the impact of the
relative priority given to rented accommodation by rural
local authorities and the disproportionate effect of some
housing expenditure cuts on rural housing problems.
Larkin argues that local housing need should be met when
and where it exists, and that conventional physical
planning policies mitigate against the groups with the most
serious housing problems, by making it more difficult to
build cheap rented accommodation in villages.

Heller considers the quality of health services
available to the residents of rural areas in Chapter 6.
His analysis demonstrates that the level of health services,
and access to health facilities in rural areas is often
lower than in towns. This relative deprivation is due in
part to the pattern of resource allocation, which favours

a limited number of centres of excellence rather than community care and preventive medicine, and in part to the increasing remoteness of facilities. Heller also defines the groups whose interests are being served by the present health service system, which tends to work against the interests of those most in need in both rural and urban areas.

In Chapter 7 Watkins examines the nature and extent of educational disadvantage in village schools. Pupils in remote rural areas often suffer from inadequate school buildings, insufficient resources, low aspriations, and from a lack of stimulus from children of the same age. Watkins suggests that there are real pockets of rural disadvantage which produce similar low levels of educational attainment as can be recognised in the inner city areas of Britain. The additional rural hazard is remoteness, which makes access to compensating facilities difficult, and is an obstacle to the professional renewal of the teaching profession. Special forms of educational provision for rural areas are discussed, and the implications of educational deprivation for national policy are outlined.

Chapter 8 also describes the problems of limited access to opportunities, this time to recreational facilities in rural areas. Ventris, drawing on material from recent surveys carried out mainly in East Anglia, presents the results of a systematic analysis of accessibility to a wide range of leisure facilities. He contrasts the differing patterns of both participation and investment in rural recreation and cultural activities in rural Britain, by comparison with the urban areas.

From Chapter 9 onwards there is a change in the general emphasis of the book. Whereas Chapters 2-8 are concerned primarily with the origins and nature of rural deprivation, and the extent to which different forms of disadvantage are experienced by particular groups in rural areas, the following chapters explore ways of coping with the problems identified, including the role of both public authorities, voluntary agencies, and private individuals.

In Chapter 9, Shaw and Stockford take 'social planning' as their central theme, and begin by summarising the various ideas on which this elusive concept is based, and the legislative framework for social planning in rural areas. The chapter examines the degree of influence over social change which local authorities can expect to have in a rural area in the context of their statutory responsibility for environmental planning and personal social services. The particular problems involved in formulating and implementing rural settlement plans and in providing personal social services to a scattered rural population are discussed. Finally the potential of a coordinated approach to achieve the social aims of Planning and Social Services authorities is assessed.

Moseley looks at the extent to which rural 'transport' is part of a wider problem in Chapter 10 which draws on the study of rural transport he directed for the Department of the Environment. Moseley looks at the causes, consequences and policy implications of the deterioration in rural

accessibility which, he argues, forces attention as much
upon rural services as upon modes of travel. The chapter
examines certain myths about rural mobility, and identifies
the fragmentation of effort which appears to be directed
towards the alleviation of the rural accessibility
problems. A managerial approach is put forward in which
resource allocation by the various bodies is assessed in
the context of defined accessibility objectives, and
several practical suggestions are made by which public
authorities and private initiative can help to overcome
the problems.

In Chapter 11 Clark and Unwin consider the non-
physical aspects of rural communications, in the form of
information delivery. They describe the nature of the
community information system in rural areas, and the type
of information needs which exist, on the basis of a sample
study in part of Lincolnshire. Clark and Unwin consider
alternative ways of providing information to rural
residents, and pay special attention to the possible application of developments in telecommunications technology
in helping to overcome the problems created by remoteness
from fixed points of information provision.

Some practical examples of local self-help in the
dissemination of information are also described in Chapter
12. On the basis of her experience as a Countryside
Officer with a Rural Community Council, Richardson cites
firsthand evidence of the increasing problems of gaining
access to information, services, and facilities in the
Welsh Border. Against this background three innovations
initiated by one Rural Community Council are explored and
evaluated. These include a scheme of voluntary village
representatives who act as local reference points for
information advice and help, voluntary social car schemes
for emergency trips, and surveys of village services
carried out by local groups.

The final chapter attempts to present an overview by the
editor of both the problems of rural deprivation set out in
the earlier chapters, and of the various ways of tackling
these difficulties mentioned in the latter part of the book.
I begin by looking at the problems of defining what is
meant by 'deprivation' in the context of social well-being
and at the relevance of the various attempts to measure
'rurality'. I consider the changing attitude towards the
rural areas of Britain and the implications of the continuing preoccupation with the multiple deprivation to be
found in the inner city, given the relative evidence of
'urban' and 'rural' deprivation. The form of the rural
deprivation cycle in contemporary Britain is described, and
three components are identified: household, opportunity,
and mobility deprivation. Some conclusions are drawn about
the social planning and support roles of public agencies in
coping with these problems, and about the role of voluntary
organisations. The nature of the service provided by local
authorities, the potential resource of voluntary activity,
and the scope for self-help are examined in relation to the
evidence of rural deprivation.

Each chapter is referenced, but does not pretend to
include a full bibliography: other works have recently

provided general surveys of the literature.[19]   There are strong links between each of the individual chapters which together amount to a comprehensive framework of essays in social problems and social planning.

The individual chapters are, however, written from different - and sometimes conflicting - standpoints; in this respect they reflect the varying attitudes to be found towards social issues in contemporary Britain.

REFERENCES AND NOTES

1. Report of the Committee on Land Utilisation in Rural Areas (The Scott Report), 1942.   Other major contributions to the debate on land resources include G.P. Wibberley, Agriculture and Urban Growth, 1959;   R.H. Best and J.T. Coppock, The Changing Use of Land in Britain, 1962;   M .C. Whitby et al., Rural Resource Development, 1974;   on agricultural land, the publications of the Centre of Agricultural Strategy at Reading, from 1976 onwards, and the Countryside Review Committee's paper on Food Production in the Countryside, 1977;   on the landscape impact, the Countryside Commission's report on New Agricultural Landscapes, 1974.

2. H.E. Bracey, Social Provision in Rural Wiltshire, 1952.

3. See, for example, J. Saville, Rural Depopulation in England and Wales, 1957;   J.W. House, Rural N.E. England, 1951-56;   and H.M. Treasury, Report of an Inter-Departmental Study Group on Rural Depopulation, 1976.

4. R. Blythe, Akenfield, Portrait of an English Village, Allen Lane, 1969.

5. G. Ewart Evans, Ask the Fellows Who Cut the Hay, Faber, 1956.

6. R. Frankenberg, Communities in Britain, Penguin, 1966.

7. R.E. Pahl, Urbs in Rure: The Metropolitan Fringe in Hertfordshire, London School of Economics, Geography Papers LL, 1965.

8. Much recent and current academic work is summarised in H. Newby (ed) Social Change in the Rural World: International Research in Rural Studies, Wiley, 1978.

9. G.E. Cherry (ed), Rural Planning Problems, Leonard Hill, 1976.

10. The first significant contribution was the paper by M. Dower, The Challenge of Leisure, Civic Trust, 1965. This was followed by Leisure in the Countryside, HMSO (Cmnd 2928), 1966;   J.A. Patmore Land and Leisure, David + Charles, 1970;   and several works in the mid-1970s, e.g. J.T. Coppock and B.S. Duffield, Recreation in the Countryside, McMillan, 1975.

11. Department of the Environment, Studies of *Rural Transport in Devon* and *Rural Transport in West Suffolk,* 1971.

12. Rural Depopulation, 1976, *op cit.*

13. 'The Countryside in 1970', *Reports of Study Groups,* 1965. This series of conferences was sponsored by the Council for Nature, the Royal Society of Arts, and the Nature Conservancy. The later works include H.E. Bracey, *People in the Countryside,* Routledge & Kegan Paul, 1970; R.J. Green, *Country Planning,* Manchester University Press, 1971; A. Thorburn, *Planning Villages,* Estates Gazette, 1971; A. Gilg, *Countryside Planning,* David + Charles, 1978.

14. G.E. Cherry, 1976, *op cit.*

15. *Rural Communities,* Report of the Countryside Review Committee, HMSO, 1977.

16. W.M. Williams, *Gosforth, the Sociology of an English Village,* Routledge & Kegan Paul, 1956; R.E. Pahl, *Urbs in Rure: The Metropolitan Fringe in Hertfordshire,* London School of Economics, 1964; P. Ambrose, *The Quiet Revolution,* 1974; H. Newby et al., *A Study of Farmers in East Anglia,* London, 1978.

17. See especially M.J. Moseley et al., *Rural Transport and Accessibility,* Final Report to the Department of the Environment, Centre of East Anglian Studies, Norwich, 1978.

18. The conferences and seminars included the following: Rural Problems and Rural Planning, North Wales Rural Group (Bangor, 1976); Social Indicators and Community Profiles in Rural Areas, Social Services Research Group (Norwich, 1976); Community Development in Countryside Planning, University of Manchester Department of Town and Country Planning (Manchester, 1977); Rural Poverty and Planning, Child Poverty Action Group (Colchester, 1977); Rural Deprivation and Social Planning, East of England Branch of the Royal Town Planning Institute (Norwich, 1977). The extensive press coverage included an unprecedented sequence of letters to *The Times* on village problems during August and September 1978.

19. See for example, M.J. Moseley et al (1977), *op cit,* Volume 2, and the full bibliographies contained in G.E. Cherry (1976) *op cit.*

2

THE ECONOMIC AND POLITICAL BASIS
OF RURAL DEPRIVATION: A CASE STUDY

David Rose, Peter Saunders, Howard Newby and Colin Bell

INTRODUCTION

This chapter presents some of the findings of a study
conducted between 1973 and 1976 at the University of Essex
concerning large scale farmers in East Anglia.[1] In the
context of an analysis of the nature and perpetuation of
rural deprivation, the most relevant aspect of this
research relates to our study of the role of farmers and
landowners in local politics in Suffolk.[2]
     The main contention of the argument here is that farmers
and landowners dominate rural local government as effectively as they did in the past; and that, among other
things, this has observable consequences in terms of rural
deprivation. Notwithstanding the fact that farmers and
landowners on local councils claim to be concerned with
performing a service for the community, and with discharging
the obligations which they see as attached to their privileged position in rural society, we wish to argue that an
examination of the operation of political routines in
Suffolk reveals another picture. For what farmers and landowners perceive as being 'in the public interest' more
generally reflects *their* values, *their* beliefs and *their*
ideologies, and thus indirectly furthers their interests to
the detriment of less powerful and less prosperous groups.
Moreover our analysis leads us to believe that the problems
of rural deprivation, as with all forms of social deprivation in whatever geographical milieux, are far more
intractable than some would believe.
     We should, however, sound one note of caution at the
outset. There has in recent years been a renewed interest
among social scientists in the problem of identifying and
explaining the role of the State in a capitalist economy,
and this debate has considerable implications for any
analysis of local politics. In the argument which follows,
we have implicitly adopted what Pahl refers to as a
'managerialist' perspective.[3]   In other words we have

focussed on the values and actions of key 'gatekeepers' in the political system, not necessarily as 'independent variables', but as intervening variables mediating and actively influencing the impact of national policy and economic market forces on the local population. As Pahl notes, these 'managers' (and we should stress that we include in this category both local authority officers *and* strategically-placed elected members) do not themselves *cause* deprivation, but their actions are important since the scope of local decision-making is by no means totally restricted and determined. Many national policies, for example, are permissive rather than mandatory (e.g. the recent Community Land Act), and many others leave consider-able scope for local inventiveness and initiative in determining how the policy is to be applied. Similarly, although dependent upon private capital for their revenue, local managers remain important as allocators of this revenue: a decision to spend money on the police rather than on public housing, for example, entails obvious redistributive implications.

Our argument, in this paper, therefore, is premissed on the view that those in institutionally-defined positions of power in rural areas can and do have an important role to play in exacerbating or reducing rural deprivation, but that they alone cannot provide an adequate explanation for the continuation of such deprivation. While their casual responsibility is limited by the actions of central govern-ment and the consequences of a market economy in land, labour, housing and so on over which they have relatively little control, it is nevertheless the case that, within their restricted range of discretion, they can profoundly influence the life-chances of different sections of the local population. This, then, is the rationale for studying who they are and what they do - or fail to do.

FARMERS, LANDOWNERS AND RURAL POLITICS

Few would seek to deny that landownership has always been a crucial power resource.[4] However, the decline in the relative importance of agriculture in the overall economy has perhaps beguiled us into believing that landownership is not as important politically as in the past. While this might be argued for the national level, at the local level landowners and farmers continue to dominate politically in many rural areas in Britain, including East Anglia.

In 1967, the Royal Commission on Local Government in England and Wales found that 35% of rural district coun-cillors were farmers.[5] In 1973 we conducted our own survey of council membership in East Anglia. This revealed that 21% of *all* councillors were farmers, this figure rising to 31% in the case of the Rural Districts. Adding in elements of the wider agricultural interest we were able to account for 42% of rural district councillors and 29% of county councillors. In themselves figures like these mean little, however. More important is the question of who occupies positions of strategic importance on councils such as

committee chairmanships and membership of key committees.[6]
Once again the agricultural interest was well represented.
For example, 30% of committee chairmanships on the county
councils were held by farmers. When we examined the type
of farmers on councils we discovered it was those with the
largest farms who were best represented. Indeed many of
them occupied other important positions in the community -
such as J.P.s and membership of the local health authority.
In Suffolk the reorganisation of local government seems to
have affected the position only marginally.

It was on Suffolk that we concentrated our attention
for a more detailed analysis of the political power of
farmers and landowners. In particular we looked at Suffolk
County Council and the Mid-Suffolk and Suffolk Coastal
District Councils, and the Councils which they succeeded.
At County Council level 16% of members were farmers but,
interestingly, the following strategic positions were all
held by farmers or landowners at the time of the study in
1975; chairman, vice-chairman, leader of the council and
the chairmen of all the key committees, i.e., planning,
education, social services, finance and policy and
resources. A similar picture emerged in Mid-Suffolk, but
Suffolk Coastal (an amalganation of rural and urban
authorities) was far less dominated by the agricultural
interest.

Nevertheless, at the most such evidence provides only a
prima facie case concerning the power of farmers and landowners in rural politics. We can certainly say on this
basis alone that they appear to have a tremendous political
potential[7] but the question remains as to how this potential
is realised, if at all. Even if landowners do occupy and
use key positions within local authorities, we cannot
assume that they exercise power in their own interests. As
Giddens points out, simply because someone emanates from a
particular class it does not follow that he will only
promote the interests of that class.[8] We must ask not only
who exercises power, but in whose benefit is it exercised;
who decides is of rather less consequence than *what* is
decided (or *not* decided).

It was with these considerations in mind that we searched
for issues which had arisen in local politics in Suffolk,
which had generated conflict and debate, and which involved
farmers opposing or being opposed by others. Immediately we
came upon an obstacle to this decision making approach: it
appeared there were no such issues in Suffolk. From a
concern with political *conflict,* we had to turn our attention to political *quiescence*. This involved examining the
routine exercising of political power in the county in order
to answer a crucial question concerning political stability.
Was political stability and tranquility in Suffolk to be
explained by the fact that all groups in the county were
satisfied that the system operated to the benefit of the
whole community? Or could it be explained by the fact that
political power had been used to engineer a wholly spurious
consensus? Could groups like farmers and landowners be so
in control that they could effectively prevent the emergence
of serious opposition? We sought to answer these questions
by seeing who benefitted from the operation of the local

political system.

To ask the question 'who benefits?' is, of course, to presuppose what the interests of different groups might be; in other words it involves the researcher in assessing *objective interests*.[9] Put simply, we can only know whether a group has benefited from a given exercise of power if we know its interests and, by extension, what would be likely to further or hinder them. It could be argued that there is no real problem here insofar as groups state their interests, but that would be rather naive. What people *believe* to be in their interests may not be what they *state* to be in their interests. We would rather argue that it is justifiable for the researcher to try and *infer* the objective interests of groups in particular contexts.

For example, it could reasonably be argued that, in a market economy, it is in peoples' interests to maximise their economic benefits and to minimise their costs - other things being equal. We could extend the argument by saying that it is in the interests of employers to sponsor and support policies which, deliberately or otherwise, result in the maintenance of cheap labour supplies. It should be noted that this is *not* to say that employers who support such policies do so for this express purpose but it is to argue that the *effect* of their support, whatever their particular aims and motives, is to advance their interests as employers while disadvantaging the interests of their employees. Similarly, it could be argued that it is in the objective interests of relatively prosperous sections of the population to support low public expenditure policies on the part of their local councils. This ensures a low rate of property taxation but at the same time it disadvantages the least prosperous section of the population who could be expected to obtain the greatest benefit from increased public expenditure on social services, housing, and education. Such statements can, of course, be made independently of the professed motives and preference of the groups concerned, or of whether they have articulated any preferences at all.

Following this logic we began to assess who gained and who lost from the routine exercise of political power in Suffolk. The overall pattern quickly became apparent: a persistent and pervasive bias had been, and continued to be, generated through county and district policies to the cumulative advantage of the relatively prosperous and already advantaged (and especially landowners and farmers) and to the distinct disadvantage of the already disadvantaged groups. We could illustrate this by reference to the whole range of local authority policies. This analysis, however, concentrates on the issue of planning policies as they relate to the preservation of the environment. We wish to argue that, in their effects, and regardless of their intentions, some planning policies in Suffolk have been socially regressive in their redistributive effects.

PLANNING, HOUSING AND THE FARMING INTEREST[10]

The planners, farmers and councillors in Suffolk to whom we

spoke all stressed that the relationship between them was essentially one of harmony and cooperation. The sympathy with which planning officers viewed farmers' interests and the informality of the relationship was stressed on all sides. Underpinning this close and informal liaison is a fundamental article of faith subscribed to equally by both parties - namely that Suffolk's principal industry is agriculture, and that anything which benefits the county's farmers must, *ipso facto,* benefit the community as a whole. In this sense the agricultural interest and the public interest were evidently seen to be synonymous. Indeed it can be argued that the identification of the two by planners has led at times to a marked reluctance on the part of local authorities to invoke the powers they have in order to force farmers to observe regulations which may hinder the profitability of agricultural enterprises. A case in point concerns the voluntary agreements reached with the National Farmers Union and the County Landowners' Association in relation to development in Dedham Vale. But in terms of rural deprivation the relationship has more serious consequences.

Let us take the case of housing. Local planning policies have affected the overall distribution of housing resources in the county. To be specific, Suffolk has not been exempt from the alleged problems of draconian restrictions on new residential development in rural areas. Insofar as this produces an artificial scarcity of private housing, it may add to inflationary pressures on house prices. To some extent - how far we cannot assess - this has resulted in some of the indigenous population being priced out of the housing market in their local villages through competition from mainly professional and managerial newcomers. The pressure for week-end homes for urbanites adds to the problem, as does the fact that urbanites can afford to pay higher rents in the private rented sector for holiday homes and weekend cottages. Suffolk, perhaps because conservation policies have succeeded in retaining truly rural character, has attracted prosperous newcomers in increasing numbers. For the local working population, and especially those in low paid work like agriculture and parts of the service sector, there remains the possibility of local authority housing.

Council house building in Suffolk is hamstrung by restrictions in the rural areas - some self-imposed, some unavoidable. The low rate policies that have been pursued throughout the county have, for example, resulted in a situation where, in the eight years prior to the reorganisation of local government, local authorities in East Suffolk built council houses at only half the East Anglian regional rate, despite the existence of lengthy waiting lists.[11] This situation was not aided by a combination of central government housing cost yardsticks and local anti-rural development policies. Cost yardsticks have recently been so tight that local authorities find it well-nigh impossible to build houses other than in large (by rural standards) estates and to a uniform design. Apart from the fact that such developments raise the ire of local protection societies on the grounds that it would be detrimental to the character of the village, they would anyway conflict with county council strategic planning policy. This certainly appeared to be the case in the former East Suffolk area before reorganization. Any new housing estate development was made very difficult in the rural areas.

One largely unforeseen consequence of such policies can be easily identified; low paid local workers were frequently denied the opportunity of living in the village in which they were born and raised, or in a village close to their employment - a frequently voiced complaint in rural Suffolk. For one particular group, agricultural workers, the combined effect of these changes in the housing market has been to push an increasing proportion into tied housing. It is interesting to note here that one of the principal objections voiced by farmers and landowners to recent changes in the tied cottage system was precisely the shortage of municipal accommodation in rural areas. Yet this shortage has been brought about by the low expenditure and restrictive development policies pursued by themselves and their representatives who dominated rural councils.

All of these effects are compounded in the case of any area which is regarded an environmentally precious. This was made clear by the Suffolk and Essex planning authorities in their 1966 *Survey of Dedham Vale* and in their subsequent 1968 *Proposals*. Despite the fact that less than three new council houses per year had been built in the Vale since the war, the planners stipulated that even this modest level should stop. Future generations of the indigenous low paid population would thus have to find either existing tied or extremely scarce rented accommodation in their home area or emigrate.

The effect of such restrictive development policies has, then, not merely been to preserve the *status quo* in such areas but has been *redistributive*. Moreover such redistribution has been socially regressive: at one extreme those in expensively priced private housing have seen their environment retained or even enhanced; while at the other low paid workers have been forced to leave the area.

A similar case can be made out in the case of industrial development which could have a marked effect on wage levels.[12] Here one of the consequences of a policy of environmental conservation has been the preservation of a low wage rural economy - with obvious advantages to local employers, and especially to farmers. Farmers in Suffolk are among the most prosperous in the country, and yet agricultural wage rates are among the lowest.[13]

Whatever the motives of those involved in making such policies, the effect is undeniable: an alliance of landed and environmental interests has resulted in vigorous anti-development policies which have not only preserved hedgerows and views, but also low wages and inadequate housing provision. To put it another way, in the routine operation of their established policies, local councils in Suffolk can be seen to have consistently generated a bias in favour of the objective interests of farmers and landowners and again those of the already deprived members of the rural working class.[14]

OTHER ASPECTS OF RURAL DEPRIVATION

Although we have concentrated our attention on the socially
regressive nature of environmental planning policies, we
could well have discussed social services or education.
The fact is that politicians in Suffolk are obsessed with
the maintenance of low rates. This is no new phenomenon to
be laid at the door of the monetarist policies of the
present (or any other) Government. Indeed it has a long
history, as many councillors will agree. In 1975/76 only
six counties levied a lower rate than Suffolk; while in
the previous year only four counties spent less per capita
on education and social services, and none spent less on
libraries. Only in two areas does Suffolk's expenditure
rise above average spending for England and Wales - for
the police and on roads.
    In the context of this discussion we would claim that
such low levels of expenditure involve few costs for the
already advantaged. For example, over half of all councillors for East Anglia attended private schools, and in
many cases so do their children. Would they personally be
hit by low levels of expenditure on education, or by cuts
in the service? Similarly, the prosperous - many farmers,
landowners, and the professional middle class - make little
use of the social services. When, as happened in 1974/75,
in Suffolk, domestic help for the elderly and nursery
provision for the young are cut back, it is not they or
their parents or children who would be likely to be affected.
When the level of expenditure on temporary accommodation
stands at a fraction of the average for all counties, it is
not they, in their owner-occupied homes, who have to worry.
On the contrary, the lower the rate the less they stand to
lose; and so we come back to the notion of objective
interests.

CONCLUSIONS

The argument advanced in this chapter is *not* that the power
of economically and socially dominant groups such as the
farmers in Suffolk is used by them in a cynical way to
pursue their own interests. However, their intentions are
neither here nor there. The fact remains that the *effects*
of the routine use of power is such that the already disadvantaged are further disadvantaged. We have discussed
elsewhere the mechanisms by which the powerful maintain
their power and avoid opposition and here we offer only a
brief conclusion.
    In the final analysis rural deprivation (like any other
form of social deprivation) is a phenomenon of the social
structure. For all we might wish to improve accessibility
to and information about services, or to improve the
services themselves, we cannot forget that the real problems
are more basic: they lie in the rural social structure. If
we really wish to tackle rural deprivation in a radical way,
far more needs to be done than improving rural bus services.
What it really involves is being willing to challenge
traditional social definitions concerning such matters as

the public interest; to challenge those who, consciously or not, help to perpetuate social deprivation.

We have summarised the existing position in Suffolk by the phrase 'the non-politics of the *status quo*'. In rural areas one frequently encounters a deeply entrenched view that politics should not enter local government. The job of the council is to pursue the 'public interest', and the 'public interest' is not seen as problematic but obvious. In Suffolk both Conservative and Labour councillors accept this view so that potentially contentious issues are avoided and effective opposition to the landed elite is rarely raised. Labour councillors in Suffolk are evidently among the most respectable in the country! There can be few Conservative dominated councils in England, for example, which are prepared to fill three out of five committee chairmanships with Labour members, but it recently happened on one District council in Suffolk.

Because everyone is assumed to be on the same side, any opposition which does occur is usually dismissed by Labour and Conservatives as the work of politically motivated troublemakers. There is no way that disadvantaged groups can be heard as long as, for example, problems like shortage of housing are seen as those of individual families rather than as political issues.

Hence the consequence of 'keeping politics out of local government' are that the powerful not only continue to govern in their own interests, but do so unopposed. The genuinely-held belief of farmer-councillors that they are working in the communal interest, and that their policies are non-political (whatever that may mean), is continually re-affirmed through the conspicuous lack of overt public hostility or opposition to local authority policies. What the landowning groups either cannot or will not see is that policies which perpetuate the *status quo* are just as 'political' as those that seek to change it. More seriously, politicians at both national and local level, including those in the Labour Party, have equally failed to understand the true nature of the non-politics of the *status quo*. In our society we tend only to see radicals as 'political'; but in pursuit of their interests farmers and landowners are as militant as coalminers. The major difference is that, at any rate on the evidence in Suffolk, the landowners are more successful!

REFERENCES AND NOTES

1. Since this essay can only give a very impressionistic account of our research, the following additional publications should be referred to for more detail: C. Bell and H. Newby, Capitalist Farmers in The British Class Structure , *Sociologia Ruralis,* January 1974, pp.85-107; H. Newby *et al.,* Field Work in Clare Le Vay (ed.) *The Designing and Interpretation of Questionnaires,* Aberystwyth, University College of Wales Department of Agricultural Economics, 1975, pp.45-73; D. Rose *et al.,* Ideologies of Property: A case study,

Sociological Review, Vol. 24, No. 4, November 1976, pp.699-730; D. Rose *et al.,* Land Tenure and Official Statistics , *Journal of Agricultural Economics,* Vol. XXVIII, No. 1, January 1977, pp.69-75; H. Newby *et al,* Farmers Attitudes to Conservation', *Countryside Recreation Review,* Vol. 2, 1977, pp.23-30; P. Saunders *et al.,* Rural Community and Rural Community Power , in H, Newby (ed.) *International Perspectives in Rural Sociology,* Chichester, Wiley, 1978, pp.56-85; H. Newby *et al., Property, Paternalism and Power: A Study of Farmers in East Anglia,* London, Hutchinson, 1978. Our research on farmers was financed by the Social Science Research Council.

2. For details see P. Saunders *et al., op. cit.,* and H. Newby *et al., op. cit.,* 1978, Chapter 6. We should stress that our research considered only the situation in Suffolk. We are aware that other counties in East Anglia may well exhibit differences from Suffolk. Indeed we are conscious of certain differences between the former East and West Suffolk counties which we allude to in other work.

3. R. Pahl, *Whose City?,* Harmondsworth, Penguin 1975, Chapter 13. Se also P. Norman, Managerialism: A review of recent work , in the Centre for Environmental Studies, *Proceedings of the Conference on Urban Change and Conflict,* London: CES 1975, pp.62-86, who reviews the changes in the concept and evaluates it in the light of recent criticisms.

4. See, for example, D. Rose, *Land Tenure and Large Scale Farming in East Anglia,* University of Essex, Department of Sociology, 1975.

5. L. Moss and S. Parker, *The Local Government Councillor,* London, HMSO, 1967.

6. For the importance of such 'gatekeepers' in the study of power, see A. Pettigrew, 'Information Control as a Power Resource', *Sociology,* 6, 1972, pp.187-204.

7. See for example, R. Martin, The Concept of Power: A Critical Defence , *British Journal of Sociology,* Vol. 22, 1971, pp.240-256.

8. A. Giddens, Preface in P. Stanworth and A. Giddens, *Elites and Power in British Society,* London, Cambridge University Press, 1974, P.xii.

9. For a discussion of objective interests see S. Likes, *Power: A Radical View,* London, Macmillan, 1975.

10. For a more extended discussion see H. Newby, *et al., op. cit.,* 1977.

11. For example, in the years 1966-73 an average of 1.3 local authority dwellings per 1000 population per year were built by authorities in East Suffolk, compared with 5.6 private dwellings and an East Anglian average of 2.7 and 6.6 respectively. (Figures computed from Local Housing Statistics, 1966-73, Department of the Environment.) Lack of building cannot be explained

by lack of demand; we estimated that as many as 10,000 families may be waiting for houses in Suffolk. Nor can it be explained by lack of sites since they are found for private developments. Rather it reflects low expenditure policies (see below) and planning policies.

12. A. Lemon, *Planning and the Future of Small Towns in East Anglia,* Regional Studies Association, Discussion paper 3, 1975.

13. H. Newby, The Low Earnings of Agricultural Workers: A Sociological Approach , *Journal of Agricultural Economics,* Vol. XXIII, 1972, pp.15-24; H. Newby, *The Deferential Worker,* London, Allen Lane, 1977, Chapter 3.

14. Concern for the environment in fact appears more passive and negative than active and positive, as a review of council expenditure on relevant items indicates. Expenditure on preservation of buildings and amenities in rural areas amounted to £74.85 per 1000 population compared with an England and Wales average of £104.64. Nor are outsiders particularly encouraged to come and look at the beauties of the environment preserved on their behalf - expenditure on promotion of tourism was £7.37 per 1000 population compared with a national average of £10.35.

15. See P. Saunders *et al.,* *op. cit.,* 1978.

3

RURAL INCOMES

Ceri Thomas and Stephen Winyard

INTRODUCTION

Low income households live in both rural and urban areas.
So far research and debate has concentrated almost exclusively on the poor in cities. The reasons for this are
clear. First, inner-city poverty is more visible; the
slums and decaying schools of our major cities have caught
the attention of politicians, journalists, and the public
alike. Second, the urban poor are often seen as a threat
to social order. Rising crime rates, particularly amongst
the young, are largely a problem for city areas. Third,
historically our perception of poverty has been an urban
one, based on the work of Booth, Dickens, and Rowntree.
This continues today; as an EEC report recently noted,
'The image of poverty is an urban image'.

The Government response to the rediscovery of inner-
city poverty in the second half of the 1960s was a number
of area-based policies, for example Educational Priority
Areas and Community Development Projects. These were
designed to tackle the highest concentrations of poverty.
We are currently witnessing a reaction to this approach.
In particular a number of researchers have reminded us that
most of the poor do not live in these 'special areas' and
that narrowly focussed policies cannot hope to solve the
problem of inequality that is to be found nationwide.

This chapter is concerned with the much less visible
problem of low incomes in rural areas. Rowntree wrote
about this in 1913,[1] but there has been little attention
given to it since that date. One probable explanation of
the neglect of rural aspects of income distribution has
been the lack of adequate data, and in the first section we
examine the various sources of information. The second
section looks at the extent of low incomes in rural areas.
It is clear that at a county level the western Celtic
fringe of Cornwall, Deven, Powys, and Gwynedd, rural and
remote from the British industrial core, come at the bottom

of the income ladder. Earnings are the most important
component of household incomes and in the third section we
show that low pay is a much more serious problem in rural
areas than in Britain generally. For example over one
quarter of adult men in Cornwall earned less than £50 per
week in 1977, a proportion 2½ times higher than the
national average. Farmworkers are one of the largest rural
groups to suffer from low pay and we go on to examine the
sort of hardships which they and their families face
because of the level of farm wages. Social security
benefits are the second most important component of household income and the next section is devoted to an examination of how they operate in a rural context. The final
section focusses on rural Wales as an illustration of the
relationship between low incomes and rural deprivation.
We look initially at the distribution of income within
rural areas and in particular at the pattern of income
inequality. Turning to the broader ramifications of this
inequality we adopt a social indicator approach (using data
from the 1971 Census of Population) and find that similar
dimensions of social deprivation exist in rural Wales as in
the declining areas of the South Wales coalfield.

INCOME DATA SOURCES

A major difficulty in analysing rural incomes is the lack
of suitable information. At least four official surveys
can be used but they each have a number of deficiencies.
Table 3.1 summarises the main features of these data
sources.
        The most serious problem for our purposes undoubtedly
concerns the spatial classification of income. The surveys
all use administrative divisions, either the planning
'region' or county; they do not distinguish rural areas.
It is therefore necessary to identify a number of predominantly rural regions and counties. Looking first at
'regions' it was decided intuitively that the South West
and East Anglia best approximate to rural regions, that is
they contain no major concentrations of population and
industry.[2] As regards counties, Cornwall, Devon, Norfolk,
Gwynedd, Powys, and Clwyd probably come closest to being
true rural areas; again they contain relatively little in
the way of large-scale industry and few large towns. In
this chapter we will wherever possible concentrate on these
rural counties. The planning regions are a less satisfactory unit for analysis, and because of their sheer size,
the 'rural effect' can be easily swamped by other factors.
        The other weaknesses of these official data sources are
more widely recognised and have been examined by a number
of different researchers. In this essay we look briefly
at the Inland Revenue Survey of Personal Incomes (SPI) and
at the Department of Employment New Earnings Survey (NES)
since they offer a county breakdown of income data. The
Royal Commission on the Distribution of Income and Wealth
in a recent report[3] has identified eight characteristics of
the SPI which limit its usefulness in studies of the
distribution of income. Perhaps of greatest importance to

Table 3.1. Main sources of data on the
distribution of income

	INLAND REVENUE SURVEY OF PERSONAL INCOMES (SPI)	DEPARTMENT OF EMPLOYMENT FAMILY EXPENDITURE SURVEY (FES)	CSO BLUE BOOK TABLES	DEPARTMENT OF EMPLOYMENT, NEW EARNINGS SURVEY (NES)
:OME UNIT :D	Tax Unit (individual or married couple with or without children)	Household	Tax Unit (As for SPI)	Individual Employee
PULATION VERED	Units with incomes above the effective tax exemption limit	Private Households	All Married couples and single people	Employees in employment with earnings above tax examption level
RIOD TO ICH INCOME LATES	Tax Year	Normal Week	Financial Year	One week in April
FINITION INCOME	Total Net Income: taxable incomes (before tax) from all sources after allowable deductions	Gross Weekly Income and other incomes averaged over year and social security payments and imputed rent and educational grants	As for SPI social security benefits and grants	Total Gross Earnings (including OT and PBR)
ATIAL ASSIFICATION INCOME	Regional and County (place of residence)	Region (place of residence)	National (place of work)	Region and County (place of work)
URCE	Random Sample of tax returns. 120,000 tax units	Interview of Random sample of households 11,000 sample, approx 70 per cent response	Based on SPI supplemented by FES and DHSS data	1% random sample of employees based on Pay As You Earn (PAYE) numbers

a study of low incomes is that the survey leaves out certain
categories of income that are not liable to tax, in particular national insurance sickness and unemployment benefit.
Some low income households will therefore be excluded.
Working in the opposite direction however is the inclusion
of part-year earners; that is people who start work or die
during the tax year and women who change their marital
status.   A third problem with the SPI concerns its treatment
of self-employed incomes.   They are only included in the
survey after capital allowances and allowable bank interest

23

have been deducted. This can lead to some understatement
of incomes. A fourth problem concerns income in kind.
The Inland Revenue believes that not all such income is
reported and that which is may be under-valued. No attempt
has yet been made to calculate the combined effect of the
various weaknesses of the SPI. Certainly it would not be
possible to say whether they bias rural incomes upwards or
downwards by comparison with urban incomes. The Central
Statistical Office estimates are adjusted to allow for
some of these deficiencies but no regional classification
of income is given.
    Turning to the NES there are far fewer problems. The
survey was specifically designed to collect earnings data
whereas the SPI is only a by-product of an administrative
process. The NES provides a detailed breakdowns of all
earnings by industry, occupation, age, sex, and collective
bargaining agreement, although, as is almost inevitable
with sparsely populated rural areas, the sample sizes are
frequently too small to allow sufficiently accurate (i.e.
publishable) estimates to be made by the Government
statisticians.

VARIATIONS IN EARNINGS

To what extent are low incomes a problem in rural areas?
As we have seen there is no one source of data that is
ideal for answering this question, but because it provides
a classification of income by county, we shall make use of
the SPI.
    Table 3.2 sets out the average total net income of the
different planning regions for 1974/75 and their ranking

Table 3.2. Average total net income by
             region/country

Region or Country	£	1974/5 Ranking	1970/1 Ranking	1968/9 Ranking
South East	2868	1	1	1
East Anglia	2643	2	4	4
Yorks & Humberside	2534	3	5	6
West Midlands	2616	4	2	2
East Midlands	2603	5	6	3
Scotland	2602	6	7	8
South West	2535	7	3	5
Wales	2527	8	10	10
North	2526	9	9	9
North West	2479	10	8	7
U.K.	2661			

Source: Inland Revenue Statistics (Survey of Personal Incomes) 1977
         and preceding years.

for selected years since 1968.   It is difficult to draw any
firm conclusions about differences in income between
regions because of their sheer size;   a good deal of
blurring takes place in the aggregation of incomes.
Perhaps the strongest point to emerge is the generally
lower incomes of the traditional high unemployment areas of
the North, North West, and Wales.   A depressed economy in
these areas will mean that not only are fewer jobs available but will also mean lower incomes for those in work.
The South West, one of our 'rural' regions, has experienced
a decline in its relative position in recent years, due in
part to a reduction in job opportunities.   East Anglia on
the other hand has improved its ranking in the first half
of the 1970s.   Here its proximity to the relatively buoyant
economy of the South East will have played a part.
     Turning now to the level of income by county a rather
clearer picture of low income in peripheral areas emerges.
In Table 3.3 we have set out the ten counties with the
lowest average incomes in England and Wales.

Table 3.3.   Average net income in low
income counties 1974/5

	£
Gwynedd	2275
Cornwall	2309
Isle of Wight	2313
Powys	2343
Lancashire	2401
Devon	2404
Norfolk	2426
Clwyd	2453
Durham	2502
Avon	2514

Source: Inland Revenue Statistics 1977
(Survey of Personal Income)

     The Inland Revenue data therefore suggest that personal
incomes in rural areas are generally lower than in urban
areas.   There are many possible explanations for this,
including the higher proportion of pensionable households
and the greater importance of self employment such as
family farms which may (or may not) underestimate the value
of incomes compared to employment incomes.   Working in the
opposite direction is the tendency for high earners in town
jobs to reside in villages and be registered as such in the
SPI, thus artificially raising the aggregate income of the
rural areas.
     The New Earnings Survey however, based on the pay of
individuals at their place of employment is perhaps a more
accurate guide to the prosperity of the rural economy.
There is no doubt that men tend to earn less in rural than
in urban situations.   Unfortunately, the NES is less comprehensive in its analysis of regional effects than it is

of other industrial factors such as the occupation or
predominant negotiating body of the employees. Table 3.4
compares the pay of men and women in two predominantly
rural areas in relation to the Great Britain average. Men
emerge as comparatively low paid in the South West and
East Anglia, although women appear to suffer less from
location. This may arise because with women generally low
paid throughout the country and dependent upon either legal
minimum wages or minima in voluntary agreements there is
less scope for women to be adversely affected in rural
areas alone. Even so the pay of women in these regions is
significantly lower than the average (though not as low as
in the East Midlands or Yorkshire/Humberside).

Table 3.4. Earnings in the South West and East
Anglia relative to the national average

Gross average weekly and hourly earnings in the two regions of four
categories of employees are shown as a percentage of the average for
Great Britain in 1977. Regional rankings are given in parentheses.

| Employee Category | South West | | East Anglia | |
	Weekly %	Hourly %	Weekly %	Hourly %
Manual Men	91.5 (10)	93.4 (9)	92.6 (9)	92.7 (10)
Non-manual Men	94.5 (7)	97.3 (2)	93.1 (10)	90.3 (10)
Manual Women	97.5 (8)	97.5 (8)	97.9 (7)	99.1 (5)
Non-manual Women	96.1 (7)	99.8 (3)	94.8 (8)	91.2 (10)

Source: New Earnings Survey, Part E 1977, Department of Employment.

Are these lower earnings simply a function of the
concentration of jobs in low paying industries in rural
areas - such as agriculture and service industries - or is
there a distinct 'rural' effect ensuring lower pay for
equivalent jobs in similar industries? The NES in fact
provides support for both these views (see Table 3.5). In
East Anglia for example over 10 per cent of the sample of
male manual workers were employed in the low paying
'agriculture, forestry, fishing' industry group (compared
to a GB figure of 2.4 per cent). Indeed apart from transport and construction this was the biggest employer.
However, even in this nationally low paying industry the
East Anglian employees earn below the average. Another low
paying industrial group, distributive trades, employs 8 per
cent of the East Anglian male manual workforce (compared to
5.7 per cent nationally) although at least in this case
earnings approach the national average.
The South West provides evidence of the other explanation - the rural effect - since 16 out of the 19 industries
for which there was published data revealed lower than
average hourly earnings in that region. The very low

Table 3.5.   Relative earnings in the South West
and East Anglia by industry

Average gross hourly earnings of full time manual men (21 and over) in
the two rural regions are shown as a proportion of the average for
Great Britain in April 1977.

INDUSTRY	EAST ANGLIA	SOUTH WEST
All industries	92.7	93.4
Agriculture	98.6	96.8
Mining and Quarrying	-	86.9
Food and Drink	95.6	93.3
Chemicals	-	98.1
Mechanical Engineering	91.9	93.0
Electrical Engineering	-	91.2
Shipbuilding	-	93.5
Vehicles	96.9	94.2
Textiles	-	108.1
Timber		90.4
Paper	94.1	94.0
Other Manufacturing	-	113.9
Construction	92.7	90.6
Gas, Electricity, Water	-	98.8
Transport and Communications	95.9	96.7
Distributive Trades	99.6	94.8
Professional and Scientific	97.6	97.6
Miscellaneous Services	97.4	90.2
Public Administration	-	94.7

Source: New Earnings Survey, Part E 1977, Department of Employment.

earnings figure for the mining and quarrying industry in
the South West reflects the progress of earnings in coal
mining found in other regions, leaving the smaller
quarrying and mining enterprises of the South West far
behind.   A concentration of employment in agriculture is a
less adequate explanation of low earnings in the South West
(3.9 per cent of male manual employment).   Construction was
the largest employer (13.3 per cent) and while at the
national level was not a low paying industry in this region
hourly earnings in construction amounted to only 90.6 per
cent (and weekly earnings only 87.2 per cent) of the
national average for the industry.   In addition, of course,
construction is notoriously sensitive to recessions and cuts

in public expenditure making the South West economy
particularly vulnerable.

The data in Table 3.5 relate to the Manual Men category
of employees, and it is unfortunate that the NES fails to
publish sufficiently detailed information for the three
other main groups of employees to permit a comprehensive
analysis. The NES publishes information on regional average hourly earnings for only the following number of the
27 industrial groupings:

	South West	East Anglia
Non-manual Men	8	1
Manual Women	4	1
Non-manual Women	6	4

A similarly explanatory exercise was not therefore attempted
for these other categories of workers.

The precise extent of any low pay problems in rural
areas is obviously concealed by average earnings figures
for the regions. Unpublished data from the New Earnings
Survey portray a more well defined pattern for individual
counties. In Great Britain as a whole, 10.8 per cent men
over 21 years who worked full-time earned less than £50 per
week gross and could therefore be defined as low paid. The
criteria by which a wage is defined as 'low' is described
in detail in a recent report by Jill Sullivan (1977)[4], and
the £50 gross threshold is adopted here for the purpose of
analysis.

At a county scale it is evident from Table 3.6 that
rural women compare more favourably with their urban counterparts than do men. The importance of minimum wages for
women nationally has already been cited as an explanation
of this. In addition the lower (though rapidly rising)
female activity rates reduce the concentrations of low paid
female jobs in rural areas, and it is noticeable that
insufficient women were located by the NES in counties like
Gwynedd, Dyfed, Cornwall, Borders and Dumfries and Galloway
to allow reliable estimates to be released. Given the much
lower earnings of women generally it is not surprising that
the £50 figure should prove a less discriminating test for
women than for men.

FARM WAGES

Since farmworkers represent probably the largest purely
rural workforce, and because, in many respects, this group
illustrates the definitive characteristics of the low paid
it is worth examining farm wages in more detail. The farmworker's wages, while ostensibly a matter between him and
his employer, are generally governed not by individual or
collective bargaining but by the statutory Agricultural
Wages Board - an institution made up of representatives from
employers and employees in the industry whose differences
are resolved by 'independent members' whose job is to
conciliate. Direct bargaining remains a long unattained
goal of the farmworkers union, the NUAAW, though the

Table 3.6.   Proportion of low paid workers in
             selected counties

The table shows the proportion of full-time men and
women earning less than £50 gross in certain counties in
England and Wales, and Regions in Scotland.

MEN	%	WOMEN	%
Cornwall	26.5	Lincolnshire	74.7
Borders	23.6	Central	71.6
Dunfries and Galloway	22.4	Northants	71.5
Devon	21.4	Humberside	70.7
Dyfed (excl. Llanelli)	20.9	Staffordshire	68.6
Gwynedd	19.5	Leicestershire	68.3
Tayside	18.3	Warwickshire	67.9
E. Sussex	18.1	Durham	67.8
Highland	17.7	Lancashire	67.4
Isle of Wight	17.7	Norfolk	67.2
Hereford and Worcester	17.2	West Yorks	66.6
North Yorks	17.1	Tayside	66.6
Somerset	16.0	South Yorks	66.3
Avon	15.2	Lothian	65.5
Lincolnshire	14.9	Nottinghamshire	65.3
Suffolk	14.8	E. Sussex	64.9
Dorset	14.6	Hereford and Worcester	64.8
Cambridgeshire	14.1	Dorset	64.2
W. Sussex	13.7	Greater Manchester	64.1
Lancashire	13.7	Wiltshire	64.1
GREAT BRITAIN	10.8	GREAT BRITAIN	58.0
ENGLAND	10.5	ENGLAND	57.3
WALES	11.6	WALES	60.7
SCOTLAND	12.6	SCOTLAND	62.7

Source: Based on unpublished data from the New Earnings
Survey 1977, Department of Employment.

statutory system of wage setting is shared by most of the
other low paying industries in this country: retailing,
catering and clothing manufacture.
    The low relative pay in agriculture and horticulture is
demonstrated by the NES which lists the average weekly wage
for manual men at £54.7 compared to the 'all industries'
figure of £71.5.   The proportion of those who could be

described as low paid is accordingly very high, 44.4 per cent earning less than £50 per week (compared to 12.4 per cent for all industries).

Apologists for the industry, including farmers and the National Farmers' Union, frequently remind us that employees often receive free or cheap food and accommodation, and we consider this later, but at this point it is important simply to point out that the value of such benefits, as defined by the Wages Order of the Agricultural Wages Board, is *included* in the New Earnings Survey figures. Indeed this dubious privilege is almost the sole preserve of agricultural and catering workers as this extract from the 1977 NES questionnaire reveals:

'Notes:
> (iii) do not include the value of benefits in kind, except as in (iv) below.
> (iv) for agricultural, catering, etc., workers only, include the reckonable value, laid down in the appropriate wages order, of accommodation, meals etc., provided by the employer.'

(New Earnings Survey, Part A, 1977.)

The general exclusion of the value of luncheon vouchers, subsidised canteens, company cars, mileage allowances, non-contributory pensions and so on, combined with the inclusion of the non-wage benefits of the farm work force tend to conceal the very significant differences which exist between the pay in manufacturing (and particularly managerial occupations) and that in agriculture. The ability of the industry to pay a living wage has long been a sensitive issue. H.R. Wagstaff, in evidence to the Royal Commission on the Distribution of Income and Wealth (the Low Income Reference), has stressed that while many small farms cannot afford to employ full-time workers (and seldom do) this fact is used by the industry to justify the continuance of low wages on the larger, more profitable lowland farms who employ the majority of farmworkers at present and who could well afford to pay higher wages. From calculations based on 1971/72 figures Wagstaff estimated that a 30 per cent increase in wages would raise the cost of food in the shops by only about 1 per cent and the Retail Price Index as a whole only 0.2 per cent.

What sort of life can agricultural workers secure from these earnings? It is not easy to give an accurate answer to this question. As the report *Low Pay on the Farm* (1975) noted: 'no attempt is made by the relevant Government Departments, or indeed by the Agricultural Wages Board itself, to see whether farmworkers and their families (have) a decent standard of living'.[4] In an attempt to fill this gap the Low Pay Unit carried out a small survey of the living standards of agricultural families.

The first issue examined by the Unit was the impact of taxation and benefits. Twenty or so years ago this would not have been a problem for families. However, because of the failure of successive Chancellors of the Exchequer to raise the tax threshold in line with earnings, a growing number of low paid workers have been pulled into the direct taxation system. In the mid fifties a family with two young children did not pay tax until they were earning

slightly above the average wage. In April 1977 their tax
threshold was £31.40, rather less than half of average
earnings. Thus even though they receive a very low wage,
farmworkers hand over a significant proportion of it to
the Inland Revenue.

One response of governments to the poverty of low wage
earners with families has been to extend the range and
value of means-tested benefits; indeed in 1976 twenty per
cent of male headed households receiving Family Income
Supplement (FIS) worked in agriculture. But the overlap
of taxation and means-tested benefits has created the
problem of the 'poverty trap'. The trap means that many
low wage earners end up worse off after a pay increase.
The reason is that out of every extra pound earned the low
wage earner pays about 41p (April 1977) in tax and national
insurance contributions. In addition the low paid worker
loses means-tested benefits which carry a high marginal
'tax' rate since the benefit is withdrawn as income rises.
FIS for example, is paid at half the difference between
gross earnings and the prescribed limit. This means that
an extra £1 earned will involve the loss of 50p FIS.
Similarly a family may lose its right to free school meals
and welfare milk with a pay increase and thus experience a
further serious reduction in its disposable income.

Tax, national insurance, and the loss of FIS alone can
create a marginal tax rate for the low paid farmworker of
over 90 per cent. As has already been noted farmworkers
comprise one in five of all male-headed families receiving
FIS. However, the Secretary of State for Social Services
in 1976 argued that 'the poverty trap exists more in theory
than in practice. This is because free school meals, free
welfare milk and FIS are granted for a whole year during
which no increase in income has to be reported'.[6] What
truth is there in this argument? In its evidence to the
Royal Commission on the Distribution of Income and Wealth,
the Low Pay Unit noted that it is very sensitive to the
dates at which families first claim benefits and at which
limits are uprated. Taking the case of an agricultural
worker with two children and paid the basic AWB rate, and
assuming that this family claimed FIS for the first time
in April 1972, we find that their initial FIS payment of
£3.20 fell over the next three years until April 1975 when
they were no longer entitled to receive any FIS payment at
all. However if they waited until July 1975 they could
reclaim when the FIS limits went up. The Low Pay Unit's
survey found a number of families who had experienced a fall
in family income following a pay increase. To these
families the problem was far from a theoretical one.
Indeed one family, the Daltons, had asked the farmer not to
pay the 1975 increase, though this is not to say that they
preferred to rely on means-tested benefits rather than on
the wage earned by Mr. Dalton. As Mrs. Dalton argued,
'there shouldn't be any need for Family Income Supplement,
it's just subsidising low wages.'[7]

The second issue that the Unit examined was the contribution made by various fringe benefits to family income. It
is widely believed that low earnings are not important in
agriculture because families receive free food, fuel and

housing. What evidence is there to support this argument? One of the most detailed enquiries into fringe benefits in agriculture was carried out by the National Board for Prices and Incomes (NBPI) in 1967. It found that the importance of cheap food had decreased due to increasing crop specialisation and concluded that the overall value of benefits in kind to farmworkers were 'relatively small and certainly too insignificant to require serious modification to the conclusion reached on the basis of the figures on earnings'.[8] The Low Pay Unit survey, carried out in 1975, confirmed this finding with free or cheap food adding a little less than £1 per week to family income. The Ministry of Agriculture's *Wages and Employment Enquiry* also supports this picture: in 1976 payments in kind (excluding housing) contributed 63p to average weekly earnings.

The other benefit that is traditionally associated with agriculture is the tied cottage. Approximately half of all full-time farmworkers live in housing owned by their employer and most pay a low rent. A farmer can deduct £1.50 a week from a worker's wage for the cottage and this will be less than the rent for a comparable local authority house. However, most farmworkers living in local authority accommodation will be entitled to a rent rebate, thus the gap between net rent and the £1.50 will be small. Subsidised housing provided by the farmer does increase family income, but again by only a small amount, perhaps £2 per week. On the other hand life in a tied cottage continues to have drawbacks despite the introduction of security of tenure. These are discussed in detail by Andrew Larkin in Chapter 5.

The available evidence thus suggests that fringe benefits make only a small contribution to family income. It is not surprising therefore that the LPU's survey found families struggling to make ends meet. Indeed *Low Pay on the Farm* identified certain additional expenditure that farmworkers face that are less of a problem to the poor in urban areas. For example food prices are significantly higher in the country. More importantly public transport is wholly inadequate which means that a car is a necessity. This obviously takes a large chunk out of family income and will be discussed in greater detail below. To get some idea of the extent of hardship amongst farmworkers the Low Pay Unit asked which of certain items the families had to do without. Low wages meant that eight out of ten families could not afford a regular evening out; six out of ten had not had a holiday away from home in the previous year and a similar proportion regularly bought clothes secondhand or from a jumble sale. Three out of ten families in the survey had gone to bed early in the previous winter to save fuel. Admittedly this sample was small, including only 110 families, but none of the critics of the survey has yet looked at a large number of families. In the absence of any large scale survey, these findings of significant hardship must stand.

BENEFITS

After income from employment the second most important
source of household income is social security benefits.
They account for a slightly higher proportion of average
weekly income in East Anglia and the South West than is
the case nationally. The significance of benefits in the
context of farmworkers has already been mentioned, but two
wider questions are of relevance here. First, are more
people dependent on social security benefits in rural areas
than elsewhere and second, is there any spatial variation
in the amount of benefit paid?

It is not easy to give a definite answer to the first
question. The available information covers certain types
of benefit and not others. However the Government has
recently published figures for the number of supplementary
benefit (SB) recipients by region. Overall something like
one in eleven of the population (claimants and their
dependents) are dependent on SB which together with
National Insurance Benefits form the basis of Britain's
income maintenance system. In addition, the SB rates laid
down by Parliament each autumn are generally accepted as
the official poverty line. It might therefore be thought
that the proportion of the population receiving SB in an
area would give a clear indication of the extent of poverty.
However two points should be noted. First, significant
numbers of people are known to be living below the poverty
line; the most important group are those receiving flat
rate National Insurance benefits who do not claim SB. In
1976 it was estimated that $\frac{3}{4}$ million retirement pensioners
had an income below their SB entitlement. Second, as we
have already noted, an important cause of poverty is low
wages. The figures for the proportion of the population
claiming SB in a region will therefore be only a very
approximate measure of poverty.

The low income regions that were identified from the
Survey of Personal Incomes again stand out strongly in
Table 3.7. The North West, the North, and Wales, which are
badly affected by demand-deficient and structural unemployment, have a significantly higher proportion of their
population dependent on SB than elsewhere. East Anglia has
the lowest proportion of SB recipients whilst the South
West is fourth lowest and is significantly below the
national average. This is also broadly consistent with
their ranking in the income 'league'.

The second question to be tackled here is whether there
is any spatial variation in the amount of benefit paid. Do
social security claimants in rural areas receive less than
their counterparts in towns? Looking again at SB and
National Insurance benefits it should be noted that the
basic rates do not vary between different parts of the
country. However in the case of SB the housing costs of
virtually all claimants (either rent or mortgage interest)
are paid in full by the Supplementary Benefits Commission
in addition to the scale rates. The Commission has recognised that the cost of housing varies considerably between
different parts of the country and that it would be
difficult and possibly unfair to deal with them through a

Table 3.7.   Supplementary benefit by region 1977

REGION	SB BENEFICIARIES PER 1,000 POPULATION	NUMBER OF SB BENEFICIARIES (Thousands)
North West	75	494
Wales	74	205
North	74	230
Yorks & Humberside	64	312
Scotland	61	322
West Midlands	61	313
South West	56	240
East Midlands	54	200
South East (including GLC)	51	868
East Anglia	44	80
Great Britain	60	3264

Source: Hansard, 6th December, 1977.

single flat-rate benefit.

The principle would seem to be clear; when there is significant variation between areas in an important item of expenditure the Commission should make special provision for this. If it fails to do so claimants living in high cost areas will suffer. The special treatment of housing favours the urban poor. However we can find no special provision to take account of those items that figure disproportionately in the cost of living of the rural poor. In particular there is the high cost of rural transport. Claimants living in the country have to pay for this out of their normal scale rates and given that the Chairman of the SBC has recently described these rates as 'barely adequate' the failure to make special provision undoubtedly causes some hardship.

The Family Expenditure Survey (1976) confirms that there is a significant variation in expenditure on housing between urban and rural areas. Households in Greater London spent 19 per cent of their income on housing compared to the 14 per cent spent by households in low density areas. However, expenditure on transport also varies: it amounts to 12 per cent in London, and is about 15 per cent in low density areas. Not only therefore is there considerable variation in the cost of personal mobility, but this element of household expenditure is often more important in rural areas than housing, for which the SB element is elastic. Thus, while town dwellers may substitute transport costs with housing costs and be compensated for this if required to claim SB, the rural dweller, in conversely

swapping housing costs for transport costs, receives no
such financial compensation. In the absence of widespread
concessionary public transport schemes for pensioners and
claimants, particularly in rural areas, this rigidity in
SB rates discriminates against people in rural areas. A
recent Department of Transport report found that the highest amounts spent on bus fares for the elderly were by the
Greater London Council and metropolitan authorities(£16.50
per head on average). The non-metropolitan authorities,
particularly in East Anglia and the South West and Wales
spent the least, averaging £4.25 per head .[9]

DISTRIBUTION OF INCOME: A CASE STUDY OF WALES

(i) The incomes profile

In reviewing average personal incomes in England and Wales,
it was demonstrated that rural areas and particularly the
western Celtic fringe figured badly in the Inland Revenue's
estimates. This is obviously far from a novel finding.
For example, Rawstron and Coates (1971) came to the same
conclusion, using data from 1949/50 up to 1964/65.[10] At
that time the counties that now comprise Gwynedd in North
Wales, perhaps the most economically remote part of Wales,
had an average income of 90-94 per cent of the national
average. A decade later, far from showing signs of
catching up with the rest of Britain, Gwynedd has apparently fallen further behind with an average income of only
85.5 per cent of the national figure at £2,275 for 1974/75.
Powys, the county of rural mid-Wales, stands at 88 per cent
of the average, while Dyfed in West and South West Wales
approaches the mean at 95.8 per cent.
     Before examining how the smaller incomes in these areas
are distributed, it is important to consider what types of
income are involved in this total net figure. Many factors
give rise to unequal distributions of income, and differences revealed in snapshot surveys need not necessarily
imply injustice. Certain tax units (or families) would of
course manifest different needs, through family size,
location or other particular circumstances. As Tony
Atkinson pointed out, 'It is possible that income differences correspond to differences in age, as where people
have saved for their retirement, or to longer periods of
training'.[11]
     In the context of rural Wales there are distinct
differences in the profile of total income from that of the
UK in general, which in part are a reflection of a peculiar
demographic structure - a markedly ageing population with
19.4 per cent (Powys) 21.5 per cent (Gwynedd) and 18.6 per
cent (Dyfed) of the population over pensionable age,
compared with the UK average of 16 per cent.
     Rawstron and Coates (1971) devoted considerable atten-
tion to the income classified under Schedule E by the Inland
Revenue (mainly wages and salaries). In 1974/75 income of
this type accounted for 81.3 per cent (including wife's
income) of the total personal income of the UK as a whole.
In Wales such income was less important (see Table 3.8) at

Rural deprivation

Table 3.8. Make-up of total personal income in
rural Wales, Wales and U.K. (1974/5)

	Dyfed %	Gwynedd %	Powys %	Wales %	U.K. %
Profits and Professional Earnings (Schedule D)	17.6	14.0	24.4	8.9	7.5
Employment Income - excluding wife's	60.2	60.7	49.7	69.9	70.5
(Schedule E) - wife's	10.2	9.4	6.9	11.0	10.8
Pensions - occupational	1.5	3.8	4.1	2.2	2.3
- retirement	2.7	3.9	4.7	2.6	2.6
Family Allowances	0.5	0.6	0.8	0.5	0.5
Total Investment Income	7.3	7.6	9.4	4.8	5.8
Total	100.0	100.0	100.0	100.0	100.0

Source: Inland Revenue Statistics 1977 (Survey of Personal Incomes)

79.9 per cent and in rural counties like Gwynedd (70.1 per cent), Dyfed (70.4 per cent) and Powys (56.6 per cent) much less important. In Powys for example where employment income (excluding wife's) amounts to less than half of the total it seems particularly unsatisfactory to explain variations or inequalities solely in terms of the distribution of this category of income. In Powys investment income represented 9.4 per cent of total income (compared to 4.8 per cent for Wales and 5.8 per cent in the UK). Similarly in Powys nearly one quarter of total income came from profits and professional earnings, under Schedule D, and again the UK figure was much lower at 7.5 per cent. Clearly this reflects the importance of small family farms and businesses in rural Wales, but work has yet to be undertaken on the extent to which this sector of the local income has expanded or contracted, and, in a more political sphere, to what extent this income is indigenous to the Welsh rural economy or is simply a reflection of the wider residential patterns of, for example, English urban employees or employers.

The minor role of Welsh wives in contributing to rural income, at least as defined by the Inland Revenue, is shown strikingly by Table 3.9. Finally, a major component which is of particular importance in rural Wales is the income from occupational and retirement pensions. While the balance between the two types of pension remains fairly constant it is clear that pensions are of considerably greater importance in these areas than for the country as a whole - it is remarkable, for example, that pensions in Powys are almost as significant in the total income as profits and professional earnings, pensions and total investment income combined in Gwent (Monmouthshire).

Table 3.9. Average income by category in rural
Wales, Wales and U.K. (1974/5)

Income Category	Dyfed %	Gwynedd %	Powys %	Wales %	U.K. %
Profits and Professional Earnings (Schedule D)	2,155	1,908	1,725	2,032	2,313
Employment Income - excluding wife's	2,130	1,884	1,835	2,201	2,283
Schedule E - wife's	1,187	1,044	738	1,030	1,027
Pensions - occupational	513	850	700	593	648
- retirement	608	627	667	588	596
Family Allowances	67	71	88	71	71
Total Investment Income	415	432	500	407	505
Total net	2,549	2,275	2,343	2,527	2,661

Source: Inland Revenue Statistics 1977 (Survey of Personal Incomes)

How do these constituents of income themselves vary in
their value in rural Wales? In keeping with employment
incomes being less significant in rural areas, they are
also lower (as our examination of earnings and the New
Earnings Survey would suggest). But, in addition, the level
of profits (Schedule D), which were of marked importance,
tend also to be significantly lower - in Powys, for
example, only ¾ of the UK average; Gwynedd too revealed a
level of profits which paralleled its lowly position in
terms of total income.
        Unfortunately it is not possible to evaluate how equally
or unequally these different elements are distributed within
sub-regions such as the Welsh rural counties. The Royal
Commission on the Distribution of Income and Wealth noted
that investment income in the SPI, at least for 1972-3 and
earlier years, had been understated, indeed 'the Central
Statistical Office estimated that in 1972-3, investment
income in the SPI was only about 86 per cent of the investment income implied as being received by households in the
National Accounts ..'[12]   It was hoped that the unified tax
system operative in April 1973 would improve the accuracy
of the estimates. The tables in the Royal Commission's
Report show, however, how unequally investment income is
distributed in comparison to the distribution of earned
income. The top 10 per cent received 62.9 per cent of all
investment income compared to only 26 per cent of earned
income. Furthermore judging by the previous year's figures
investments were becoming more concentrated among the rich
while earnings were being more equally distributed.
Although the SPI figures for Wales in 1974/5 lack this
detail of presentation, it is estimated that in Wales 64.2
per cent of all investment income accrued to 13 per cent of
the tax units. A hypothesis which remains to be tested is

whether the relative importance and value of investment in rural areas is accompanied by the highly unequal distribution by the national statistics. Such a relationship combined with a predominance of retirement pensions would predict a highly unequal distribution of what is any way a smaller local income in rural Wales. Is there any evidence of this?

An attempt has been made to portray graphically[13] the respective inequalities in income in rural Wales (the counties of Dyfed, Gwynedd and Powys combined) compared to the UK as a whole. In considering Figure 3.1 it should be remembered that a situation of income equality would be portrayed by a simple diagonal line (i.e., where 40 per cent of the population receive 40 per cent of the total income). In the cases we describe the curve falls significantly below the diagonal, with 40 per cent of the population receiving approximately 20 per cent of the income. The marked similarity of the two curves in Figure 3.1 suggests similar patterns of income distribution in the two areas, though as we have stated, the average income is much lower in rural Wales.

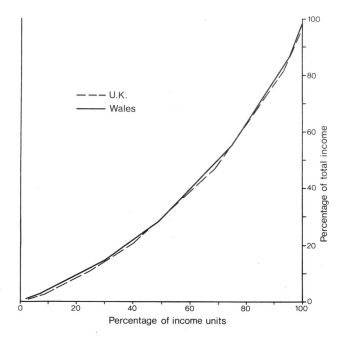

Figure 3.1. Lorenz curve of income: United Kingdom and rural Wales 1974-5.

The technique has certain limitations - not least is the effect of the arbitrary location of benchmarks (income/population reference points) which is governed by statistics as published. Second, it is necessary to estimate the total amount of income in each category for individual counties.

We have assumed that the average income within each income
band is the same for each county as it is for the whole of
Wales (for which figures are published). By multiplying
this estimate by the number of cases in each county we
arrive at an estimate of the missing figure for the total
income in each band. This process of estimation inevitably
leads to some small error - the estimate is least accurate
in Gwynedd where the inferred total income represented
only 97.8 per cent of the published figure. On the other
hand the estimates for Dyfed and Powys exaggerated the
published data - but by less than 2 per cent. Clearly
greater error may well occur in individual income bands
during the course of the estimation and the results should
for this reason be considered suggestive rather than
definitive.
      The profile of economic inequality described here
provides little support for the often held belief in a
'classless' Welsh idyll, though obviously the distribution
of social status may follow a totally different pattern.
In terms of income derived from wages, pensions and wealth
Figure 3.1 shows that rural Wales differs only marginally
from the distribution in the UK as a whole.

(ii)   'Levels of living' in rural Wales

Having reviewed sources of data feeding into the system of
rural incomes we broaden the perspective to consider
income through the lens of 'levels of living'.[14]
      An attempt was made to examine the dimensions of this
well-being through the use of 1971 population census data
for the whole of Wales according to the 168 pre-organisation
local authorities, without any explicit 'income' variable.
Principal Components Analysis (PCA) was used to compress 32
variables, for which there were measurements for each area,
into a much smaller number of uncorrelated components which
'explain' much of the substance or 'variance' of the data.[15]
      Three principal components emerged which explained just
under half the variance (45.2%), and the characteristics of
all the components are described in the Appendix to this
chapter. Component 1, as is often the case, was a general
factor with many variables being strongly associated with
it either positively or negatively. Perhaps the most
striking feature of this component was the importance of old
age or retirement variables, which highlight first the
coastal strip of the North Walian 'Costa Geriatrica', and
second, the small islands of urban life in the extensive
rural sea of Mid Wales. Such towns as Llandrindod Wells,
Bala, Newcastle Emlyn and Llandovery scored highly on this
first component reflecting their ageing population, low
birth rates and their roles as retirement destinations for
surrounding rural areas. Low 'levels of living' in rural
Wales are, however, more clearly portrayed by the composite
maps of the second and third components (Figures 3.2 and
3.3).
      The second component we may call an 'urban/rural'
component with high positive loadings for variables such as
households without cars, travel to work by bus or train,
population density, married women working, and rate rebates

39

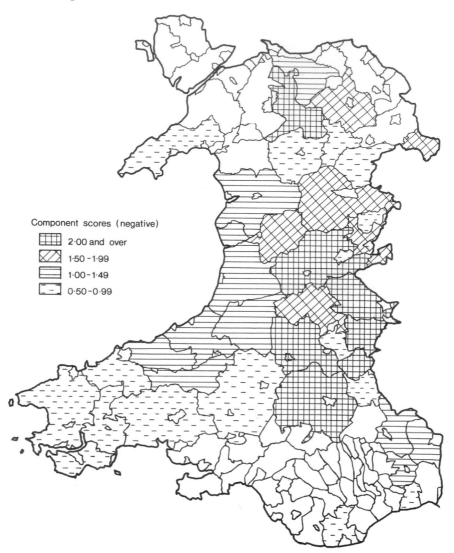

Component scores (negative)

▦ 2·00 and over

▨ 1·50 – 1·99

▤ 1·00 – 1·49

▱ 0·50 – 0·99

Figure 3.2. 'Rurality' in Wales 1971 (based on principal
  components analysis – component II)

per hundred households. The appearance of rate rebates on
this component provides some support for the idea that
various welfare benefits often go unclaimed by households
who would be eligible. Approximately 80 per cent of such
rebates are to pensioners (nationally). The age profile
of rural Wales would therefore predict a high percentage of
rate rebate provision in these areas. This is far from the
case and ignoring the possibility that pensioner households
in rural Wales are significantly more affluent with minimal
rate bills, it suggests that the problem of take-up of

means tested benefits may be particularly serious in rural Wales. On the negative or rural side, high loadings were recorded for the numbers employed in agriculture, along with the process of short-move migration by pensioners.[16] Although this component demonstrates, with some element of statistical rigour the areas which may be regarded as rural, Figure 3.2 shows that Snowdonia in particular is not included as rural by these definitions! The mountainous area around Snowdon - Gwyrfai RD - in fact had only 5.8 per cent of its population employed in agriculture. Builth RD (44 per cent); Tregaron RD (44 per cent) and Knighton RD (65 per cent) were typical of the areas defined as 'rural' by this analysis - all had very high proportions of their workforce working in agriculture. The largest industry in Gwyrfai RD was, in fact, distributive services employing over 20 per cent of the economically active adults working and resident in the area. It could be argued therefore that the component is predominantly 'agriculture' rather than 'rural' in its nature when areas of fairly low density are excluded. However to call an economy agricultural when it is founded on the provision of services for tourists, and on large scale capital projects, such as road building and power station construction, would also perhaps be misleading.

Component three was termed a 'class' factor because it was most clearly influenced by variables associated with further education, social class (as defined by the occupation of the head of household), car use for work and the number of households with exclusive use of three basic amenities, WC, hot and cold water and bath. Furthermore the loading of 'in-migration' on this component suggested that areas with high positive scores could be termed 'attractive' (and, conversely, areas with high negative scores 'unattractive'). Figure 3.3 shows the areas manifesting a high negative score on this component - and they clearly fall into two main blocks. First, the so-called 'heads of the valleys' from Glyncorrwg in West Glamorgan, via the Rhondda and Merthyr Tydfil to Abertillery in the East. These are the areas of industrial decay in South Wales - Glyncorrwg for example was the site selected for Wales' Community Development Project on the basis of its special need. The remaining block spans most of Mid Wales and while occupying a much greater geographical area, concerns fewer households. It stretches from Penllyn (around Bala) in the north to Builth in the south. They are typically areas of poor quality housing with over one-third of the houses lacking one of the basic amenities (Llanfyllin RD, New Radnor RD, Tregaron RD, Machynlleth RD). This may also be combined in certain cases with overcrowding (i.e. more persons than rooms per household) - Penllyn for example registered 7.2 per cent of its households as over-crowded, compared to an average for the 168 areas of 4.4. per cent. Rural depopulation was measured in this component by the change in population 1961-1971 accounted for by migration, and again areas like Penllyn in Merioneth were seen to be gravely affected by this problem - with out-migration running at over 2 per cent per year. Finally, social class, as defined by social economic group was a

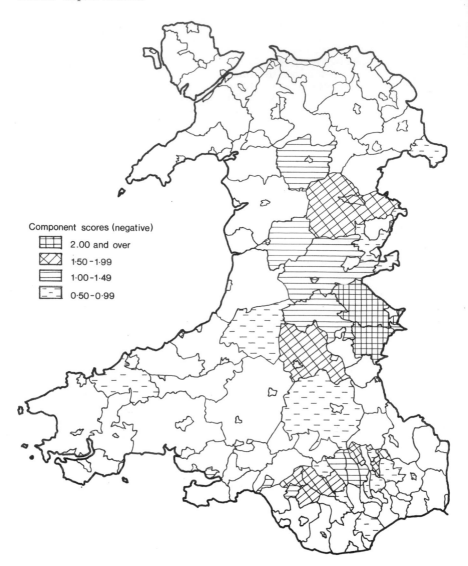

Figure 3.3. 'Class' in Wales 1971 (based on principal
    components analysis - component III).

significant element in the component although the loadings
of +0.356 for males in social class I and II (professional
and managerial occupations) and -0.278 for males in social
class IV and V (semi-skilled and unskilled occupations)
are not particularly high. In rural areas the most
important influence on the number of males in class IV and
V was the number of agricultural workers (socio-economic
group 15, transferred into social class IV). The areas
with relatively high numbers of farm workers tended therefore to receive high 'negative' scores on component two

(Penllyn RD 12.5%, Builth RD 10.4%, Fordern RD 11.4%, Llanfyllin RD 11.7%, Presteigne RD 11.4%, Knighton RD 15.7%, New Radnor RD 11.3% and Painscastle RD 10.5%).

However, it must be emphasised that large areas of income-related 'deprivation' are not revealed by this type of analysis. For example, small-scale family dairy farmers have been classified in social class III, and may even be included in social class II, and it has been shown elsewhere[17] that large proportions of these small farms are 'too small to give full time employment and an adequate income to the average farmer'. This problem is most acute in Cardiganshire, Carmarthenshire and North Wales (the Lleyn peninsula, Anglesey and Merioneth) and the incongruence of the two spatial patterns signifies perhaps the inability of census indicators - which are predominantly based on urban values - to estimate adequately levels of living in remote rural areas, where the proportion of 'own account' farmers is high. The other reservation to be stressed concerns the data itself. Many of the variables measuring occupation and economic and social class refer to only a 10% sample in the 1971 census. This need not cause too many problems in densely populated urban areas, but in rural areas with smaller populations a 10 per cent sample may lead to more extreme distributions across variables and these will be reflected in component scores for the rural areas, some of which in Radnor, for example, had populations of less than 2,000 individuals (Presteigne RD, New Radnor RD, Colwyn RD and Painscastle RD) so that the very high component scores of 'over 2' should be regarded with a degree of caution. From the above sketch of levels of living in Wales, based on the dimensions measured by the population census, it is evident that rural Wales suffers

Table 3.10. Unemployment - the 'worst thirty areas'
May 1977

Rank	Area	Males	Rank	Area	Females
4th	Tenby	20.4	7th	Milford Haven	13.6
5th	Cardigan	20.3	10th	Pembroke Dock	12.3
9th	Lampeter	18.5	14th	Blaenau Ffestiniog	11.3
11th	Rhyl	18.0	21st	Cardigan	10.0
13th	Milford Haven	17.1	22nd	Holyhead	9.7
16th	Tywyn	16.2	25th	Lampeter	9.5
19th	Pembroke Dock	15.5	30th	Tywyn	9.2
25th	Holyhead	14.6			
27th	Fishguard	14.2			

Source: Hansard 20th June, 1977.

from the same type of decaying social fabric as the older
parts of South Wales. To this already disturbing picture
may be added high rates of unemployment, as well as the
low average earnings mentioned at the beginning of this
Chapter. Of the worst 30 areas of male unemployment in the
UK in May 1977 9 were found in rural and coastal Wales
(see Table 3.10). This relationship between deprivation
and rural unemployment is explored more fully in the next
chapter.

CONCLUSIONS

We have, in this chapter, attempted to locate rural areas
on the national income ladders as defined by personal
income (SPI) and earnings (NES). The incongruence of the
findings from the surveys was marked at the regional level,
where, for example, East Anglia ranked highly according to
personal income and on low dependence on Supplementary
Benefits, but was at the bottom of the earnings league for
male and most female employees. In East Anglia the
orthodox relationship between surplus labour supply
(unemployment) and low wages seemed less explanatory than
the role of agriculture as a low paying 'wage leader'.
Furthermore, in common with rural Wales, employment income
was of less importance, and profits and investment income
of greater importance than the overall profile for the UK.
Unlike rural Wales, however, investment income and to a
lesser extent profits and professional earnings were of
much higher relative value in East Anglia. The South West
offered evidence of low wages across the whole range of
industries which was accounted for by the remoteness of the
region from the centres of investment decision-making and
the more sophisticated spheres of company activity (such
as research and development).
     Concentrating on one large occupational group of low
paid rural workers, farmworkers, we outlined the often
disastrous effects of the overlap of two forms of social
policy - direct taxation and the welfare state - in pushing
thousands of agricultural workers' families into the
poverty trap. The low level of labour organisation and the
absence of any significant collective bargaining in the
industry has preserved the necessity for statutory wage
regulation. The lack of union recognition in turn may well
deny the farmworker other employment rights - such as
access to the Fair Wages principle in the Employment
Protection Act 1975 (Schedule II).
     In our discussion of the spatial bias of welfare bene-
fits we suggested that the elastic provision for housing
costs contrasts with the standard element of Supplementary
Benefit intended to cover the cost of personal mobility
irrespective of the varying need.
     In focusing on Wales we sought to utilise a broad
approach to the variations in local 'levels of living' in a
rural context via a statistical method that previously has
been popular among academics in identifying and mapping
urban deprivation. In particular, it was suggested that
large parts of rural Wales suffered from similar symptoms

of social and economic decay which are generally viewed as definitive of the problems of the declining industrial communities of the coal mining 'heads of the valleys'. On the other hand the analysis, which was heavily dependent on the variables in the Census of Population, 1971, did not identify the areas of small unprofitable family enterprise which, if they were outside the UK, would be termed 'peasant farms'.

The articulation of these themes of rural incomes has been almost wholly derived from various Government surveys whose results impinge on the subject of rural income without actually being designed for the necessary measurement. As such the findings here reflect the values and short-comings of those surveys - like the exclusion of employees who earn less than the tax threshold from the New Earnings Survey. This chapter has been unapologetically empirical in its flavour for the reasons outlined in the intro-duction - simply to compensate for the lack of attention to the problems of low 'rural' incomes in the past, and in part to counter-balance the obfuscatory obsession with low incomes in 'the inner city'. Both geographical expressions, however, contain an element of deception if used in attempting to explain social and economic 'problems'. As we know, the poor are always with us, but they are also everywhere with us.

REFERENCES AND NOTES

1. B. Seebohm Rowntree and M. Kendall, *How the Labourer Lives,* Nelson & Son, 1913.

2. A solution to the problem of objectively defining and measuring changes in rurality has been proposed by Paul J. Cloke in *An Index of Rurality for England and Wales , Regional Studies,* Vol. II, pp 31-46, 1977. He made use of a principal components analysis of selected discriminating variables in the population census and produced a spatial pattern which largely supports the intuitive selection of rural regions adopted here.

3. Royal Commission on the Distribution of Industry and Wealth, *Report No. 5,* Third Report on the Standing Reference, Appendix C, Cmnd 6999, H.M.S.O., 1977.

4. Jill Sullivan, *Low Pay Report,* Bulletin No. 17, Low Pay Unit, October, 1977.

5. M. Brown and S. Winyard, *Low Pay on the Farm,* Low Pay Unit, London, 1975.

6. Quoted in *Community Care,* June 23rd, 1976.

7. This issue is explored more fully in an article by Chris Pond: *Soaking the Poor - A Report on the Poverty Trap,* Bulletin No. 18, Low Pay Unit, February, 1978.

8. National Board for Prices and Incomes, *Report No. 25,* Cmnd 3199, H.M.S.O., 1967.

Rural deprivation

8. National Board for Prices and Incomes, *Report No. 25,* Cmnd 3199, H.M.S.O., 1967.

9. Quoted in *New Society,* 29th September, 1977.

10. B.E. Coates and E.M. Rawstron, *Regional Variations in Britain,* Studies in Economic and Social Geography, Batsford, 1971.

11. A.B. Atkinson, *The Economics of Inequality,* Oxford University Press, 1975.

12. Royal Commission on the Distribution of Income and Wealth, *Report No. 4,* Second Report on the Standing Reference, 1977.

13. The use of the Lorenz Curve to describe the distribution of income is discussed more fully by A.B. Atkinson, *The Economics of Inequality,* (ibid) pp. 15-17.

14. Spatial variations in 'levels of living' are fully discussed in P.L. Knox, *Social Well Being - A Spatial Perspective,* Clarendon Press, Oxford, 1975.

15. Principal components analysis, a variant of factor analysis, is fully described in S. Daultrey, Principal Components Analysis , *Concepts and Techniques in Modern Geography No. 8,* Geo Abstracts Ltd., 1976. The technique has been made accessible by the use of such computer package programmes as the Statistical Package for the Social Sciences which was used in this particular application.

16. This variable, entitled 'within migrants over pensionable age' refers to the number of pensioners who have moved household in the previous 5 years without crossing a local authority boundary. It is a substantially different form of household mobility from the traditional retirement migration which involves a long distance move to the coastal resorts, for example.

17. *A Strategy for Rural Wales,* Welsh Council, H.M.S.O., 1971.

ACKNOWLEDGEMENTS

The sections on rural Wales were written by Ceri Thomas alone and are derivative of postgraduate research undertaken at the Geography Department, UCW Aberystwyth. The author would like to thank Professor H. Carter and Mr. W.J. Edwards for their encouragement and supervision and the Social Science Research Council for their financial support during the course of this research.

APPENDIX TO CHAPTER 3 overleaf

Characteristics of the principal components: component loadings and eigenvalues

Variable	I	II	III	IV	V	VI	VII
1 % Households 1+ persons per room	-544						+393
2 % Rate Rebates	+592	+466					
3 % Households with three amenities			+585	-511			
4 Rateable Value					-843		
5 % Owner Occupier					-843		
6 % Retirement Age	+847						
7 % Without Cars		+842					
8 % Welsh Speaking	+460				+964		+495
9 Births 1973 as % Population Estimates 1973							
10 Deaths 1973 as % Population Estimates 1973	+744						
11 % Within migrants in social class I and II						+643	
12 % Within migrants in social class IV and V						-865	
13 % Travel to work by car	-364		+782				
14 % Travel to work by bus	-368	+667					
15 % Travel to work walk/none	+563				+561		
16 Persons per hectare		+559					
17 % Employed in agriculture		-831	-309				
18 % With A Levels/ONC employed			+719				
19 % Immigrants over pensionable age	+428			+559		+307	

	LIFE CYCLE	URBAN/RURAL	CLASS	GROWTH DECAY	HOUSING TENURE	SOCIAL CLASS	FEMALE ACTIVITY/WELSH
20 % Immigrants in social class I and II							
21 % Immigrants in social class IV and V							
22 % Within migrants over pensionable age	+534	-398				-369	
23 % Population under five				+918			
24 % Unemployed		+502					+473
25 % Married women working more than 8 hours a week							-714
26 % Married women inactive under 60 years age	-313						+723
27 % Econ act. and rtd males in social class I and II	+368	-354	+356			+465	
28 % Econ act. and rtd males in social class IV and V						-388	
29 Population Increase/Decrease - Natural	-849						
30 Population Increase/Decrease - Migration			+805				
31 % Local Authority Housing	-378	+319			+726		
32 Shops per 1000 population	+761						
% of Variance explained	20.3	12.9	12.0	8.5	6.2	5.0	4.5
% of Variance explained (cumulative)	20.3	33.2	45.2	53.7	59.9	64.9	69.4
Eigenvalues	6.48	4.13	3.85	2.73	1.98	1.61	1.45

(Varimax – Rotation)

Notes:
1) Component loadings describe the relationship between the components and the original variables. They are in fact correlation coefficients and range from perfect positive correlation (+1.0) through no association (0.0) to the perfect negative correlation (-1.0).
2) It must be stressed that the exercise is a form of *ecological* correlation and any inference that the relationship between variables is *causal* (eg. pensioners speak Welsh or Welsh speakers will be pensioners) must be regarded with suspicion.

49

4

RURAL EMPLOYMENT: PROBLEMS AND PLANNING

John Packman

INTRODUCTION: EMPLOYMENT CHARACTERISTICS OF RURAL AREAS

This chapter demonstrates that the seriousness of rural
employment problems has not been matched by the attention
which they have received in the past, and that the time
is clearly ripe to attempt to provide more jobs in rural
areas. Consideration is initially given to the employment
characteristics of rural areas which differentiate them
from urban areas. The social problems derived from these
are then examined followed by an assessment of the need
for additional jobs and the potential for creating them.
Finally, the existing roles of the planning agencies
involved in rural employment and the policies they could
pursue are reviewed.
    The employment problems of rural areas have been
recognised to some extent with the inclusion of the most
deprived areas in the government 'Assisted Areas' (Figure
4.1). However, not all of the areas in which agriculture
is important in the local employment structure are included
(Figure 4.2). Table 4.1 shows that Norfolk, Lincolnshire
and Salop, which are not wholly included in the Assisted
Areas, also had higher than average unemployment rates in
1977. Much of the case study material in this chapter
relates to these counties.
    Rural employment is characterised by structural
imbalance, low economic potential and poor accessibility,
and these are discussed separately below.

(i) Structural characteristics

Figure 4.2 shows that most 'rural' areas have higher proportions of their total labour force than the national
average employed in agriculture and this is the most basic
structural characteristic of the rural labour force. Since
the mid-fifties increased mechanisation and rationalisation

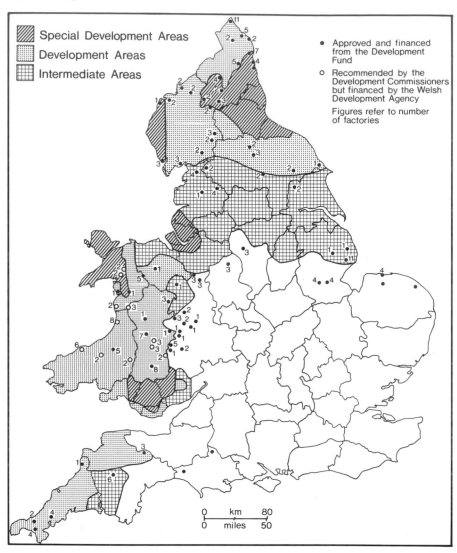

Figure 4.1. Assisted areas and Development Commission
    Projects 1977. Source: Thirty-fifth Report of the
    Development Commission.[1]

has led to a dramatic decline in the size of the agricultural labour force: 329,000 workers have left the
industry, a 52% decline, in the period 1955-77.[3] Perhaps
more significantly the number of full-time workers has
fallen by 308,000, a 64% drop (Figure 4.3).
    In Norfolk, the number of full-time agricultural
workers dropped by nearly 70%, from 32,000 in 1951 to only

Table 4.1.   Total unemployment for rural counties
not wholly included in the Assisted Areas, 1977.

County	January 1977	June 1977	December 1977
Berkshire	3.6	3.7	3.7
Oxfordshire	4.8	4.7	4.5
Cambridgeshire	4.5	4.8	4.5
Norfolk	6.2	6.1	6.3
Suffolk	5.0	5.0	5.0
Gloucestershire	5.4	5.6	5.4
Somerset	5.4	5.4	5.6
Wiltshire	5.6	5.6	5.6
Hereford/Worcester	5.3	5.2	5.8
Salop	6.4	6.6	7.1
Warwickshire	N/A	N/A	N/A
Leicestershire	4.7	4.8	4.4
Lincolnshire	6.5	6.9	6.6
Northamptonshire	5.1	4.8	4.5
Great Britain	6.0%	6.0%	6.1%

Source : Department of Employment Gazette

10,000 in 1975, at an average rate of 3% per annum.[4]   The
mid 1960s was the period of greatest decline,with the
change between 1964 and 1966 rising to over 7% per annum.
This can be compared with the fall in agricultural employment in Lincolnshire, which has 11% of its work force
employed in agriculture, but where the decline has been
less rapid because of the intensive nature of the farming.
The major decline here has been in the number of hired
workers, and the number of regular male hired workers per
holding fell from 1.6 in 1960 to 1.24 in 1974.[5]
    There is evidence that labour shedding from agriculture
will continue and that there may soon be shortages of
skilled labour since the industry is failing to attract and
retain young workers. This may have contributed to the
increase in the number of seasonal and casual workers in
the mid 1970s. The increase in mechanisation has lent
itself to more use of contract labour, often through firms
providing specialist services, such as aerial spraying,
manure spreading and land drainage.
    In addition to this 'direct' agricultural employment
in the rural counties there is also other employment, in
food processing, agricultural machinery and engineering,
and transport services, which is either heavily dependent
upon local agricultural produce, or directly serves

Figure 4.2.   Agricultural employment in England and Wales
   1975 (Location quotients by county).   Source: Abstract
   of Regional Statistics 1976.[2]

$$\text{Location Quotient} = \frac{\text{Percentage of employment in agriculture in County}}{\text{Percentage of employment in agriculture in England and Wales}}$$

the local agricultural industry. For example, in Norfolk
it is estimated that this 'indirect' agricultural
employment probably amounts to a further 6% of the
total labour force,[4] on top of the 7% directly employed
in farming. While the expansion of agricultural-
related industries has to some extent offset in numerical

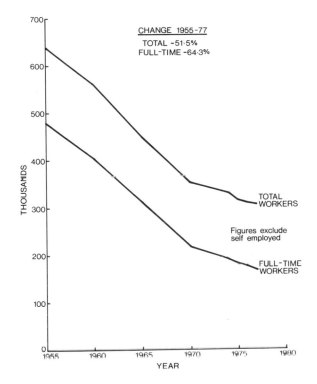

Figure 4.3. Agricultural labour force 1955-1977 England
    and Wales, Source: Ministry of Agriculture census
    returns.

terms the decline in 'direct' employment, the former have
been mainly seasonal jobs for women in urban centres,
whereas the jobs lost have been full-time jobs for men in
the remoter rural areas. There is also scope for increased
mechanisation in the food processing/packaging industries
and thus the number of female jobs is threatened.

The second structural characteristic of rural areas,
the under-representation of manufacturing industry, is
partly due to their remoteness and partly to lack of raw
materials. Table 4.2 gives the proportion of workers in 3
rural counties.[4,6,7]

However, in the period 1971-75 manufacturing employment
increased in all three of these counties at a time when
nationally it was static or declining (Table 4.3). In
Norfolk and Salop this was particularly marked and this
trend reflects partly the success of the Thetford and King's
Lynn Town Expansion Schemes and Telford New Town.

The third characteristic is the under-representation of
service employment in rural areas. This sector of employment has shown the greatest growth nationally in recent
years and it counterbalanced falls in employment in the
primary and manufacturing sectors. However, service jobs

55

Table 4.2.   Manufacturing labour in selected
counties 1975

	% in production industries (S.I.C.s II - XXI)
Lincolnshire	35.3
Norfolk	37.2
Salop	39.8
England and Wales	41.85

Source: Structure Plan Report of Survey

Table 4.3.   Employment change by sector in
selected counties 1971-5

	Primary	Manufacture	Service	Total
Lincolnshire	-1107 - 1.3%	+1269 +0.7%	+ 7977 + 2.0%	+ 8139 + 1.2%
Norfolk	-2431 -11.1%	+1485 +2.1%	+24226 +18.3%	+23280 +10.3%
Salop	-1511 -14.7%	+1645 +3.7%	+ 7458 +12.3%	+ 7592 + 6.6%

Source: Structure Plan Report of Survey

have been located mainly in major urban centres with a
large proportion of them taken by women. In Norfolk two
thirds of all new service jobs created between 1961-71 were
taken by women and 85% went to the two major centres of
Norwich and Great Yarmouth.
     The net effect of these changes has been a growth in
employment in urban centres at the expense of the rural areas.

(ii) Low economic potential

The peripheral location of many rural areas and their poor
external communications make them relatively unattractive to
many employers and firms outside these areas. In particular,
lowland rural areas not included in the 'Assisted Areas' are
unable to offer the incentives of the development and intermediate areas. Policy changes by central government in
respect of Inner City Areas will make the attraction of
industry to rural areas more difficult. The recently
announced Department of the Environment Inner City Programme
provides considerable funds to retain industry in inner city
areas. In 1977 the 'partnership schemes' included £22
million for Inner London Boroughs alone and in the case of
the 'docklands' an estimated 18% of the total £17m allocated
is to be ear-marked for 'employment support'.[8]

The migration of firms to rural areas in the late 1960s and early 1970s was encouraged by government policy and a buoyant economy.[9]   A substantial proportion of these firms were branch factories vulnerable to closure in times of economic recession.   For example, forty-eight of the 113 firms which moved to Cornwall between 1961 and 1975 were new branches (employing mainly women) responsible for nearly two-thirds of the additional employment.[10]   In Norfolk redundancies at four branch factories in 1975 owned by the same electronics company at Fakenham, Cromer, Aylsham and Harleston involved the loss of over 250 jobs.

In rural areas the limited manufacturing sector is characterised by the dominance of a relatively small range of industries and there often exists a limited number of dominant firms.   In one small town in Norfolk, of the 8 manufacturing firms with more than five employees, two employ three-quarters of the total number, one providing predominantly male employment, and the other female.   This illustrates the small and narrow manufacturing base on which the fortunes of an area often depend.

(iii)   Poor accessibility to employment centres

The dispersed nature of rural populations creates problems which are largely absent from suburban and urban environments.   The inadequacy of public transport and the high cost of both public and private transport frequently preclude acceptance of a job, and increase the mismatch between the jobs available and the location and skills of the unemployed.

In Norfolk the closure of 96 railway stations since the early 1950s has reduced the rail network to 30% of the mileage in operation at the time of maximum extent, and the number of bus miles has declined by 30% since then.   The net result is that almost one third of the village population does not now have a journey to work public transport service.[11]   The picture in Salop is similar, with over 2,000 people living in 20 parishes with no bus service at all and a further 14,000 people living in the 57 parishes with a less than daily bus service.[6]   The accessibility problem is discussed more fully in Chapter 10.

Car ownership rates are higher in rural areas than the national average (Norfolk had 0.31 cars per person in 1977 compared to the national average 0.25), but it is inevitable that rural public transport and car ownership patterns result in certain social groups being disadvantaged in terms of employment opportunities, particularly married women, school leavers and the low paid.   Moreover, poor access to employment centres also has implications for information on jobs.   The Manpower Services Commission has been concentrating its services in urban Job Centres, and this has meant the closure of some of the smaller employment offices, thereby placing rural dwellers at a great disadvantage when competing for jobs.

Rural deprivation

SOCIAL PROBLEMS RELATED TO EMPLOYMENT

Unemployment rates in the remoter rural areas tend to be
higher than the national average as is shown in Figure 4.4.
Also, within counties, the most isolated rural areas have
the highest unemployment rates. In Norfolk, for example,
the average male unemployment rate in December 1977 for
the urban exchanges was 7.3% (Norwich 6.4%, Thetford
5.4%, Great Yarmouth 9.5%, Kings Lynn 7.8%), whereas the
average for the rural exchanges was 10.5% (Cromer 14.6%,
Dereham 10.9%, Diss 7.7%, Downham Market 7.1%, Fakenham 9.0%,

Figure 4.4. Average total unemployment rates (January, June
    and December) 1977 by county. Source: Department of
    Employment Gazette.

Hunstanton 13.8%, North Walsham 8.4%, Swaffham 12.3%).
Four social groups have shown themselves to be particularly
susceptible to unemployment in rural areas as the economic
recession has deepened in the 1970s: the young, the old,
women and the unskilled.

(i) *The young*. Rural areas have followed closely the
national trend of rising unemployment among school leavers.
In Norfolk the number of school leavers registered at
careers offices has risen from 330 in October 1972 to 1,250
in October 1977,[12] though this recent increase is partly
due to an absolute increase in the number of young people
reaching school leaving age. The duration of unemployment
among the young is also increasing and there is a danger
that if they do not receive a training in a job soon
after leaving school, they may join the ranks of the future
long-term unskilled unemployed.

The lack of local job opportunities offering apprentice-
ships and professional training clearly contributes to the
outmigration of young people from rural areas. For example
Table 4.4. shows the age breakdown of net migration flows
for Shropshire in the period 1961-71. The three rural
areas of Oswestry, South Shropshire and North Shropshire
show large losses in the 15-24 age group.

(ii) *The old*. Generally, in the more rural areas of
Britain the proportion of the rural unemployed who are of
age 50 or over is above the national average, reflecting
mainly the age structure of the population in these areas.
For example, in Lincolnshire in July 1977 22.0% of the
total unemployed were aged over 50, compared with 19.0% in
Great Britain. While Special Programmes for the young
unemployed are in preparation, very little is being done to
help the unemployed aged over 50, although it is recognised
that in a period of rising unemployment and shortage of
jobs, the persons in this age group experience most
difficulty in finding a job.

(iii) *Women*. Women account for an increasing proportion of registered unemployment. In Norfolk they represented only 12% of total unemployment in January 1971,
though the figure had risen to 22% by January 1978. This
is a reflection of increasing female activity, a greater
awareness of a woman's right to claim unemployment benefit,
the seasonal nature of many female jobs and the greater
propensity for employers to lay women off first in times of
economic recession. Many of the female jobs lost have been
through the closure of branch factories. These were set up
to exploit the large female labour pool in times when women
could be employed at relatively low wages.

Low activity rates and the incidence of seasonal work in
rural areas hide the extent of the lack of opportunities and
there is evidence of considerable *under* employment, in
addition to the level of unemployment shown by official
registers.

Activity rates define the proportion of the population
over the age of 15 who are in paid employment, or who are
prevented from working through illness or are seeking work,
and female activity rates are lower than the national
average in rural areas. In Great Britain as a whole 42.4%

of women were economically active in 1971 compared to 37.9%
in Norfolk, 38.0% in Lincolnshire and 40.5% in Salop.
Recent analysis stresses 'opportunity factors' - the
availability of jobs locally, the means of travel to them
and the provision of day-care facilities - as being crucial.
The main difficulty appears to be the distance between many
homes and the nearest employment centre which makes travel
to and from work costly and inconvenient, if not impossible.
This is supported by age-specific activity rates for Salop[6],
which show that activity rates for all groups, and particularly for married women, are lower in the more rural
districts. For example, the activity rate for married
women aged 25-34 in 1971 was 38.4% for Great Britain but
34.1 for Shropshire, and while it was 35.3 in Shrewsbury
the figure fell to 30.5 in Oswestry.

   Agriculture and tourism, important sources of employment in rural areas, are subject to marked seasonal
variation in labour need, and this is reflected in higher
unemployment rates in the winter months. However, because
a large number of seasonal employees, especially women and
older men who work part-time or full-time in the summer,
do not register as employed in the winter months, the
higher unemployment figures for January do not represent
fully the level of under-employment.

   (iv) *The unskilled*. The majority of the unemployed
in rural areas are in the semi-skilled and unskilled categories. They are the most difficult to place and their
duration of unemployment has risen. The longer they are
without employment the more difficult it is to place them.
Many of the firms who have moved to rural areas require
skilled labour, in direct contrast to the abilities offered
by the majority of the unemployed.

Table 4.4.   Age structure of net migrants as a % of
     total migration movements between 1961 and 1971

% in each age group

	Area	0-14	15-24	25-44	45-64	65+
Population 1961	Shropshire	23.5	14.9	25.7	24.3	11.5
Net migrants	Shropshire	19.8	4.0	45.1	17.8	13.4
	Bridgnorth	- 7.7	1.5	63.3	15.3	12.1
	North Shropshire	-22.1	-45.3	5.9	7.0	19.8
	Oswestry	-15.0	-32.4	0.1	21.8	30.7
	Shrewsbury	25.8	2.0	39.5	22.0	10.7
	South Shropshire	-11.0	-44.2	- 5.8	17.5	21.4
	Wrekin	27.8	19.6	37.4	10.4	4.8

Source: Salop Structure Plan Report of Survey

THE NEED FOR NEW JOBS IN RURAL AREAS

There are sound economic and urgent social reasons why
existing rural industries should be assisted and new enterprises encouraged.   This encouragement requires a positive
effort on the part of public authorities, and despite the
problems there are several arguments to justify regional
policies aimed at stemming rural decline.   These have been
well surveyed by Gilg:[13]
   (i)   Unequal standards of living and other general
   inequalities give rise to rifts and divisions in society.
   (ii)   Agricultural and other similar basic jobs cannot by
   themselves support economically efficient communities.

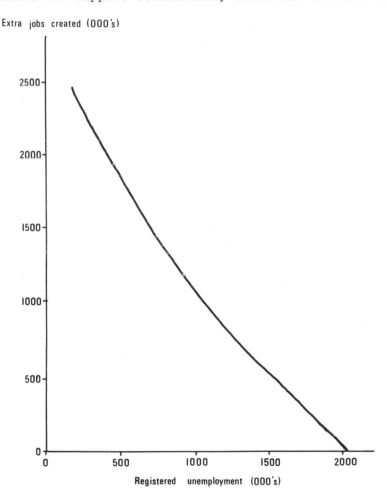

Extra jobs created (000's)

Registered   unemployment   (000's)

Figure 4.5.   The national job gap curve, 1981.   The chart
   shows the number of jobs required to achieve various
   levels of registered unemployment in 1981.
   Source: Manpower Services Commission Review and Plan
   1977.

(iii)   Most of these areas have substantial reserves of labour which if brought into employment would not only boost the Gross National Product, but would also save Government expenditure on unemployment and other state benefits.

(iv)   A continued exodus of people and jobs from the remote to the already overcrowded urban areas would lead to a further intensification of congestion in these areas.

(v)   These areas contain a good deal of social capital which, in a period of low economic growth, is very expensive to replace and reconstruct in another location.

(vi)   Finally, most people living in these areas do not want to leave, and many who have left would return given the chance.

The need to create more jobs in the rural areas is all the more pressing because of the anticipated changes in the labour supply and demand at a national level. Demographic trends and activity rate assumptions indicate that there will be a considerable rise in the number of people seeking employment. The Manpower Services Commission expects 1.34 million additional jobs (5% increase) to be required in the period 1976-1981 to reduce registered unemployment to 800,000.[14] The relationship between jobs needed and unemployment is summarised by the 'job-gap' curve shown in Figure 4.5.

The national position is exacerbated in rural areas because low female activity rates encompass a potential increase in labour supply exceeding the national average. Moseley[15] has calculated for East Anglia that on the basis of the 1971 census data a further 25,000 women would have to be at work for the female activity rate to equal that of Great Britain.

The development of the silicon chip and mini-computer could substantially reduce future labour demand, particularly in the service sector,[16] the very areas where recent job growth has been concentrated. One recent report suggested that unemployment may approach five million by the 1990s.[17] In rural areas marginal enterprises could be the first to go out of business if urban factories and offices invest in the new technology.

AGENCIES AND POLICIES

The problems identified above can be tackled in three ways:

(1)   Improving accessibility (in its widest sense) to alternative job opportunities in the existing employment centres.

(2)   Assisting local employers to expand and take on more workers.

(3)   Attracting new employment into the area.

The first of these approaches could include indirect measures such as the organisation and provision of play groups and nursery schools to enable married women to work, as well as the more obvious transport initiatives, which are examined in Chapter 10. This chapter concentrates on the promotion of new and existing industry.

Agencies and policies concerned with employment promotion can be divided into two:
(i) Those mainly concerned with development, for example, the attraction of industry by advertising, the construction of advance factories and provision of loans and rent-free periods, in order to create more local jobs.
(ii) Those mainly concerned with manpower i.e. aimed at either matching labour supply and demand or reducing labour supply, including training programmes and the work of the Manpower Services Commission.[18]
Figure 4.6 illustrates the multiplicity of agencies in Norfolk involved in development and manpower policy, and the links between them. Three bodies in particular, acting on a local level, are developing their roles in rural areas, and these are considered below:

(a) The Development Commission

The Commission advises the Department of the Environment on applications for advances from the Development Fund, calculated to benefit, directly or indirectly, the rural economy. The Development Fund is voted annually by Parliament and stood at £7.2 million in the year 1977/78. The Commission tackles rural revival in three broad ways.
First the construction of small factory premises (1,500 to 10,000 feet) in selected growth points is aimed at stimulating local employment growth. Factory building is undertaken within the Government's Assisted Areas by the English Industrial Estates Corporation on the Commission's behalf, and elsewhere by the Council for Small Industries in Rural Areas (CoSIRA). The construction of 420 factories has been approved (see Figure 4.1) of which 62 have been built. All but six of the factories have been let immediately 'creating jobs' at a rate of £1,500 to £3,000 a job.[19] The Government's interdepartmental report on rural depopulation[20] indicated that 2,500 jobs per annum will need to be created in the rural areas of the country in the next fifteen years. The current factory building programme already exceeds £7½ million and the total financial allocation has been recently raised to £17m for 1978/79.
Most building programmes are based on 5-year Action Plans prepared by local authorities. For example, the Action Plan for North Norfolk was submitted by the local authorities in November 1976 and confirmed by the Development Commission in March 1977. Construction has already begun on two 6,000 square feet 'nursery clusters' of factory units at Wells and at North Walsham, and in 1978/79 a further 15,500 square feet of factory units will be constructed in Fakenham and North Walsham. Action Plans are now set within the context of Special Investment Areas relating to zones of identified need, in terms of job opportunities. The most recent to be designated (1978) is that for the Fenland of Cambridgeshire and Norfolk, which provides for factory building in 6 centres.[21] Smaller 'pockets of need' are also identified.

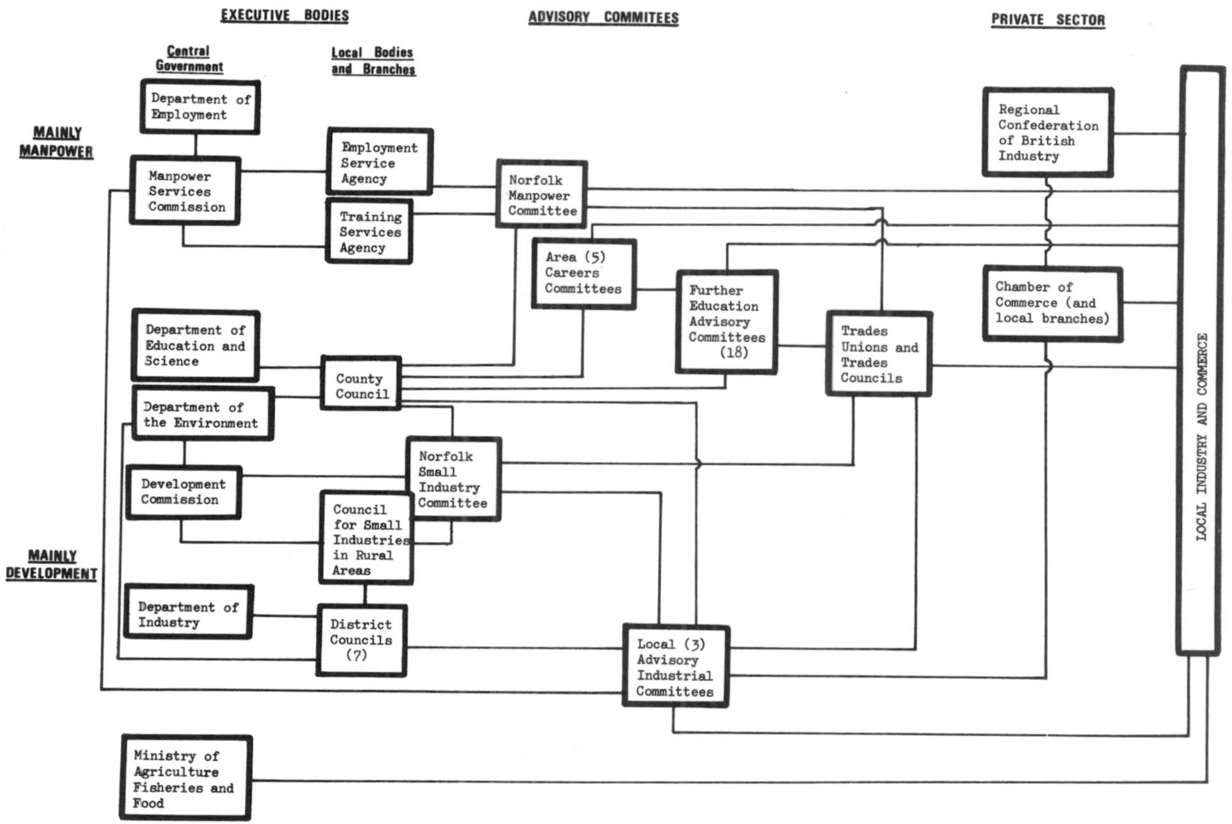

Figure 4.6. Employment and industry : links between agencies in Norfolk, 1977.
Source: Industry and Employment in Norfolk, Report of Norfolk County Planning Officer (1978)

In other counties, the Development Commission has been active over a much longer period. In Lincolnshire, for example, in 1970 the Alford- Horncastle- Spilsby area was selected as a 'trigger area' for assistance and in 1973 the Kirton- Swineshead - Gosberton -Donnington area was similarly designated. So far, six factories (a total of 30,000 square feet) have been built, one in Horncastle and five in Spilsby employing 145 people and representing an investment of £150,000. Four other factories have recently been approved at Alford, Spilsby, Louth and Kirton representing 3,906 square metres (42,000 square feet) of floorspace capable of employing upwards of 100 people and likely to cost over £350,000. Similarly,in Salop, Development Commission schemes are already in hand at Bishop's Castle, Church Stretton, Craven Arms, Market Drayton and Whitchurch.

CoSIRA, acting as agent for the Development Commission has a representative in every county providing business management and technical advice. In addition it provides loans to small firms from a fund totalling over £11 million in 1978. In Lincolnshire, for example, 16 enterprises have been assisted, providing jobs for about 200 people with a capital investment of £164,000 in building loans.

The Commission also gives financial support to several voluntary or self-governing organisations providing rural areas with a variety of services. In particular, the National Council of Social Service, Rural Community Councils and National Federation of Women's Institutes are encouraged.

(b) County Councils

In addition to providing the Careers Advisory Service for school leavers, County Councils, in their Structure Plans, have emphasised employment problems and included policies to assist rural employment.

e.g. *Salop County Structure Plan Draft Written Statement September 1977:*

Policy No 10   The County Council will support the active promotion of employment opportunities in the County.

Norfolk County Structure Plan Written Statement February 1977:

Paragraph 3.3.24   Workshop-scale industries in the Rural Areas will be encouraged.

Lincolnshire Structure Plan 'The Consultation Document' 1977:

Paragraph 7.136   'The County Council will provide, and will encourage the District Councils to provide financial and technical assistance to promote and accommodate new employment in towns.'

Central government has recently encouraged local authorities to play a stronger role im promoting industrial development:

'First, authorities can initiate proposals to acquire sites under the community land scheme. Secondly, local authorities with substantial land holdings will wish to

re-appraise them and to consider the release of such
land for industrial use where there is a demand for it.
Local authorities may play a useful role in partnership
with developers in the developing and letting of industrial estates particularly for small and medium sized
firms. Where proposals to carry out industrial development may be frustrated by lack of public funds to provide
the requisite infrastructure, authorities should, where
appropriate, consider encouraging the developers to assist
with this provision.'[22]

It is against this background that special reports on
employment and industry have been considered by many County
Councils, including Lincolnshire, Salop and Norfolk,
suggesting more active involvement by the Councils. In
Lincolnshire £1,000 has been allocated for advertising as a
first step, in Salop approval has been given for the appointment of an Employment Promotion Officer while Norfolk
County Council[23] has accepted a range of recommendations
relating to increased priority for industry, particularly
in the rural areas.

The greatest potential for the County Councils involved
is probably in co-ordinating the action of the various
bodies and using their existing powers in respect of high-
ways and transportation and education.

The co-ordination role is recognised in most rural
Structure Plans[24] and in Lincolnshire a Joint Development
Committee of County and District Council representatives
was started in 1975. A similar joint working party of
County and District Council Officers exists in most rural
counties, while in Salop a prime role of the Employment
Promotion Officer is expected to be that of co-ordinating
District and County activity.

(c) District Councils

The intensity of District Council involvement in industrial
promotion and development varies considerably, often depending on the situation inherited from pre-reorganisation
authorities and the presence of Town Development or New
Town Schemes. In Norfolk, for example, two of the most
active of the rural District Councils are West Norfolk and
Breckland which include the Town Expansion Schemes at King's
Lynn and Thetford, together with North Norfolk, which includes a former Rural District (Walsingham) which was
heavily committed to industrial development. All three
Councils publicise the advantages of their respective
Districts, buy land, and build and let factories.

In Lincolnshire, only one District, East Lindsey, has
built its own factories, while in rural Salop, Oswestry is
the most active District, being within an Assisted Area;
the District Council pursues a vigorous industrial promotion campaign and owns industrial land.

District Councils, in their capacity as housing
authorities can and often do provide additional incentives
to prospective employers in the form of key-worker housing,
and this is the case with most rural Districts in Norfolk,
Lincolnshire and Salop. A few rural authorities are also

directly assisting local industry to promote its own sales
of goods and services, usually at a 'workshop' - scale.
For example, in addition to assisting local craft industry
through the development control system, North Norfolk
District Council are providing a Small Industries Exhibition Centre at Holt to display locally-made furniture,
pottery etc.

CONCLUSIONS

Four factors influencing the national labour market are
likely to maintain a high rate of unemployment, relative to
past levels, in the 1980s:
    (a)   Slow recovery of the national economy;
    (b)   Increased size of the potential labour force;
    (c)   Structural changes in industry and commerce;
    (d)   Mechanisation and rationalisation.
    In rural areas this situation will be exacerbated by
the special characteristics outlined above and there is
therefore a considerable need for local action.
    Local authority planners will have two roles in this
situation, as advocates and co-ordinators.

(i) Advocacy

Planners will have to justify to elected members at district and county level any financial involvement in the
industrial development and employment field, to assist the
private sector and particularly small firms. Further
submissions to the Development Commission may well be
necessary to supplement local authority resources. Also
the plight of rural areas needs to be stressed to central
government in the bid to ensure that national resources are
distributed so as to reflect rural priorities.

(ii) Co-ordination

Local authority planning departments will increasingly have
to take on the co-ordination of action in employment at a
local level. They already have contacts with other
relevant bodies, and these will have to be widened and
strengthened. The task will involve the acquisition of new
skills and knowledge particularly related to financial
arrangements and the demands of industry.

REFERENCES AND NOTES

1.   *Thirty Fifth Report of the Development Commissioners,*
    H.M.S.O., 1977.

2.   *Regional Statistics (No.12)* H.M.S.O., 1976.

3.   *Agricultural Returns for England and Wales,* Ministry of
    Agriculture, Fisheries and Food, August 1977.

4. *Structure Plan Written Statement and Report of Survey,* Norfolk County Council, March 1977.

5. *Lincolnshire Structure Plan, Background Paper: Agriculture,* Lincolnshire County Council, 1976.

6. *Salop Structure Plan Draft Written Statement and Report of Survey,* Salop County Council, September 1977.

7. *Lincolnshire Structure Plan, Background Paper: Employment and Industry,* Lincolnshire County Council, 1976. See also *Background Paper on Existing Policies,* Lincolnshire County Council, 1976.

8. Michael Whitbread, *Programmes for Inner City Regeneration: The Search for Priorities,* Department of the Environment, 1977.

9. *The Direct Impact of the Relocation of Manufacturing Firms from London to the New and Expanded Towns,* Department of Industry Research and Planning Unit for South-East England, 1976.

10. *Background Paper, County Conference on Unemployment,* Cornwall County Council, April 1977.

11. M.J. Moseley, R.G. Harman, O.B. Coles, and M.B. Spencer, *Rural Transport and Accessibility,* Centre of East Anglian Studies, University of East Anglia, 1977.

12. *First Monitoring Report,* Norfolk County Council, December 1977.

13. Andrew W. Gilg, Rural Employment, in *Rural Planning Problems,* ed G.E. Cherry, 1976.

14. *M.S.C. Review and Plan 1977,* Manpower Services Commission, 1977.

15. M.J. Moseley, *Female Activity Rates in East Anglia, Regional Studies Vol. 12(3),* 1978.

16. C. Hines, *The 'Chips' are Down,* A Discussion Paper , Earth Resources Limited, April 1978.

17. *Economic Policy Review,* University of Cambridge Department of Applied Economics, No 4, March 1978.

18. *Towards a Comprehensive Manpower Policy,* Manpower Services Commission, 1976.

19. *'Rural Development Issues and Problems in East Anglia',* a seminar sponsored by the East Anglia Economic Planning Council and CoSIRA, January 1978.

20. *Rural Depopulation,* Report of an Interdepartmental Study Group, H.M. Treasury, 1976.

21. *Action Plan for Proposed Fens Special Investment Area,* Cambridgeshire County Council, November 1977.

22. *Local Government and the Industrial Strategy,* Department of the Environment *CIRCULAR 71/77.*

23. *Industry and Employment in Norfolk,* Report of County
    Planning Officer to Norfolk County Planning and
    Transportation Committee, February 1978, and to
    Policy and Resources Committee, June 1978.

24. Structure Plan Consultation Document, Lincolnshire
    County Council, 1977.

5

RURAL HOUSING AND HOUSING NEEDS

Andrew Larkin

INTRODUCTION : HOUSING AID EXPERIENCE

The housing problems of the lower income groups in rural
areas have long been neglected by both central and local
government. A major reason for this neglect of rural
housing policy is the fact that local housing needs in
rural areas are not as clearly identifiable as they are in
the major urban areas. By definition the rural parts of
Britain do not contain street after street of decaying
overcrowded houses, otherwise they would not be 'rural'
areas. Yet there is no doubt that there are very real
housing problems in rural Britain. Overcrowding, sub-
standard property, and lack of security of tenure do exist
in small towns and villages and in some areas exist to a
proportionately greater extent than in cities and the
larger country towns.
In 1976 Shelter organised a Housing Aid Tour in Dorset,
operating housing aid surgeries in thirteen different
centres, eleven of which were small towns servicing a
surrounding rural area, including the towns of Blandford
Forum, Sherbourne and Shaftesbury. This operation provided
firm evidence that the poor who are badly housed in rural
areas often suffer greater hardship than their urban
counterparts. There were young families living with their
parents who had been on housing waiting lists for about ten
years, whilst their children grew up in more and more
cramped surroundings. There were parents who had ended up
walking the streets with their children as a result of the
homelessness policies being operated by councils in that
area. There were families and young couples who were
living in winter let accommodation, gaining a brief respite
of independence before eviction and a return to overcrowding and perhaps a caravan site over the summer. There
were families living in rural slums, usually isolated
privately rented cottages with no basic amenities, which
had suffered years of neglect and would probably be rented

out until the point was reached when even the most desperate would not take them. Then they would be either left empty to fall down, or be sold into owner occupation and then improved. This sequence may well be peculiar to the rural areas, and it seems that the most likely way in which improvement takes place is via that process of through movement into owner occupation. The rural areas, like the towns, have seen a reduction in the amount of privately rented housing, but rented accommodation in the rural areas is often not improved and is kept as rented accommodation. Such cases, although they may be isolated examples in any particular village or rural town, when they are brought together, form a picture of general neglect of rural housing problems which has lasted for decades.

RURAL HOUSING NEED AND RENTED ACCOMMODATION

A rough statistical picture of the extent of housing problems in rural areas for those who cannot afford to purchase private accommodation is given by an examination of waiting lists for local authority accommodation.[1] It is important to remember that such figures can only be used as an approximate guide to housing need, since the criteria used by local housing authorities tend to vary widely. Local authorities may also exclude large numbers of people from these waiting lists, by means of residential qualif- ication criteria and rules which prevent certain categories from applying. In the author's experience, such restric- tions tend to be more common and more draconian in rural than in urban areas. Bearing in mind these caveats the picture presented by local housing waiting lists is shown in Table 5.1. There are more people in obvious housing

Table 5.1. Applicants for local authority housing:
England and Wales 1975

Number of Applicants (Households)		% of Total Applicants
Urban stress areas:	597,590	47%
Non stress areas:	661,639	53%
Total	1,249,229	100%

need outside the nationally recognised (urban) stress areas in this country than there are inside those stress areas. The figures in Table 5.1 are the latest available at the time of writing, following the publication in August 1976 of the Department of the Environment Circular 80/76, which imposed restrictions on local authority building programmes. Since that time the relative numbers have changed slightly with the transfer of some authorities from the 'non stress' list to the 'stress area' list. Whilst it is not possible

accurately to analyse the numbers of applicants for council
housing from the so-called 'non stress' areas, in terms of
the numbers from truly rural areas and the numbers from
second ranking towns and cities, the very fact that more
than 53% of applicants live outside the areas of greatest
stress must lead to the conclusion that real housing need
almost certainly exists in the countryside. The evidence
presented in this essay suggests that policies do not exist
to meet this need. If the proportion of households on the
waiting list is measured for particular areas, then
certainly some rural areas do show equal amounts of housing
stress to that found in inner city housing authorities
(see Table 5.2).

Table 5.2. Proportion of households on housing
waiting lists - 1976: selected examples

Authority	Total Households (000s)	Households on Waiting List	
'Urban'			%
Manchester	177.40	14,063	8%
Salford	93.37	5,307	6%
Birmingham	380.02	31,000	8%
Hammersmith	60.37	3,932	7%
'Rural'			
Derwentside	31.95	4,462	14%
New Forest	48.31	4,344	9%
Tonbridge and Malling	33.18	3,600	11%

It is a widely accepted premise that the poorest people
in housing need can only find adequate accommodation in the
rented sector. This is especially true given the restrictive lending policies of building societies and the severe
cutbacks in finance available for local authority lending
for house purchase which have occurred in the 1970s. Even
the schemes which are supposed to promote home ownership
for the less well-off, such as the arrangement by which
local authorities can recommend people to building societies,
have scarcely been used to their full extent by rural
authorities. For example, almost the whole of the mortgage
allocation for Berkshire in 1976/77 was taken up by Reading,
and not by the surrounding rural housing authorities.
Given this reliance of the poor on rented accommodation,
the low income groups in the rural areas are particularly
badly placed because of the overall shortage of rented
accommodation in their areas. The supply of rural housing
in Britain has never favourably compared with the urban
areas. Even when, as before the First World War, privately
rented accommodation comprised about 90% of all housing,
the vast majority of the stock was in urban areas, and,

apart from tied accommodation, country areas generally
lacked such rented dwellings. The decline in the private
rented sector has hit rural areas particularly hard. We
have now reached a position where there are virtually no
permanent regulated lettings in rural areas. The only
lettings that are often available are by wealthy owner
occupiers who may, for example, spend a year abroad and let
their house out at a rent beyond the reach of the lower
income families. As regards local authority accommodation
the rural areas are equally poorly provided for. Traditionally the proportion of council housing in such areas has
been low and some councils appear to be deliberately
adopting policies to keep it so. In Fareham in Hampshire,
for example, the local council has decreed that the present
position, where exactly 14% of the total stock is council
housing, is adequate and they are even ensuring that this
ratio will continue by requiring that, on certain large new
housing estates, only 14% on that estate can be council
housing.

Table 5.3. Council housing stock and building
performance comparing types of area 1974/75

County	Local Authority Housing Stock per 1000 households	New Local Authority houses started 1974/75 per 1000 households	Ratio of households on waiting lists to Local Authority houses built
Buckinghamshire			
Urban	298	10	4 : 1
Urban/Rural	255	24	2.5 : 1
Rural	184	10	7 : 1
Hampshire			
Urban	273	11	2.7 : 1
Urban/Rural	240	8	6.3 : 1
Rural	180	7	9 : 1
Berkshire			
Urban	210	17	3.5 : 1
Rural	165	5	8 : 1

This pattern of low priority for council housing is seen
plainly within the mainly rural counties, by comparing the
local authorities' stock and the building programme of the
urban areas within those counties with the remaining rural
areas. (For this purpose, these terms are defined in
relation to the population pattern of Urban District councils
before local government re-organisation in 1974, i.e. 'urban'
means a district composed almost totally of the population
of a former 'urban district', 'urban/rural' describes a
district which is composed of an amalgamation of former urban

and rural districts, but where the urban population pred-
ominates; and 'rural', in this context, is where the
population of former Rural Districts forms the majority).
The results of such a comparison for three rural counties in
the South-east of England are given in Table 5.3. Of
course, it can be argued that there is a lower proportion
of families in the lower income groups in the rural areas
and therefore there is a reduced need for council accommodation. But if one looks at the ratio of the waiting lists
from those rural areas to the number of council houses that
are being built in a particular year, and over a number of
years, then a very similar pattern can be discerned (Table
5.3).

Having given some rough indications of the extent of
housing need amongst the poor in rural areas, it is important to consider the ways in which those housing needs are
manifested. Just as urban areas have their characteristic
ghettos of decaying multi-occupied rented accommodation, so
too in rural areas, there are characteristic types of
accommodation which tend to be used by the most vulnerable
and underprivileged groups in rural society. Some of these
types of accommodation are described below.

TYPES OF ACCOMMODATION

(a) Tied accommodation

This type of accommodation has traditionally been prevalent
in rural areas, chiefly in the form of agricultural tied
cottages. Agricultural workers have now been given a large
degree of security of tenure by the Rent (Agriculture) Act
of 1976. However, the evils of insecurity in tied accommodation still exist for large numbers of families in rural
areas. In particular, people employed for domestic or
general maintenance and gardening duties, and provided with
accommodation, are often vulnerable to the whims of their
employers. Shelter have been involved in numerous cases
where the conditions of employment and the demands made of
the worker were changed to such a degree that they even-
tually became too onerous and termination of employment and
subsequent eviction took place.

(b) Caravans

Rural areas abound in caravan sites, many of them the
subject of little planning control. In many ways they are
the true ghettos of the rural poor since, however inadequate
they may be, they have far easier access than other forms
of housing tenure. In some rural districts, like South
Oxfordshire, more than 10% of all 'permanent' dwellings are
caravans. Some rural councils tend to use their own or
private caravan sites as dumping grounds for homeless
families and their so-called problem families.[2] Out of
desperation and relative ease of access, some people in
rural areas are paying extortionate sums for basically
decrepit accommodation on caravan sites. For example, in

1977 this author visited a family on a caravan site at
Otteshaw in Surrey. They had paid £2,000 for a caravan
which was so damp that their clothes and bedding became
rotten with mildew in winter. Out of their weekly income
of £43 a week, they were repaying loans for the purchase
of this caravan at a rate of £21 a week plus a site rent of
£3 per week, plus £1 a week rates and £5 a week electricity
purchased from the site owner. That was the direct result
of their having been on the local council's waiting list
for several years while living with their parents and the
situation having become intolerable. Even if the local
District Council were to agree to house this couple they
would still be left with the massive outstanding debt on
the caravan to settle.

The Isle of Wight Shelter group has recently published
a short report[3] on the conditions encountered in caravan
sites on the island, including the supposedly 'holiday'
sites, many of which had become permanent dumping grounds
for the homeless. These sites had often been recommended
by the local housing authorities to desperate families,
even though those same local authorities should be enforcing
planning regulations on such sites, requiring the sites to
close over the winter. The writer visited two holiday
caravan sites at the end of 1977, and both were still open:
they were full up with homeless families who had been
referred there by the District housing department and/or
the County social services department. The local planning
department have apparently turned a blind eye because they
do not want deliberately to create the need to rehouse
dozens of homeless families each winter. It is strictly
illegal for such holiday sites to be used as houses over
the winter, and yet there is evidence that this happens in
many areas of seasonal holiday accommodation.

(c) Winter lets

In a similar way to caravans winter-let accommodation is
often used as an accessible, if temporary, expedient by the
rural poor. In the experience of Shelter, winter lets, such
as holiday accommodation let on a temporary basis out of
season, are normally taken by local families who live for
the rest of the year in adequate housing, often moving from
one holiday let caravan to another throughout the summer.
This writer has met families in Dorset who have followed
such a pattern for over ten years without any local
authority taking responsibility for their permanent rehousing.
Winter lets, apart from frequent overcharging for fairly
basic accommodation, are in this sense not, in themselves, to
be criticised. They are symptoms, rather than causes of
insecure housing, chiefly because many rural authorities
ignore the needs of people who have to resort to them for
want of a better choice. For example, the West Dorset
District Council refuses to house people evicted from winter
lets unless they qualified for rehousing prior to entering
such accommodation - in which case, presumably, they would
have opted for council accommodation anyway.

THE DRIFT FROM THE VILLAGES

Some work which has been done in West Oxfordshire illustrates the way in which policies can penalise village
applicants for council housing as against applicants from
towns within the same District.[4] Firstly, an analysis of
the waiting list for local authority accommodation establishes that in a significant number of villages the demand
for accommodation is as high as in the towns (see Table 5.4).

Table 5.4. West Oxfordshire: proportion of households
on waiting lists in towns and selected villages

Settlement	Estimated Population 1974	Number of households on waiting list	Proportion of Total Households on Waiting List
Towns			
Chipping Horton	5,320	208	10%
Carterton	8,330	207	6%
Witney	13,990	602	11%
Villages			
Bampton	2,160	73	8%
Burford	1,610	94	15%
Clanfield	720	38	13%
Salford	320	15	12%
Stonesfield	1,280	45	9%

Table 5.5. West Oxfordshire: areas of rehousing of
applicants for a council house 1975/76

Village applicants rehoused - 44% of total applicants (151) rehoused

Rehoused in:	Same village	- 80 (52%)
	Another village	- 46 (30%)
	Town	- 25 (18%)

Town applicants rehoused - 56% of total applicants (186) rehoused

Rehoused in:	Same town	- 133 (71%)
	Another town	- 7 (5%)
	Village	- 46 (24%)

Total on waiting list	: 2,121
Village applicants	: 956 (45%)
Town applicants	: 1,165 (55%)

Rural deprivation

Secondly, if we look at the proposed building programme for 1975/76 and 1976/77 we find the following pattern. For 27% of applicants there were going to be no houses built locally; for a further 5% there would be less than 10% built locally; for 14% of applicants there were less than 20% of dwellings to be built locally, and for 4% of applicants there were less than 30% of dwellings to be built locally. For 3% of applicants there were less than 40% of dwellings to be built locally. Thus for 49% of all applicants, between 0% and 40% only of dwellings were proposed to be built locally. Of the proposed dwellings in the Council's building programme, 67% were to be built in the 3 main towns, whereas only 42% of the applicants came from those towns. A study of allocations over an 11 month period in 1975/76 shows a similar pattern of disadvantage to the village applicants, in that a lesser proportion could hope to be rehoused within their own village. The actual figures and proportions are given in Table 5.5.

THE FUTURE: HOUSING STRATEGY AND STRUCTURE PLANNING

It has been established that rural areas already suffer in that a disproportionately low proportion of overall national spending on housing tends to flow to such areas. The most recent government strategy, of arbitrarily delineating stress areas (based on widely inaccurate data for priority spending) at the expense of rural areas only serves to exacerbate this disadvantaged position. Some rural housing authorities have been trying to meet local needs by pur-chasing property in villages, but the municipalisation budgets for that purpose have been drastically reduced in the mid-1970s. The most savage cut, however, has been in the already inadequate house building programmes of rural authorities. Many areas have been left with only a single major project to serve the housing needs of widely dispersed areas, thus exacerbating the trend illustrated above in West Oxfordshire. An illustration of the cuts resulting from central government policy in three different District Council areas in Southeast England is given in Table 5.6.

Table 5.6. Approved housing programmes 1977/78
some examples

Authority	Schemes submitted for approval of D.O.E. for 1977/78	Schemes Approved by D.O.E.	
		Number	Percentage
Waverley (Surrey)	327 units	118 units	36%
Wokingham	537 units	185 units	35%
Windsor and Maidenhead	311 units	129 units	41%

In addition to the above trends in housing policy, the longer term Structure Planning process is tending to reinforce the housing deprivation of rural areas by making it virtually impossible to build cheap rented accommodation in the vast majority of villages. With overwhelming monotony the Structure Plans of rural counties propose a strict limitation on development in rural settlements.[5] Time after time villages are divided into 3 categories. Typically they are identified by such terms as 'potential development centres', 'restraint villages' and villages for 'local needs' only. The argument is that the provision of services in rural areas is so costly that residential development should be concentrated in a small number of the service centres. The logic is that the rural settlements become no-go areas for the working classes since they do not have a sufficient populus to justify support for regular public transport and basic services: a logical sequence which is likely to become a self-fulfilling prophecy. It also has to be accepted that allowing housing development for 'local needs only' will not necessarily go to meet those local needs. Experience shows that it is the poor in rural areas who are pushed out as limited new housing development pushes up house prices. As the Suffolk Structure Plan simply states, 'the listing of large numbers of minor centres and small villages where housing development is to be related to the needs of the local community cannot of itself ensure that the housing permitted will become available to local people...'. The operation of a free market in land and housing means that some of these houses in the villages will inevitably be occupied by people from outside the village and it is surely not rural parochialism to conjecture that the outsiders are likely to be both relatively well-off, and from urban areas, and will displace the poor in many rural settlements. Indeed the restriction on development will help to push up local land values and thus ensure that any housing that is built is of a high standard and beyond the reach of workers in lower income groups. Such development policies tend to be reinforced by the lack of positive policies towards services. The one welcome exception to this approach which the writer has found is in the Norfolk Structure Plan,[7] which envisages large numbers of rural service centres in a positive effort to solve many rural problems, including housing, where they exist, and not just export them to the second ranking county and market towns.

REFERENCES AND NOTES

1. *The Case against the Housing Cuts,* Shelter, 1976.

2. *Caravans in Bordon,* Shelter, 1970.

3. *The Hidden Homeless,* Report of the Isle of Wight, Shelter Group, 1977.

4. *Housing Committee Minutes,* West Oxfordshire District Council.

Rural deprivation

5. M. Rawson and A. Rogers, *Rural Housing and Structure Plans*, Countryside Planning Unit, Wye College, University of London, 1976.

6. Suffolk C.C., *Suffolk County Structure Plan*, 1977.

7. Norfolk C.C., *Norfolk Structure Plan*, 1977.

6

RURAL HEALTH AND HEALTH SERVICES

Tom Heller

INTRODUCTION: THE RURAL PROBLEM

Health service provision in the rural areas of England is
often inadequate and poor access, even to those facilities
that are provided, compounds the problems for people living
in these areas. A recent nationwide survey of health
service provision in rural areas[1] unsurprisingly concluded
that:
> 'the problems experienced by country dwellers in gaining
> access to health care facilities appear to have three
> main causes:
> (a)　transport difficulties arising from the high cost of
> 　　　travel and inadequate public transport;
> (b)　shortage of medical services;
> (c)　centralisation of medical services.'

Of the 226 settlements included in this survey with a
population size of below 500 people:
87% had no doctor's surgery
99% had no chemist
100% had no dentist
100% had no optician.

A large proportion of the first hand comments which are
quoted in this survey indicate that the quality of many of
the facilities that do exist in rural areas is often very
poor and only rudimentary facilities are provided:
> 'The village has an hour long surgery in the local church
> every Monday: there are no facilities, and no running
> water. The doctor can only attend to children or minor
> illnesses, and the group practice is 3 miles away.'
> 'The sub-surgery is in a private house: there is no
> waiting room and there are no examination facilities.'

It is evident that similar deficiencies in both the
quantity and the quality of domiciliary support services,
provided by both health and personal social service departments, are frequently found in rural areas.

Rural deprivation

The problems of gaining access to health care facilities cause the most additional hardship for those
families which are in the greatest need of supportive servic(
services. Within rural communities the problem of access
to facilities of all types is much worse for certain social
groups than for others, and medical facilities are no
exception. In general terms it can be shown that those
groups who are potentially most in need of health care
facilities have the greatest problems of access. The study
of rural transport and accessibility by Dr. Moseley described in Chapter 10 clearly demonstrates that within rural
communities women have much poorer access to all types of
facilities than 'economically active men'.[2] The lower
income groups have similar difficulties, while the elderly
population has the greatest problem of all. It is well
accepted that these are exactly the groups within society
who suffer the bulk of mortality and excess morbidity. The
same survey presents a depressing picture of multiple deprivation among some groups in rural areas, and especially
amongst the elderly: 65% of the 'elderly households' did
not own a car, and less than 30% of all the elderly people
included in the survey 'nearly always had a car available
for their use'. Eight additional factors were surveyed in
the Moseley study all of which are indirectly associated
with the quality of health and health services likely to be
enjoyed by rural residents; these factors were as follows:
    No bus in the parish
    No shop
    Someone in the household physically handicapped
    Income below £1,000 (survey done 1975/76)
    No telephone
    No public telephone within 5 minutes walk
    No bicycle
    No fridge
    Of the elderly households without a car 67% suffered
three or more of these additional factors and 22% suffered
5 or more additional factors. When considering the policy
options for rural transportation it is evident that even
the most optimistic forecast will leave those most in need
of services without adequate access to health service
facilities. Predictions of what is actually likely to
happen to transportation in rural areas in the future
suggest that the problems outlined will almost certainly
get worse. For example, none of the alternative long term
strategies postulated in the Moseley report would result in
a satisfactory level of access to health services (Figure
6.1).
    By any standards access to health services will continue
to remain low in rural areas and the poor accessibility for
the elderly people in particular ensures that the effective
level of services for this group is even lower than a
survey of facilities provided would indicate. The elderly
are, of course, disproportionately represented in the two
most 'rural' English regions, the Southwest and East Anglia.

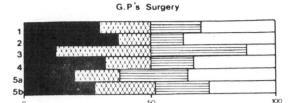

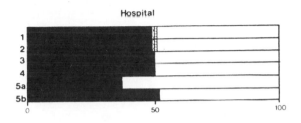

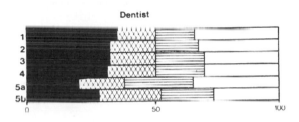

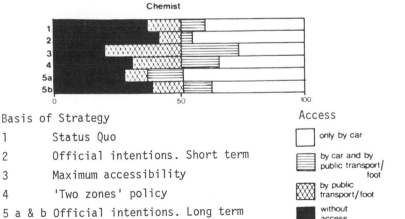

Basis of Strategy

1   Status Quo

2   Official intentions. Short term

3   Maximum accessibility

4   'Two zones' policy

5 a & b Official intentions. Long term

Access

☐ only by car

by car and by public transport/foot

by public transport/foot

without access

Figure 6.1. The North Walsham area: Six possible future planning strategies (numbered 1–5b) compared in terms of the access they afford to different kinds of health facilities. Source: Moseley *et al*. (1976)

Rural deprivation

LEVELS OF PROVISION

Health service statistics demonstrate that provision in
rural areas per head of population is often very far below
the national average. A case study of the distribution of
caring facilities in East Anglia[3] showed clearly that this
large rural region is grossly underprovided in health
facilities of all types. Even within the region there is a
concentration of expenditure on a few 'centres of excellence', and in the main urban centres, which exacerbates the
problem of low levels of provision in the remote rural
areas. For instance, in 1975/76 Addenbrookes Hospital in
Cambridge - which has only 678 beds - received virtually
the same budget as the entire health services (hospitals,
community and preventive services etc.) for the 342,000
people living in the largely rural health districts of
King's Lynn and Great Yarmouth and Waveney. The Addenbrookes budget was itself about half that of the average
for London teaching hospitals (See Table 6.1).

Table 6.1. Concentration of resources
in 'centres of excellence'

Service	Annual Revenue Allocation £ 000
Average London teaching hospital costs, 1973/74	11,773
Addenbrookes Hospital (678 beds including 178 regional speciality) 1975/76	6,542
King's Lynn Health District (population 167,000) all services 1975/76	3,542
Great Yarmouth and Waveney Health District (population 175,000) all services 1975/76	3,700

Source: Heller (1976)

Table 6.2.shows that all of the rural Health Districts
of East Anglia have expenditures of both hospital and
community facilities very far below the national average
per capita. The people living in these rural districts are
in receipt of very poor services, typified by much longer
waiting lists for surgery, as shown in Table 6.3. In the
most rural districts, such as those based on Great Yarmouth
and King's Lynn in Norfolk, patients have to travel to
other districts for many forms of treatment more frequently
than people living in well endowed districts, even within
the East Anglian region. This type of intra-regional
variation can be found in other parts of England.

Table 6.2.   Revenue allocation per
head of population

% Difference of East Anglia from National Average 1974

Health District	Hospital Services	Community Services
Cambridge	-13.4	-50.5
Peterborough	-40.8	-70.6
Great Yarmouth	-51.2	-61.7
Kings Lynn	-51.9	-63.6
Norwich	-17.8	-53.7
Bury	-22.6	-56.9
Ipswich	-22.0	-49.5
East Anglia Region	-27.2	-56.4

Source: Heller (1976).

Table 6.3.   Intra-regional variations in health
services provision: East Anglia (1973/74)

Criterion	Health Districts		
	Cambridge	Great Yarmouth	King's Lynn
Acute waiting list per 1,000	7.7	15.6	10.8
Hospital Revenue: per capita % difference from national mean	-13.4	-51.2	-51.9
Capital expenditure per head: 1948-74	£61.47	£10.90	£20.32
Staff per 1,000 population:			
Medical	0.76	0.42	0.40
Nursing	5.46	3.60	3.83
% of patients treated outside district	12	23	21

Source: Heller (1976)

The Department of Health and Social Security has
recently published a report on geographical resource allocation throughout the health service. This report[4], which
studies the problem of *Sharing Resources for Health in
England,* unfortunately ignores the particular cost implications of providing services in rural areas. Although
weighting is given for the additional costs of employing

staff in London, no mention is made of the special problems
of rural areas in England. Even the proposed ambulance
service costings ignore the increased distances which are
an inevitable corollary of providing a service in rural
areas where the population is widely dispersed.

PATTERNS OF RESOURCE DISTRIBUTION

It would appear self-evident that the situation outlined
for rural areas can only be analysed in relation to the
total problems of service provision throughout the country.
Concentration on the 'problems' in deprived rural (or urban)
areas *as if they were a geographical feature* is highly
dangerous. [5] It is important to study in their historical
context the social and political forces that create the
total picture and which resist change towards more equitable resource allocation. It will only then be possible to
demonstrate in whose interest the present patterns work,
and begin a discussion on strategies that might be required
to influence effectively the forces producing such adverse
conditions.
     It is possible to identify two major patterns of
resource distribution which are present in the health
services throughout the world:
     1. Health services are becoming increasingly urban-
based, capital and skill intensive, based on high technology interventions and focussed largely on the curative
aspects of health care. The obvious corollary is that
rural, preventive and caring services are becoming
increasingly starved of resources.
     2. Those most in need of health care resources are least
likely to have adequate access to them. Areas with high
concentrations of 'marginalised' population, or of the
lower income groups, who suffer the bulk of health care
problems, are provided with the most deficient services.
This 'inverse care law' which was first described by
Julian Tudor Hart for general practitioner services [6] has
now been demonstrated to exist for services of all types. [7]
     These patterns are produced by a variety of forces at
work creating the actual shape and distribution of service
delivery. It is possible to identify the four major forces,
relating to the conflict between medical practitioners and
administrators, to commercial interests, to the media, and
to the membership of health authorities.
     Firstly, within the health service itself the major
dynamic at present remains the struggle between the medical
profession and the administrative group. Over some issues
the interests of these two groups are quite opposite. For
instance the interests of the administrative group lie in
obtaining firm control over the decision-making machinery
of the service and the ability to determine the expenditure
on all items of health service budgets. It is evident that
the doctors will resist any attempt at eroding their
traditional areas of decision-making influence. They can be
seen to fight vociferously for the maintenance of their
right to remain the sole arbiters of all the resources at

their disposal, even when the present treatment of various conditions can be shown to be ineffective, or simply more costly than other alternatives.[8] Similarly, they resist all attempts to introduce measures that would lead to a fairer distribution of doctors throughout the country and dismiss as 'interference with their professional autonomy' procedures such as common waiting lists that would make for a more rational treatment of people awaiting surgery.

Where the interests of these two groups coincide, enormous distortions can occur in the pattern of service delivery. This has certainly been the case with much of the present striving for 'rationalisation' and in particular for centralisation of services in rural regions. It is in the interests of both the doctors and administrators to provide centralised facilities, and the current trend towards massive district general hospitals, 100% hospital confinements etc. should be viewed in this light and with the consequent effects on the services in rural areas that have been described earlier. Similarly, it is in the interests of both of these groups to avoid the introduction of more democratic features into the decision-making structure. This has produced a service in which the ordinary workers and the consumers of the service have only a minimal, muted and automatically outweighted possibility of any democratic voice in the service.[9]

Secondly, acting directly on the patterns of service provision are the commercial manufacturers and suppliers of medicines, high technology equipment and expensive buildings. It is obvious that it is in the interests of these groups to create a service which focusses on the curative, high technology end of the spectrum, thus creating a market for their products. The links between these commercial groups and the decision-makers in the service, both administrative and medical-professional, should not be underestimated. Decisions on vitally important matters of resource allocation are taken in an atmosphere of continual bombardment by irrelevant, inadequate misleading or even dangerous advertising from these commercial companies.[10] A rather flippant example from a doctor's postbag demonstrates this important point:
   'I recently received through the post three Mexican
   jumping beans together with promotional material from
   Napp Laboratories Limited, for Bradilan (tetracotinoyl
   fructose) ... The advert stated (among other things)
   that we cannot promise to make your patients jump, but
   your claudicants will be able to walk further'.

Thirdly, the media habitually exploit and emphasise the technological and curative aspects of the health case delivery spectrum. The concentration on dramatic, interventionist, rare charismatic or transplantable aspects of health services can be routinely observed. This moulds general attitudes to the service and ensures that changes to the present patterns are hard to obtain and will remain unsupported by media coverage.

Finally, the democratic entry into the health authorities is firmly controlled by members of the upper and middle income groups in whose interests the present patterns

of service tend to work.[12] Often the members of these
authorities lack full commitment to the statutory services
because they are able to be, or are already, insured
through alternative private systems such as the BUPA scheme.
The members of these health authorities, by virtue of their
class position and status as members of the authority
receive preferential treatment for themselves or family in
times of need. Similarly, the membership of the newly
created Community Health Councils is predominantly middle
or upper class and does not reflect the class structure of
the communities they purport to serve.[13]

WHOSE INTERESTS DO THE PRESENT PATTERN SERVE?

It might be interesting to sketch out simply how some
interest groups derive benefit from the patterns of service
provision that have been described.

1.   The medical profession

 - The medical profession enjoys practising technological
and interventionist medicine. The most technological
specialities enjoy the greatest kudos and greatest earning
potential.
 - With imperfect controls over their activities they are
able to practise almost wherever they wish, and to practise
and prescribe even those interventions that have been shown
to be ineffective, dangerous or simply expensive.
 - They enjoy very high earnings and are often able to
supplement their earnings from private practice or by
secretly awarded 'merit awards'.
 - They are well represented in the decision-making
machinery. Three out of six members of the District Management Team are doctors, and they are well represented on all
health authorities.
 - They are able to reproduce the present system through
their control of the entry into, and syllabus of, graduate
and post-graduate medical education.
 - They have considerable political and 'industrial'
muscle and are becoming less reticent about threatening to
use it. They use the actual or potential withdrawal of
their labour to protect their own interests and to maintain
the present patterns of service provision.
 - Sanctions against the profession are extremely weak.
The complaints procedure against doctors is firmly controlled by the medical profession at all levels.

2.   The upper social classes

 - The population grouped in the 'upper' social classes,
and those classified in the higher socio-economic groups,
tend to suffer less and to die later from all causes.
 - They have easier access to facilities of all types and
receive better treatment at those facilities than members
of groups socially distant from the providers of the service.

- They are less likely to be concerned about various charges made for services under the present system, such as prescription charges etc.
- They tend to have a disproportionate representation in the membership of all the Regional and Area Health Authorities and on Community Health Councils.
- They are able to opt out into the private system if they feel that the statutory services fall below their view of a satisfactory standard.
- Their ability to 'go private' applies to provision of all types of services, preventive and curative, as well as such services as abortion and long-term care. Group insurance provision is an increasingly common feature of middle-management remuneration schemes.
- They are also more likely to be able to provide facilities for 'self help' or 'community care'. This often depends on economic or environmental considerations. Examples might include the provision of space for elderly relatives, conversion of homes for wheelchairs and the employment of additional help.

3.   Commercial interests

- Many commercial interests are dependent on the present patterns of service provision to provide a market for their products.
- Alternative forms of private service depend on a poor quality service on the public sector and particularly on long waiting lists; who would pay if the statutory alternative was of equal standard or convenience?

4.   The State

- The technological emphasis of medical services has the effect of focussing primarily on the economically active sectors of the community. The elderly, mentally handicapped etc. are provided with poor quality facilities or left to the voluntary sector.
- Curative involvement legitimises the interventionist activities of the State. It is seen to be involved, benignly, in the welfare of the community. This high profile is more profitable than more effective (medically speaking) preventive efforts.
- The present state-operated services stimulate the economy by providing a good market for the commercial sector. Preventive activity, particularly in the prevention of industrial hazards might be expensive and could inhibit economic activity, and hence profitability and net revenue from taxation.
- The concentration on disease and individual illness distracts attention from the wider social economic and political causes of ill health, which is discussed further on the following page.

THE SOCIAL CREATION OF ILL-HEALTH

Although it is important to consider the problems of health services provision in rural areas, this should not be allowed to obscure the more important problems regarding the factors that are *creating* illness in the first place. Such factors operate in rural as well as in urban areas. There is no real doubt that there is a core of 'inevitable' disease, that would afflict a certain number of people whatever type of society is in existence. This is responsive to the usual techniques of detection, diagnosis and clinical management, and there can be no serious doubt that some of this task does require the very obvious benefits of appropriate technological intervention. However, the exact size of this 'core' of inevitable illness is hard to determine exactly, and it is probably not as large as the professional interest groups providing the service would have us believe. The excess mortality and morbidity suffered over and above this can be considered to be socially produced ill-health.

Almost the entire range of diseases presently afflict members of various social classes differentially. In almost every disease category for which statistics exist it can be seen that there is a gradient such that the members of the lower social classes suffer more from that disease, and die at a greater rate from it that members of the upper social classes. There is no evidence that this is genetically determined so it is safe to conclude that this excess mortality is caused by the particular adverse conditions of the social and physical environment available to people in manual and semi-skilled families.

In addition, there are major diseases that are actually being created by our society. There are forces at work creating the types of behaviour that are known to produce disease. Many of the so called 'modern epidemics' fall into this category. For example, we can identify the manufacturers of fast, unsafe vehicles as creating and promoting the major cause of death for 5-35 year olds. In the 35-70 age group the major killers (cardiovascular disease and cancer) are attributable to the behaviour vigorously promoted by the commercial interests of manufacturers such as the tobacco, alcoholic beverage and food processing and marketing companies.

The whole process of production which creates occupational hazards and environmental pollution is itself socially created and also ensures a large and growing health problem.

We can also identify various factors that are destroying the potential for caring and support at family and community level - in both rural and urban areas. Although one should not become too starry eyed when considering actual historical social conditions, there are certainly economic forces presently ensuring very migh mobility of the workforce, rapid demographic change in many rural areas and a destruction of many traditional forms of social organisation.

All these socially created factors are as relevant to the rural situation as to the more frequently considered urban scene. Social class variations in disease levels apply wherever they have been studied, and the major early killers even in the rural areas of Britain are the cardio-vascular diseases and cancers. The destruction of rural communities by the introduction of 'agribusiness' or 'agricapital' and the new patterns of rural life and con-comitant decrease in the caring potential of the commun-ities can be observed, while the hazards of the agricul-tural production process and the side effects of rural environmental pollution are often ignored or under-estimated in discussion on these topics. However, although measurable levels of health appear to show that the inhab-itants of rural areas are 'healthier' than their urban counterparts[14] there is insufficient statistical evidence to demonstrate that such attributes are directly caused by rurality, as distinct from social factors. The patterns that we have attempted to demonstrate, and the forces that produce these patterns are relevant to the study of health and health services in both rural and urban areas.

REFERENCES AND NOTES

1. D. Leschinsky, *Health Services in Rural Areas*, A survey of a selected sample of Women's Institute members, March, 1977.

2. Malcolm Moseley et al., *Rural Transport and Access-ibility*, Final Report to the Department of the Environment, Centre of East Anglian Studies, University of East Anglia, December 1976.

3. T.D. Heller, *The Distribution of Caring Facilities*, A Case Study of East Anglia, School of Development Studies Discussion Paper, University of East Anglia, Norwich, 1976.

4. *Sharing Resources for Health in England*, Report of the Resource Allocation Working Party, Department of Health and Social Security, HMSO, 1976.

5. P. Townsend, Area Deprivation Policies, *New Statesman*, August 6th, 1976.

6. Julian Tudor Hart, The Inverse Care Law, *The Lancet*, Vol. i, p.405, 1971.

7. M. Stacey, People who are affected by the Inverse Law of Care, *Health and Social Service Journal*, June 3rd, 1977.

8. A.L. Cochrane, *Effectiveness and Efficiency*, Nuffield Provincial Hospitals Trust, London, 1971.

9. T.D. Heller, *Restructuring the Health Service*, Croom Helm, London, 1978.

10. G.V. Stimson, Information contained in Drug Advertise-ments, *British Medical Journal*, Vol. i, p.508, 1975.

11. L.F. Prescott, Drug Promotion, *British Medical Journal*, Vol. i, p.574, 1977.

Rural deprivation

12. Julian Tudor Hart, Industry and the Health Service ,
    The Lancet, Vol. ii, p.611, 1973.

13. R. Klein, *The Politics of Consumer Representation,*
    Centre for Studies in Social Policy, London, 1977.

14. E.M. Howe, *A National Atlas of Disease Mortality in the
    United Kingdon,* London, Nelson, 1963.

7

EDUCATIONAL DISADVANTAGE IN RURAL AREAS

Roger Watkins

INTRODUCTION : URBAN V RURAL EVIDENCE

Are your chances of doing well in school affected by the
accident of where you happen to be brought up? Are you
more likely to succeed in education if you grow up in a
rural rather than an urban area? It is possible to answer
the first question with reasonable confidence without being
very sure about the answer to the second.

A number of researchers have marshalled evidence in
which it is shown that children in some regions do better
at school than the children in other regions. The most
substantial work has been by Taylor and Ayres, whose
conclusions are contained in their book *Born and Bred
Unequal*.[1] They have demonstrated convincingly that in
regional terms the educational opportunity available to
children depends to a great extent on the variety and
quality of education provided in the area in which they
live, and have argued that a number of 'non-educational'
factors in the environment' have helped to influence this
quality. These factors included the level of health
enjoyed by parents and children, the standard of social
services, local prosperity measured in terms of personal
incomes and income available to the local authority, local
opportunities for employment, social class structure,
population dynamics, and levels of literacy among parents,
relatives and employers. In particular, Taylor and Ayres
documented the differences between local authorities
1965-1966) in the amount of spending on various aspects of
education. For example, in provision for the special
education of handicapped children one former borough in the
North-west of England spent £244 per thousand of the
population, whilst a neighbouring borough spent £944.
There were similar inconsistencies in the North-east and in
the Midlands. Direct comparisons of this sort are not
always helpful (and cannot in fact be made now because of
changes in the way statistics are published) but in spite
of expressing such caution, Taylor and Ayres concluded that:

'It would seem abundantly clear that the distribution
of resources for special education requires investigation.
Over the country as a whole there is expenditure of the
order of £37 million on this sector of education but, as
in the case of other social services, it is far from
certain whether the expenditure is directed to the areas
where children are in most need. There are no national
criteria for establishing the extent of need for special
education and no national surveys of the local criteria
in use; consequently, little national planning is
possible.'

Unfortunately, Taylor and Ayres were not interested in the
urban/rural comparison and although their data clearly
established that environment influenced educational
provision and take-up, their work does not offer anything
more specific to enable an answer to be given to the second
question posed in the opening paragraph.

Byrne et al.[2] sought to show with a socio-spatial model
of educational attainment that class background, local
environmental factors, local authority policy, local
authority resources and local authority provision were
linked to measures of educational attainment including
rates of staying on and the receipt of awards for further
and higher education. They concluded that 'the level of
educational provision in local authority areas has a very
direct bearing on educational life chances of children in
these areas'. Class background still remained the dominant
influence but the way in which this interacted with the
quality of education provided, it was argued, was the
crucial question. Byrne and his colleagues are less helpful on the rural area question. The only thoroughly rural
authorities they looked at were the Welsh counties. They
noted that here 'high provision and generous patterns of
expenditure sustain exceptionally high rates of attainment'
(p.15) but wondered whether this might not be a special
case. 'It would indeed be difficult to avoid the view that
Welsh culture places a very high value on education and
that this cultural variable has historically played an
important role in the development of Welsh education. What
is not so clear however is precisely how this Welsh trad-
ition works in practice' (p.108).

Conclusions based on objective data about rural
education are clearly hard to come by. Moreover, it must
be remembered that any attempt to interpret the evidence on
these questions is dogged by a number of special difficulties. First, most available data have not been collected
with any idea of an urban/rural analysis in mind.
Secondly, within that data there may well be a confusion
between 'small' and 'rural' schools. These terms are not
necessarily synonymous since there are small schools in
urban and suburban areas as well as in the countryside.
Thirdly, there is not enough evidence, perhaps because the
issues cover sensitive political and professional areas, on
the relationship between teachers' competence and levels of
educational success or failure. However, despite the lack
of firm evidence small rural schools have been a cause of
concern on educational grounds for some time. Typically
these schools are at the primary level and have fewer than

50 pupils on roll and employ two teachers only. They are
frequently organised into two classes for children of 5-8
and 9-11 respectively. The grounds for concern relate to
the difficulty of providing enough intellectual stimulus
from peers at all age levels, of providing teachers who
can offer a full range of expertise across the curriculum
and of providing the specialised facilities which one can
expect in larger schools. To these potential disadvantages
one must add the difficulty of providing pre-school education and accessible opportunities for any follow-up to
school education in the form of further education and
training.

SCHOOLS AND TEACHERS

(i) Buildings

Both the Plowden[3] and Gittins[4] reports on primary education
recognised that there were particular difficulties for both
pupils and teachers in the remote rural areas as a result
of the condition of school buildings. Plowden found, for
example, that the buildings of many country schools 'lag
behind what is tolerable let alone what is desirable'.
(para 4.7.4). In spite of the national school-building
programme which followed the publication of the Plowdon
report, most of the inadequacies of the obsolescent rural
school buildings still remain. Both reports noted the
complaints of headteachers about rural schools without
assembly halls, without gyms, without playing fields, and
even without adequate facilities for staff discussion.
Inside those buildings Gittins found that while some very
stimulating teaching was taking place, 'small rural schools
could also be among the dullest and most dispiriting of
educational environments'. (para 7.5.1.).

(ii) Teaching staff

Many difficulties for teaching staff stem simply from the
fact that, say, Johnny aged 9 may not have any other 9 year
olds in the school with whom he can compare and challenge
himself. All the other children in the school may simply
be younger or older than he. The teacher may be drawn in
spite of himself or herself to concentrate his or her
efforts on those children who do form part of a coherent
group. It is very difficult to provide adequate opportunities for what are essentially group activities, such as
physical education, games and music in small village schools.
This point is made strongly in the recent survey of rural
education by the Schools Council.[5]
    For reasons such as these, Gittins recommended that the
minimum size for a school should be 50-60 pupils, and
Plowden in a similar recommendation expressed this as a 3
class school, with each class covering two age groups.
Both wanted a minimum of 3 teachers in each school. The
implications of this desire for at least 3 teachers on the
staff of a school draws attention to one of the potentially
most disadvantaging aspects of education in remote rural

areas, that of maintaining the quality of teaching. Some teachers, it has to be admitted, have been in rural schools for a very long time, not out of choice but simply because the schools cannot in themselves provide the career opportunities which would facilitate promotion to larger schools. The Welsh report spoke frankly of these difficulties and of the possibility of 'the isolated rural school becoming educationally stagnant' simply because of inertia among teaching staff. Gittins talked of the teacher for whom the rural school was a retreat enabling him to escape from the challenge of new ideas and experiment. 'Outstanding work' said Gittins, 'in one class of a 2 or 3 teacher school might be neutralised by indifferent or inadequate teaching in another. The personality of an individual teacher can have a disproportionate effect on children who remain in the same environment throughout their primary school education.' (para 7.5.2.).

(iii) In-service training

Saville (1977),[6] drawing on his administrative experience with a rural East Anglian authority has pointed out that applications for secondment for in-service training are received less often from rural than from urban teachers. He has described the relative isolation of teachers in village schools from their professional peers, and identified a tendency towards 'rustic reclusiveness'. This means that their initiative to look beyond the immediate educational environment may be dampened by the evident cosiness of village school life, and this applies not only to the primary sector but at the secondary school level as well. Some teachers like that have in fact been identified by Nash[7] in another recent study (1977) based on a review of 26 rural schools. Nash describes some of the teachers in those schools as 'pre-retired', though he does not give us any idea of how many teachers fall into this category. However, it is clear that there is a real danger of underestimating the complexities of the tasks facing the dedicated teacher in a village school. Harvey,[8] a former Assistant Education Officer of a largely rural county pointed out in 1973 that all teachers are expected to respond to the expanding demands of a modern school curriculum, and with languages, social sciences, instrumental music, woodwork, pottery, the one teacher in a small primary school needs the skills and knowledge of a polymath. Of course, the outstanding teacher will doubtless overcome some of these limitations, though at considerable personal cost. To meet the needs of both the 'pre-retired' and the highly dedicated teacher, the local authority clearly has an obligation to provide opportunities for professional renewal and refreshment. But once again, the difficulties of sparsely populated areas are a source of disadvantage. In a two teacher school, attendance on an in-service course by one member involves a reduction of staff of 50%, and the provision of supply teachers has been reduced in most rural authorities in the financial climate prevailing in the mid-1970s. If a course is held out of school time it might involve a journey of 60 miles there and back at the end of

a working day. This is hardly inviting even to the most
enthusiastic teacher, and would be distinctly forbidding to
those contemplating 'pre-retirement'.

Various means of taking resources to the teachers in
rural areas have been the subject of experiments by local
education authorities. A large teachers' centre in Cumbria
has developed an 'out-reach' scheme, and Normal College,
Bangor, has a custom built mobile exhibition trailer, which
is specially equipped to visit schools with materials for
one session courses on reading and language science in the
infant and primary schools, and remedial resources in the
primary school. When that vehicle does visit remote rural
areas, it apparently provokes a very good response from
local teachers.

(iv) Resources

However rewarding such experiments in 'mobile' training may
be, they are clearly only scratching the surface of a large
and intractable problem which probably needs substantial
expenditure for its solution. However, it would obviously
be unrealistic not to recognise that, when there are clear
and absolute limits on the amount of local education
authority expenditure to be shared out, then small schools
with well below the normal teacher/pupil ratio are enjoying
a subsidy at the expense of more typical schools in more
densely populated areas. It is very difficult to make
effective calculations here, but in East Anglia, it has
been estimated that children in small village schools cost
up to three times the average cost per pupil to educate.
Roy Nash[3] in a study published in 1978, based on the costs
of Welsh primary schools, calculated that when, in 1972,
the average cost of educating a child in a Welsh school was
£132 per head, per year, the comparative cost in a school
of 14 pupils was £473 per head and in a school of 11 pupils
£848 per head.

PUPILS

Turning from schools and teachers to the pupils and their
families, a number of commentators have located one of the
sources of educational disadvantage in the pathology of the
rural family. Agricultural workers certainly work long and
exhausting hours for among the lowest wages in the country,
as discussed in Chapter 3. Where income is low and consequently the quality of the housing accommodation and its
amenities are poor, there is a strong correlation with
educational failure, as many studies have shown. It is
hardly surprising therefore that childrens' early education
is sometimes neglected in rural areas, and that on entry
to primary school, country children are sometimes described
as having the greatest difficulty in finding the language
that schooling demands. It is reported from Devon, for
example[10] that teachers report difficulties with children
who have inability to receive instructions and information
because of differing accents, attitudes, vocabulary,
linguistic structures, restricted horizons and lack of

independence. However, one must say that one does not know
how that differs in quantity and quality from problems
which beset children coming into schools in the inner city
areas of Britain. Certainly it is possible to say that
the numbers receiving pre-school education are considerably
less in rural than in urban areas. One estimate has been
that 52.2% of country children received no pre-school
education, compared with 17.9% in the inner city areas.

An OECD/CERI[11] report *Basic Education and Teacher
Support in Sparsely Populated Areas in England* lends
support to the teachers who feel that children in rural
areas lack the motivation and drive for educational success:

'In the (rural) areas under discussion there are indications that parents do not always value education,
especially beyond the primary stage, as a means of self-
improvement or of escape to another sphere. Both they
and their children have comparatively modest expectations
and there is not that pressure on the children to do well
at school which is often noticeable in other, often less
agreeable, areas. The child's happiness and wellbeing is
highly regarded by the parents and schools are sometimes
asked not to push children to hard. This contentment
with one's present way of life also makes difficult the
persuasion of some children to take up further education
courses, especially if that means leaving the area, and
schools, quite deliberately, have to give the children a
taste of the outside world to spark off ambition in them'.

It is difficult to state categorically that attainment
standards are higher in urban as opposed to rural areas,
especially when satisfactory empirical studies exploring
this question are few in number. We have to go back, for
instance, to Barr[12] in 1959 who showed that there are fewer
pupils of high academic attainment and more pupils of low
academic attainment in rural as compared with urban areas.
But his own research pointed to the fact that this was a
function of the socio-economic trends in, and the structure
of the population as of any specially 'rural' characteristics. Low income can be correlated with educational under-
achievement and the published statistics show that there is
a higher proportion of low income families in the country
than in towns. This may help to explain why, in the
Ministry of Education surveys in 1950 and 1957, rural
children did not do as well as urban children in tests of
reading. But unfortunately this picture of the rural
situation is not a clear one. For instance, in a very
interesting survey published in 1977 by Kent Education
Authority[13] teachers had tested in 1975 all the 2nd year
junior pupils (a sample of over 22,000) on the basis of the
'NFER Reading Test AD.' The results were analysed in
various ways according to whether the schools were urban or
rural in location and according to their size. 'Small'
schools had up to 120 children on roll, 'medium' schools
had between 120 and 300, and 'large' schools had over 300.
Neither girls nor boys did their best in the small schools.
Girls did best in the medium sized schools. Boys did best
in the large schools. As far as the location of the schools
was concerned, it was found that boys functioned better in
urban rather than rural schools, whereas girls functioned

better in the rural rather than the urban situation.
Greater complexity still was introduced in a recent study by
Twine[14] who argued that the urban/rural dichotomy was
simplistic, and that a more meaningful model would employ a
continuum based on life-style and social behaviour. He
measured children's attitudes to school on a continuum of
traditional-rural, transitional-rural, emergent-urban and
wholly urbanised. He found that the most favourable
attitudes to school were held by children in the
traditional-rural areas from communities unaffected, in his
words, by the spread of urbanism. There was not a steady
development along that continuum but rather there was a
curvilinear relationship, a wave pattern where the worst
attitudes were held by the most urbanised areas, but in
which the transitional-urban areas provided the best
attitudes after the rural ones. He found that levels
tended to build up again during the emergent-urban phase,
though the level attained does not regain that of the
original situation. In the final stage of becoming wholly-
urbanised, school attitudes began to fall again to less
satisfactory levels.

IMPLICATIONS FOR POLICY

There is clearly a need for a more definite and a more
informed picture of the urban/rural differences in educational attainment, before firm conclusions can be drawn as
a basis for resource allocation. There is evidence that
there are major social circumstances which correlate with
the incidence of low educational attainment in *cities,* and
that to some extent these problems also exist in remote
rural areas. It has not been established either in cities
or in rural areas that these circumstances are the direct
cause of low educational attainment, but it can be confirmed that children who experience such circumstances do
not do as well in school, on the whole, as do children from
more privileged backgrounds. The indicators suggest that,
within the broad definition of rural areas, which encompass
favoured commuter villages as well as subsistence level
living, there are real pockets of social disadvantage which
produce the same low levels of educational attainment in
school as can be readily recognised in inner city areas.
The disadvantaging family circumstances include, above all,
low income and, associated with it, poor housing, social
stress, and low educational aspirations. The additional
rural hazard which compounds the problem is remoteness.
This makes access to facilities that can compensate for
educational deprivation difficult and it is an obstacle to
the professional renewal of the teaching profession.
    What can be done to offset these circumstances? Some
authorities have experimented within their own limited funds
to provide special resources. For example, the Cumbria
County Council's nursery bus scheme allows small groups of
children to enjoy some of the traditional facilities of a
school within the confines of an especially equipped
vehicle. It also provides transport to bring larger groups
together to a central village hall. There is a similar

scheme run by the Humberside authority. These are imaginitive responses to the difficulties experienced by some of the most scattered and isolated communities in England, and represent a deliberate attempt to counter the linguistic and social disadvantages noted earlier, in the Devon survey. Other authorities have similar projects in hand, and there is no doubt that more experiments would be mounted if funds were available. The sources which cities can tap such as the Urban Aid Programme and Section II[15] are of course closed to the rural local education authorities. An apparent dispute between Gwynedd and Dyfed County Councils and the Burnham Committee, about the designation of social priority schools within the counties, seriously affects the extra payments which teachers in the schools may be entitled to, but does not affect the amount of finance available for spending on disadvantaged children. There are hopes that the EEC may be able to make some funds available, but it is too early to be confident about the potential of this additional source of finance. What is needed is a clear recognition by central government of the real difficulties of access to education experienced by families in remote rural areas. The Centre for Information and Advice on Educational Disadvantage, in Manchester, is doing its best to keep the rural context of educational problems in view. Its priorities however, like those of many other agencies, will always be mainly with the inner city areas (and the Centre has a major commitment with the ethnic minority groups). However, this organisation is continuing to gather information and experience about good practice in response to rural disadvantage and it is hoped in this way to identify the gaps in provision and to suggest ways in which they might be filled. The important issue at this stage is to admit that the problem exists and to describe its main feature accurately, as a basis for the allocation of resources.

REFERENCES AND NOTES

1. G. Taylor and N. Ayres, *Born and Bred Unequal,* Longman, 1970.

2. D. Byrne, B. Williamson, B. Fletcher, *The Poverty of Education,* Martin Robertson, 1975.

3. Central Advisory Council for Education (England), *Children and their Primary Schools,* (The Plowden Report), HMSO, 1967.

4. Central Advisory Council for Education (Wales), *Primary Education in Wales,* (The Gittins Report), HMSO, 1967.

5. Schools Council, *Small Schools Study,* (internal paper, not published).

6. C. Saville, Perception of Teachers' In-Service Education Needs in Rural Areas , in *Innovation and Rural Education.* Report of the Tenth Interskola Conference on Rural Education, 1977.

7. R. Nash, The Future of the Village School, in
    Innovation and Rural Education. Report of the Tenth
    Interskola Conference on Rural Education, 1977.

8. R.M. Harvey, The Viability of the Rural School:
    Educational and Social and Financial Aspects, in
    P. Warner (ed), *Rural Education* Aspects of Education
    No. 17., University of Hull, 1973.

9. R. Nash, The One-Teacher School in *The British
    Journal of Educational Studies,* Vol XXIV, No. 1,
    February 1975.

10. Council of Europe, *The Planning of Alternative Pre-
    School Arrangements in an Area where few Pre-School
    Establishments Exist: Devon in the United Kingdom,*
    Council for Cultural Co-operation, 1977.

11. OECD/CER 1, *Basic Education and Teacher Support in
    Sparsely Populated Areas - England* (in press)

12. F. Barr, Urban and Rural Differences in Ability and
    Attainment, in *Educational Research,* Vol 1, No. 2,
    1959.

13. Kent County Council, *Interim Report on County Reading
    Survey of May 1975,* Duplicated 1977.

14. D. Twine, Some effects of the urbanisation process on
    rural school children, *Educational Studies,* Vol 1,
    No. 3.

15. Section II of the Local Government Act 1966 allows LEAs
    in areas with high concentrations of ethnic minority
    children with language difficulties to claim additional
    staffing to assist the teaching of English.

8

RECREATIONAL AND CULTURAL PROVISION
IN RURAL AREAS

Nikki Ventris

INTRODUCTION

The bulk of the literature on recreation in rural areas
turns out to be about the use of the countryside by urban
populations. Where the recreational predilections of rural
residents are treated it is often as part of an anthrop-
ological study or an oral history of a rural settlement.
For example, Frankenberg, in *Village on the Border*[1],
describes the way in which the status and power conferred
by land ownership is reinforced and re-enacted in the
committees of the Garden Produce Association and the Sheep
Dog Society. The titbits and insights into the importance
of recreation in English Rural Communities are to be found
mostly in literature, in books such as *From Lark Rise to
Candleford*[2], and *The Go Between*[3], books that portray the
rural community as a slow moving but delicately balanced
social system, largely dependent on its own resources and
connected only with the outside world at moments of personal
or national crisis.

In the same way that rural-urban differences appear to
have narrowed in the twentieth century, so the policies of
national governments and their agencies and of local
authorities for the arts and recreational provision make
no distinction between urban and rural populations, in the
way that could, and can still to some extent, be shown to
operate in the teaching syllabus of schools in the big
cities compared with those in small market towns. The
Sports Council and its regional offices do not follow a
policy of encouraging 'rural sports' for rural populations.
Nor does the Arts Council's programme seek to promote 'rural
arts'. Both start from an assumption that there is a
national culture and that the needs of all for leisure and
recreation follow national patterns. If there are differences, then these are between regions and do not reflect
any urban/rural dichotomy. One exception to this general
rule is the Development Commission and its agents, the
Council for Small Industries in Rural Areas, whose work is

based on the premise that some forms of industrial development are particularly suited to rural areas. To the extent
that the work of CoSIRA and the Development Commission is
aimed at retaining or developing specific work skills in
the countryside it may have an influence on the availability of leisure time and on the recreational preferences
of those employed in rural craft industries. It is less
likely that these influences spread across the whole rural
population.

The evidence for rural/urban differences in a recreational (or any other) context from community studies is
unclear. Certainly there are differences, but there are
also similarities between villages in the countryside and
'villages' in the cities (or there are similarities in the
ideal types used by the authors to describe these communities).[4] The policies of most of the agencies responsible
for leisure provision assume no innate differences, and
studies of participation in recreation at national and
regional level seldom bother to make a distinction between
urban and rural populations. Where they do, these can often
be explained by differences in the availability of opportunities. To take one example, gardening as an activity
appears to be more popular among residents of the smaller
towns and villages, and this may simply be a reflection of
the greater proportion of houses with gardens.

PATTERNS OF PARTICIPATION AND PROVISION

User studies of facilities in rural areas are few. This is,
of course, partly a reflection of the distribution of
facilities. A study of the Breckland Sports Centre at
Thetford in Norfolk[5] showed some results which are similar
to those obtained at facilities in the London Borough of
Islington.[6] The graph of distance against visits per
thousand population (a crude measure of participation) for
the swimming baths at Thetford and in Islington show a
marked degree of similarity (Figure 8.1). Although the
base participation rate in Islington appears to be higher,
the smoothed curves show almost identical relationships.
Given that Thetford itself is a Greater London Council
'overspill' town and that the area outside the town (more
than 3 km from the pool) is very sparsely populated and
entirely 'rural', in the sense that the settlements are all
small and there is very little employment other than
forestry and agriculture, a marked discontinuity or change
in slope might be expected. This comparison must be treated
with care, however, since the similarities may equally be
due to the statistical techniques used.

The same surveys provide other data for comparison. The
social characteristics of the users of the two pools do
vary, but this is to be expected given the differences in
the resident populations from which the users are drawn.

The similarity of the participation rates shown in
Table 8.1 in these two widely differing areas suggests that
much the same drives and constraints operate in both populations. The differences between age groups within
each set of figures also suggest that these drives

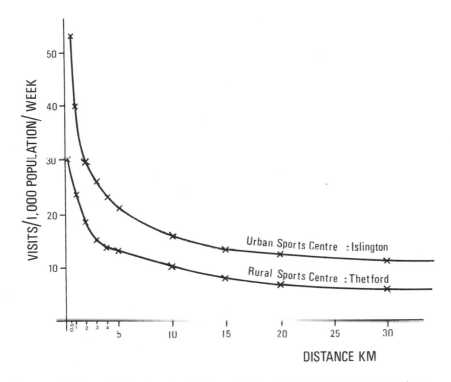

Figure 8.1. Effect of distance on visits to recreation centres.

and constraints have more to do with the individual circumstances of each user than their area of residence. More detailed analysis of both sets of data shows that not only age, but also sex and marital status have much the same influence on participation in both populations.

Again there is a suggestion that the same sets of constraints are operating in both cases, and more importantly that the constraints or influences are operating in a way that has more to do with the social background and family status of the user than the area of residence. This conclusion is made also in a study of access to recreational provision, *Fair Play for All* (1977), which compares the results of several studies.[7] The point is made very strongly that accessibility is not just a geographical measure of travel time, distance, or time-space lozenges[8] but a social measure which reflects the perception of the quality of the recreational opportunity by the potential user, his or her past experiences and the cultural context for a decision about the desirability of the recreational experience.

There is even less evidence to show the pattern of use of arts facilities by rural residents. Since many of the larger cultural attractions are located in large towns and cities, the catchment area patterns tend to show a heavy

Table 8.1.   Recreation participation rates by
age group.

% of each age group participating in recreational activities
in Islington and at the Thetford Sports Centre

Age Group	Islington (% borough population)	Thetford (% population in 15 mile radius)
0 - 9	0.8	0.6
10-14	4.8	3.0
15-19	1.6	2.6
20-24	1.1	1.1
25-29	1.0	
30-34	0.9	)1.6
35-39	0.8	
40-44	0.7	)0.9
45-59	0.4	
60-65	)0.4	)0.2
65+	)	0

dominance of urban populations. The few places where major
arts productions occur which are located in the countryside,
such as the Maltings at Snape, or Glyndebourne, were not
established to serve the needs of the local population.
Rural residents, if they are using opportunities to participate in or view the arts are likely to be doing it in
one or more of three ways: by travelling to urban centres,
or by using local facilities, which tend to be of a different kind, or through the mass media.
    It is evident from the discussion of differences in
participation that the economics of provision for recreation
in built facilities (as opposed to the development of
'natural' resources - a slightly unsure distinction) tend to
put large facilities in large settlements. So that,
although the country as a whole tends to have a hierarchy
of facilities for sport and the arts, ranging from small
multipurpose halls with simple equipment to specialist
facilities with sophisticated equipment and large spectator
areas, the residents of rural areas are likely to find that
only the larger market and county towns can satisfy the
needs of the specialist or expert.
    A study of sports provision in Norfolk[9] showed that
although the type of facility provided in the villages and
smaller towns was limited, provision for the more popular
sports appears to be at a higher (per capita) level than in
the larger towns. Access to major sports provision and
spectator facilities, however, is poor. This study had to
take account of the way in which 'facilities' could be used
for a number of different activities, so that even where
potentially available, a school gym or parish hall might
not be programmed to accommodate a particular sport.
Another limiting factor may be the availability of coaching
or leadership. These comments apply even more strongly to
any attempt to assess arts provision in the rural areas,

where 'facilities' are often less important than 'activities'. A simple count of the number of theatres, galleries and concert halls would give a very misleading impression of what went on in the countryside. On the other hand the list of events in a local newspaper in a rural county such as Norfolk shows that the professional events are all concentrated in the larger towns.

PATTERNS OF INVESTMENT

This distribution of facilities and activities is supported by or mirrored in the distribution of grants and investment by all the agencies concerned with provision for recreation: central government, local government, trusts and foundations, government agencies and commercial organisations.

In 1975-76 the Arts Council of Great Britain spent the largest proportion of its money on grants to professional orchestras, opera, ballet and drama companies and arranging exhibitions, as shown in Table 8.2.

Table 8.2. Regional Arts Associations grants from Arts Council 1975-76

	£ ,000s	% Total	popn. ,000s	% England
Eastern A.A.	183	6	4659.0	10
E. Midlands A.A.	182	6	3209.5	7
G. London A.A.	307	10	7027.6	15
Lincs & Humb. A.	171	6	1372.1	3
Merseyside A.A.	146	5	1575.5	3
Northern A.	561	19	3121.6	7
N. West A.	275	9	4977.9	11
S. East A.A.	142	5	2103.2	5
Southern A.A.	253	8	4907.3	11
S. West A.	272	9	3744.0	8
W. Midlands A.	324	10	5164.5	11
Yorkshire A.A.	206	7	4044.8	9
Total	3,022	100	45,907.0	100

Source: the Arts Council Annual Report 1976.

A relatively small proportion of the total budget went directly to the Regional Arts Associations. This sum, however, does not include the benefits of grants to national companies who toured in the regions, nor does it reflect the regional distribution of grants made by the Arts Council directly to individual companies, centres and projects.

The Sports Council capital grant is more obviously shared out between the regions (see Table 8.3). The total grant in Table 8.3 represents just over half of the capital grants made by the Sports Council in 1975-6, the remainder

Table 8.3. Regional allocation of Sports Council
grant 1975/76

	£ Grant ,000s	% Allocation total	% of population in England
Northern	111	5.6	6.8
North-west	214	10.8	14.4
Yorks and Humberside	204	10.3	10.7
East Midlands	204	10.3	8.2
West Midlands	293	14.8	11.3
East	184	9.3	10.2
Great London and South-east	409	20.7	21.7
South West	133	6.7	7.2
South-west	225	11.5	9.5
Total	1,977	100.0	100.0

going largely to the Trust Funds and a smaller amount to
the National Governing Bodies of Sport. The income from
the Trust Funds goes largely towards the running of
National Sports Centres.

Both sets of figures illustrate the regional versus
national debate which has been going on for some years,
with the regions gradually winning a larger share of the
resources in both cases. It sheds very little light on the
amount of resources deployed in rural areas.

The regional reports give a rather better idea. In the
case of East Anglia, the annual reports of the Eastern Arts
Association make it possible to estimate the way in which
money is distributed between sizes of settlements, as shown
in Table 8.4.

Table 8.4. Grants by Eastern Arts Association 1976-77

Settlement Population	% of Grant	% of Total Regional Population
Under 5,000	17 (3)*	36
5,000-10,000	6	4
10,000-20,000	2	7
20,000-50,000	35 (4)*	16
50,000-100,000	14	17
100,000 +	26	20
total grant to fixed locations	100=43	100
touring/mobile grants	13	
other, non-locational	44	
Total Grant	100	

( )* figure excluding major grants to one and two projects
Source: Eastern Arts Association

Of course, the table should not be interpreted directly to
show an urban bias since the larger settlements act as
service centres for much wider areas. There is support,
however, for the idea that the economics of provision which
restrict the larger facilities to larger settlements is
supported implicitly or explicitly by government and
government agency grant aid policies.
    At a more local level, the policies of local government
follow the same pattern (Table 8.5). In Norfolk, during
the financial year 1976-77, grant aid totalling £90,000
was made to various bodies, groups and facilities. The
area of interest covers a wide range within the sphere of
recreation, but excludes statutory local authority functions
such as libraries and museums services. Again a certain

Table 8.5. Norfolk County Council Recreation and
Arts grant aid 1976/77

Settlement population	% of grant	% Population of Norfolk
Under 5,000	4	47
5,000-10,000	0	4
10,000-20,000	35	4
20,000-50,000	23	5
50,000-100,000	0	9
100,000	38	31
Total grant to fixed locations	100=66%	
non locational grants	34%	
Total	100	100

amount of caution should be used when interpreting this
table. Not only do the County Town and market towns act as
service centres for surrounding 'rural' areas, but some
sports facilities and clubs which received grant aid are
located in the countryside though they bear the name of the
larger towns.

DISTRIBUTION OF FACILITIES: THE ACCESS PROBLEM

The existing pattern of facilities may form the framework
for the distribution of grant aid. Certainly, they are
subject to the same influences. In Norfolk the size of
settlement has a strong influence on the number and type of
facilities to be found. (Table 8.6). Taking the parish
populations (which for administrative purposes include
towns and cities up to the size of Norwich) and examining
the range of facilities available suggests a hierarchy of
provision that follows, roughly, the costs of provision.
A map of the distribution of each of these types of facilities reinforces the impression, showing how many of the
larger or more expensive facilities are concentrated in the

Table 8.6. Hierarchy of Rural recreation facilities.

Facility	Smallest settlement population
Playing field	140
Community hall	130
Badminton court	1,140
Indoor pool	10,800
Squash court	14,800
Cinema	18,900
Theatre	120,000

Table 8.7. Settlement size and recreational facilities in Norfolk.

% of Parishes having a	+100,000	+20,000	+10,000	+5,000	+1,000	<1,000
Playing field	100	100	100	100	95	50
Community hall	100	100	100	100	40	52
Badminton court	100	100	100	100	34	3
Squash court	100	50	20	22	4	1
Cinema	100	100	60	11	1	0
Indoor pool	100	100	40	0	0	0

larger towns and how few there are in the areas of small settlements. This is confirmed by Table 8.7 which shows the relationship between settlement size and provision in Norfolk.

The mapping of facilities and the tables showing the distribution of facilities by settlement size tend to give a false picture. Since the population, even in a 'rural' county such as Norfolk tends to be concentrated in the larger settlements the proportion of the population which is far from facilities is much lower than might be expected from the preceding analysis. Actual distances to facilities are shown in Table 8.8. As with the analysis of patterns of grant aid distribution the picture given of the distribution of facilities is based on 'static' provision. Many badminton 'courts' represent temporary uses of school gymnasia and community halls, so that the limiting factor on provision may be catchment populations rather than settlement size. In the same way, the village hall can also become a cinema; for a period several South Norfolk and North Suffolk parishes were served by a mobile cinema which visited once a month. Travelling theatre groups are occasional visitors to several small parishes, and, of course, there are active amateur

Table 8.8. Distance to recreational
facilities in Norfolk

Distance from a	% of population in private households more than				
	2	5	10	20	30 km
Playing field	7	0	0	0	0
Community hall	14	1	0	0	0
Badminton court	38	17	1	0	0
Squash court	72	46	22	1	0
Cinema	69	48	29	5	1
Indoor public pool	80	52	35	9	1

dramatic societies and music groups in small parishes
throughout the Eastern Region. In this the pattern of
provision has changed: a century and a half ago there were
45 theatres linked by regular touring circuits in East
Anglia, with 20 in Norfolk alone.[10]
    A theme in this discussion has been that it is diffic-
ult to distinguish between urban and rural patterns of
access to recreation; or perhaps more accurately that
'rural' and 'urban' tend to take on particular meanings in
this context. Thus a rural location may have a generally
accepted meaning when applied to a house on an agent's
list, but may not apply as easily to the way of life of the
people living in the house. A great deal will depend on
the education, occupation, place of work and access to
transport of each of the individuals within that household.
Even where the decennial census suggests that a relatively
high proportion of the population own or have access to
private transport (70% of households in parts of rural
Norfolk) there will be individuals who do not have the
recreational mobility implied by that statistic. As the
recent study of Rural Accessibility undertaken at the
University of East Anglia[11] showed, the car or van in the
family tends to be available at the weekend and in the
evenings. This is the period when the majority of the
population have their leisure and, to that extent, there is
a matching of need and provision. However, the distribution of facilities may make it difficult for several
members of the family to pursue different recreational
activities out of the house on the same evenings. Public
transport where it exists is organised primarily around the
journey to work and to a lesser extent shopping and other
day time visits to service points. Evening and weekend
recreational trips are not well served.
    For those with access to private transport and a desire
to use a particular type of facility, the journey times are
often no greater for rural residents than they would be for
urban residents to an equivalent facility. Comparison of
journey times to the swimming pools at Hornsey Road,
Islington and at the Breckland Sports Centre, Thetford, shows

Table 8.9. Travel modes to Thetford swimming pool.

	% users arriving by:				
Distance	car	m/c	bus	train	foot
Under 1 mile	44	1	0	0	48
1-2 miles	62	3	2	0	30
2-5 miles	*	*	*	*	*
5-10 miles	95	0	2	1	0
10 + miles	91	0	6	0	0

* numbers small, % misleading

similar patterns, while those for the distances are rather different.

Those who depend on public transport, and it should be remembered that a large proportion of swimmers are under twenty, either do not wish to or cannot travel long distances to pools in rural areas, as the study, again, of the users of the Thetford pools shows. (Table 8.9).

The difficulties of access to Thetford facilities do not, therefore, depend on the size of settlements and their distribution alone, since there are some groups in the population which find it relatively easy to overcome the barriers of distance. Others, however, have fewer transport resources or are prevented, by factors which have nothing to do with transport, from taking up recreational opportunities. The groups who are not aware of, and who do not wish to use, recreational facilities or opportunities offered in a formal way, are exhibiting differences in cultural norms and expectations which are related to the institutions of work and education, and are not caused by rural/urban differences. They are found in central city contexts[12] as often as rural areas. The lack of desire or ability to participate, if it is a problem,is not a rural problem.

The rural recreational 'problem' is really one for the providers, and it stems from a conscious desire, or an implicit methodology which seeks to provide all residents in a given administrative area with the same standards of service. As has been pointed out, this poses a number of problems when there are within the area wide variations in population density.

CONCLUSIONS: AGENCIES AND POLICIES

Statutory service provision in rural,areas, for example, health (Chapter 6), education (Chapter 7), and Social Services (Chapter 9), is almost always more expensive per capita, and may also be of a lower standard than that in urban areas. Recreational providers do not have to accept the same universal standards, but they are faced with a situation where the people living in villages and small market towns are able to see what sort of facilities the larger towns and cities possess, not least through the efforts of the mass media.

Ameliorative action to redress some of the imbalance in the distribution of recreational opportunities between larger and smaller settlements tends to focus on one of three aspects, location, scale or transport. In fact all three are interconnected and appear as separate approaches only because they reflect differences in the executive powers of the agencies involved in recreational provision. Local authorities, and to a lesser extent, the regional councils or committees of central government agencies and of the Water Authorities, see recreational planning as part of forward planning and, therefore, as part of a concern with the relationships between housing, employment, service provision, infrastructure investment and communications, resulting in policies and action set in a strong locational framework. There is little evidence that these policies attempt a redistribution of resources to favour the smallest settlements. What usually emerges is a compromise in which such resources as are to be made available in areas outside the largest towns and cities will be concentrated in relatively few settlements which act as local service centres. As shown in the recent study of rural access-ibility[13], such policies may increase job opportunities and help to make shopping trips or visits to the doctor easier, but they do relatively little for recreation.

The locational policies are supported by both the capital investment and grant aid policies of the same local authorities and by the decisions taken by the commercial sector, so that a series of implicit scale and locational policies emerge. Thus a hierarchy of appropriate provision is planned, in which settlements can be expected to provide a range of facilities related to their size, from playing fields and a hall at the village scale to theatres and sports centres in towns of over 50,000 inhabitants. As the analysis of grant aid distribution showed, there is nothing redistributive about these policies either; in fact the resources are concentrated on the larger settlements.

Redress in favour of smaller settlements is made by grants to support touring companies or transport subsidies to the visitors of cultural or recreational facilities. As in the case of the capital grant policies, there is an implicit scale factor in operation. The grants awarded by the Arts Council of Great Britain allow national companies to tour the provinces, while regional arts association grants allow provincial companies to tour market towns and villages. Thus the picture produced by the analysis of the distribution of grant aid by settlement size is not complete without a consideration of the effects of grants for touring.

The responses of agencies responsible for arts and sports provision are significantly different in emphasis when one examines their policies with regard to provision in areas of low population density. Arts provision tends to concentrate on funding people, whereas sports provision is geared to buildings; although there is a major fund for housing the arts, and some money for activities such as

'Sport for All' days. This difference is less evident at national or metropolitan level since much of the expenditure goes into the maintenance of centres of excellence, but seems to reflect what has been a fundamental difference in attitude which is apparent also in the way in which local authority grants are given to each sector. Those groups which are concerned about provision in rural areas are concentrating on community arts. In East Anglia, in the Southwest, Lincolnshire and the North of England, there are a number of attempts to provide villages with a variety of entertainments, based on resources available within the community, although some organisation, equipment and technical direction often have to be supplied from outside. The community arts movement is not restricted to rural areas, but is found equally in the cities. It is the equivalent in arts provision of 'Sport for All', without the publicity and support of a national campaign.

The Sports Council booklet *Provision for community recreation in rural areas*[14] lays emphasis on dual use and joint provision, multi-purpose facilities and the use of buildings surplus to other needs. It also suggests that the local authorities must give more attention to the needs of recreation in local and structure plans (Chapter 9) and in their new role of public transport coordination (Chapter 10). This area of intervention has received the least attention of all possible strategies for redressing any urban/rural disparities in provision. There have been some experiments in unconventional forms of public transport in rural areas (Chapters 10 and 13) but the extent to which they contribute to increasing accessibility to recreation depends largely on how they are organised. Schemes based on voluntary local drivers gain in flexibility and can be directed towards group trips into town in the evening or to the beach at weekends. Collective jollity is not everyone's preferred form of leisure, however, and there is obviously a more limited range of spontaneous or individual recreations available in the countryside than in the larger towns. Changes in legislation and in the policies and attitudes of central and local government which help to improve mobility are likely to improve accessibility to recreational provision.

The problems of recreational provision for rural areas have strong similarities with those experienced in other forms of service provision in rural areas and with the problems faced by the agencies responsible for recreation in urban areas. The differences are due in the first instance to the statutory framework and in the second to the geographic context. Rural residents with average or above average incomes have, effectively, available to them the same range of recreational opportunities as their urban counterparts. Those with lower incomes and those who for other reasons, such as age, do not have easy access to private transport have a different range of recreational opportunities, almost the mirror image of their urban counterparts. The universals are the pub, television and the newspapers. Because of the framework of provision and a set of more or less widely accepted constraints, policies for recreation, in the formal sense, are likely to continue

to be related to the scale of rural settlements. The
implication is that any public money directed to the smaller
settlements will be put into flexible multi-purpose facilities, into supporting travelling coaches, animateurs,
entertainers or organisers, and into improving accessibility
to existing facilities in the larger settlements. This will
still leave some groups and individuals at a relative
disadvantage and should continue to be a cause for concern
to those interested in the quality of life in rural areas.

REFERENCES AND NOTES

1. R. Frankenberg, *Village on the Border,* Cohen and West,
    1957.

2. F. Thompson, *Lark Rise to Candleford,* Penguin, 1973.

3. L.P. Hartley, *The Go-Between,* Hamish and Hamilton, 1953.

4. R. Pahl, The rural-urban continuum , in R. Pahl (ed.)
    Readings in Urban Sociology, Pergamon, 1968.

5. This survey was carried out by Norfolk County Planning
    Department in 1977.

6. J. Crofts, J. Naumann, S. Peacock, N. Ventris,
    Islington Recreation Study, Polytechnic of Central
    London, 1974.

7. M. Hillman and A. Whalley, *Fairplay for all, a study
    of access to sport and informal recreation,* P.E.P., 1977.

8. T. Carlstein, *A Time Geographic Approach to Time
    Allocation and Socio-ecological Systems,* Department of
    Geography, University of Lund, 1975.

9. *Sporting Facilities in Norfolk, Consultative Draft,*
    Planning Department, Norfolk County Council, 1978.

10. E. Grice, *Rogues and Vagabonds: or the Actors' Road to
    Respectability,* Terence Dalton, 1977.

11. M. Moseley, R. Harman, O. Coles, M. Spencer, *Rural
    Transport and Accessibility,* University of East Anglia,
    1977.

12. *Recreation and Deprivation in Inner Urban Areas,* HMSO,
    1977.

13. M. Moseley *et al., op. cit.*

14. *Provision for Community Recreation in Rural Areas,*
    Sports Council, undated.

9

THE ROLE OF STATUTORY AGENCIES
IN RURAL AREAS: PLANNING AND SOCIAL SERVICES

Martin Shaw and Dick Stockford

INTRODUCTION : CONCEPTS OF SOCIAL PLANNING

The extent to which statutory agencies can, and should,
affect the physical and social environment of communities
has long been the subject of debate. On the one hand,
charges of 'social engineering' are laid at the door of
those who consider that the duty of the statutory
agencies is to aid the evolution of the 'good' society.
At the same time, there appears to be an increasing concern
with the wider social (and environmental) implications of
the intervention of statutory agencies, with the extent to
which these agencies do or do not account for 'social
costs', and the effect of such intervention on personal
choice.
    Of course the vantage point of the critic will have
much bearing on the particular position that is taken up,
but one problem that emerges from contributions to such
forays relates not so much to the extent of interference,
or lack of it, but the extent to which statutory agencies
are able, for good or ill, to affect the quality of life of
individuals and communities.
    The central theme of this chapter is the degree of
influence over social change which local authorities can
expect to have in a rural area, in the context of their
present duties and responsibilities. In examining the
function of statutory authorities in relation to some of
the social issues in rural Britain we concentrate on what
the authorities can do, rather than on what they should do.
At the local level, two local authority agencies which
might be expected to have a particular influence on, and
concern for, the social aspects of community life, are the
Planning and Social Services Departments and Committees.
But since their expenditure together typically represents
only one-tenth of the total local authority budget,[1] their
influence is likely to be limited and, in part at least, is
deployed in attempting to assess, appraise, and subsequently

direct the efforts of various other statutory and non-
statutory bodies involved in the process of change.

In the remainder of this introductory section we
examine the ideas of 'social planning' which have developed
in response to the recognition that both Town and Country
Planning, and Social Services, as traditionally conceived,
can only hope to assist in the solution of a limited range
of social problems. This is followed by an appraisal of
the philosophy behind Planning and Social Services legislation, of the problems of achieving social objectives by
implementing rural settlement plans, and of identifying and
meeting the needs of particular social groups in rural
areas. Finally, we consider the case for a more corporate
approach by statutory agencies to rural problems.

Williams has classified concepts of social planning
into two groups,[2] based on those which equate social
planning with all planning and those which view it as an
aspect of planning. For practical purposes, however, the
following four interpretations are the most relevant. They
are set out below, starting with the broadest concepts and
ending with the narrowest view.

First, there are concepts of social planning based on
the *aims* of public agencies, defined by Eversley as those
authorities whose activities are geared to 'the pursuit of
improvements in the living standards of the (urban)
population'.[3] This implies that public authorities will
exercise a strong political advocacy role, irrespective of
the specific statutory responsibilities of the authority.
A second, and related broad view, is that social planning
is the process of integrating physical, financial, manpower
and management programmes with social ends in view. This
is the concept propounded by Cullingworth in his *Social
Content of Planning*.[4] Thirdly, some commentators view
social planning as an aspect of Town and Country Planning,
dealing with the 'social implications' of the statutory
planning process in Britain; in Cherry's words it can be
defined 'as the contributory specialism within town planning
itself, dependent on the parent subject, but with its own
coherent range of interest and study'.[5] The fourth interpretation is based on the social welfare role of public
authorities, and puts social planning within the framework
of Personal Social Services and similar agencies in Britain
rather than being allied to the formal planning process.
Certainly in America the idea of social planning has its
roots much more clearly in the activities of health and
welfare authorities than is the case in Britain.

THE LEGISLATIVE BASIS OF SOCIAL PLANNING

The task facing rural Planning and Social Services
authorities tends to differ both in degree as well as in
kind from that facing urban agencies - but the significant
differences are of degree. Clearly different phenomena do
manifest themselves, but problems of accessibility to
services, information and expectation regarding services,
costs of service provision and types of service, remain

issues in both urban and rural areas. The rural areas are, however, less populated and, as such, pose several questions more sharply, since unit costs of services almost invariably rise with the added-in costs of transport and the virtual inability of rural authorities to achieve economies of scale in capital projects.

Against this background, what legislative tools do these agencies have with which to influence community life and satisfaction?

Statutory physical planning in Britain emerged during the first half of the present century in response to *social* issues, of heavy mortality, poverty etc., but the legislation was geared to the control of *physical change*. Indeed one of the main pressures in the 1960s for the radical overhaul of the 1947 Town and Country Planning Act was the need for the planning system to have more regard for social factors. The 1968 Town and Country Planning Act and subsequent legislation therefore called for an explicit account to be taken of the social needs and problems of an area in the framing of policies. Despite this emphasis, the policies and proposals themselves were still to be focussed on 'land use' and 'development' and neither the current planning legislation for the associated Regulations[6] are specific about the social content of surveys or plans. The Department of the Environment understandably has felt it necessary to prepare a special note to examine the place and scope of social considerations in development plans.[7]

The starting point for the Development Plans note is that physcial development 'both reflects and conditions the values, problems and way of life of the population ... plans acquire their significance only insofar as they help to achieve the hopes or to solve the problems of the community with which they are concerned'. Despite this laudable view of the role of statutory plans the note's philosophy does not amount to 'social planning', however defined, and it falls clearly into the realm of dealing with the 'social implications' only of physical plans. Moreover, it can be criticised in the present context on two grounds. First, it fails totally to relate this type of local authority activity to the Social Services responsibilities of County Councils in rural areas - which reflects the total absence of such a link at central government level. Secondly, while trying to cover all levels of planning it reveals an essentially urban approach to social issues, particularly when discussing the use of indicators of social 'need'. The official Department of the Environment view of the social function of statutory planning thus distinguishes between the development *plan,* concerned with the physical environment, and the planning *process,* which provides the opportunity for considering a wide range of topics - including social issues - but goes no further than this.

In contrast the Social Services legislation is directly related, not surprisingly, to the improvement of life chances and standards for individual groups of clients. The most recent of these statutes is related to provision for children, but perhaps most significantly in terms of service provision in rural communities, the Local Authority Social Services Act of 1970 established the Social Services

Departments, which enshrined many of the principles contained in the Seebohm Report.[8] This report recommended strongly that the Personal Social Services should encourage the development of community identity, and that Departments should be involved in social planning in concert with 'other Departments of Local and Central Government concerned with the community environment', and that 'designated areas of special need should receive extra resources, comprehensively planned, in co-operation with (other) services'. There is little doubt from the Report that the special areas related much more to urban than they did to rural areas, mention being made of 'areas of rapid population turnover, high rates of delinquency, child deprivation and mental illness, and other indices of social pathology'. There can be little doubt that the development of a community-identity in an urban area presents problems, but how much more so in sparsely populated, under resourced and inaccessible rural areas?

The development of non-institutional services has been the basis of much statutory direction, central government guidance and professional thinking, since the Seebohm Committee Report was published. Much had, anyway, started before that date. For example, the philosophy behind the 1959 Mental Health Act was to diminish the in-patient population of the old Mental hospitals, and to promote the care of the mentally ill in the community. Influential guidance on the care of the mentally handicapped was issued by the Government in 1971[9] and this, too, strongly advocated the role of day and community care. Subsequent advice and legislation continued to emphasise this feature, and the recent White Paper on Priorities for Personal Social Services Spending[10] again singles out the important role of caring for clients in the community. Thus, it seems clear, that as far as central government is concerned, there is an expectation of both a planned and a community orientated service in the future.

How can this statutory framework be related to the social needs of rural areas, expecially in terms of the resources available? This is the question discussed below, in relation to the implementation of statutory plans and the provision of personal social services to rural communities.

FORMULATING AND IMPLEMENTING RURAL SETTLEMENT POLICY

The physical planning system provides one means by which public authorities can alleviate some of the difficulties posed by a scattered settlement structure and an increasingly centralised pattern of services, facilities and opportunities. In this context the forward planning and development control activities of County and District Councils can be seen as a 'preventive' approach to rural deprivation: at best, in the long-term, the planning system can help resolve some problems, and at worst can seek to avoid adding to the number of people who suffer from a lack of access to opportunities. This section examines the reasons why social factors have only rarely been given their full weight in the formulation of rural settlement plans,

and some of the problems which are involved in the implementation of statutory planning policies to achieve social
objectives.

The priorities of the early postwar County Development
Plans were closely related to the physical environmental
problems of rural Britain, and in this respect they
reflected contemporary attitudes towards rural life. In
Devon, for example, five 'guiding principles' informed the
work of those who, in 1949, were preparing the first county
plan: these objectives were to assist agriculture, to
protect the landscape, to provide facilities for tourism,
to preserve trees, and to protect mineral resources. [11]
The legacy of this type of approach is one reason why
social factors have been of little explicit significance in
most rural settlement policies. Indeed, to continue the
Devon example, the prime determinants of the pattern of
rural settlement since the mid-1960s have actually been
outside the direct control of the statutory planning system:
the provision of, or, more importantly, the lack of
provision of sewerage facilities has apparently been a more
important factor than any other in the development control
process. [12]

A second and practical influence on the social input to
the formulation of rural settlement policies is that of
resource availability. This has been conventionally translated into a cost-minimisation objective, so that where
'economic' versus 'social' arguments have arisen the former
have tended to predominate. In particular, the basis for
rural settlement policies involving the classification of
villages by size is to be found in the economies of scale
associated with the provision of various services. Recent
studies of alternative patterns of village development have
demonstrated the higher per capita cost of providing
services to housing dispersed among many small villages
(even adopting a 'marginal costing' approach, and taking
account of changes in the technology of utility services). [13]
However, none of the first round of rural Structure Plans
has attempted a full 'marginal' costing of the continued
provision (and extension) of services to small villages,
and few rural settlement strategies have been formulated on
the basis of a genuine *social* accounting framework. Such
an approach should attempt to identify who gains and who
loses as a result of planning policies - in terms of social
benefits and disbenefits, as well as in terms of the
economics of service provision.

In part, the reason for the relative neglect of social
factors at policy formulation stage is probably due simply
to the difficulty of measuring the social attributes of
policy options. Ayton (1976) has argued that a distinction
can be drawn between the measurable aspects of rural
settlement, relating to services, and the less tangible
'community' aspects. [14] This is, however, an over simplif-
ication, since the level of rural service provided
(particularly in the sphere of education) is notoriously
difficult to assess. In contrast, there are some aspects
of community development which *can* be measured, as recent
studies in Norfolk have demonstrated. [15] More effort at
assessing social consequence of village development is

essential if social factors are to be given their due
weight against the more familiar economic criteria.

Finally, the way in which planners tend to view 'need'
in rural areas helps to explain the lack of any clear
social dimension to much rural settlement policy. This is
particularly evident in the frameworks which are used as a
guideline to the location of new housing development.
Planners have frequently been criticised for their failure
to build into the policy formulation process the interests
of different social groups, and for their tendency 'to
identify with the group that can afford change, rather than
the group that needs it'.[16] Certainly, planning authorities
in rural areas have responded less to housing 'need' than to
'demand' (need backed by purchasing power). This generally
contrasts with the stance adopted by urban planners who
have tended to take a view more closely aligned to the
'need' approach of housing departments, based on the inadequacy of the existing housing stock and the size of local
authority waiting lists. It is, of course, true that the
quality of housing stock is conventionally measured in
terms of unfitness criteria which have most relevance in
urban areas, and that rural housing waiting lists are
notoriously volatile as indicators of need. Nevertheless
rural planning strategies have taken insufficient account
of the aims of local authority housing policy while
attempting to grapple with the pressures for private housebuilding. Some local authorities have tried to identify a
specifically 'local' component of need, and to make
provision for meeting that need in their overall policies.
Such attempts have received less than enthusiastic support
from central government when the Secretary of State for the
Environment has published his modifications to County
Structure Plans, partly because of the problems of using
the statutory planning system to implement a policy based
on such a concept of need: one example of the problem is
discussed below.

It is the problems of implementing 'socially-based'
policies for rural areas through the medium of the statutory planning system which accounts for much of the gap
between society's expectations of planning, and the results
in practice. In rural Britain, the fundamental changes in
employment have been largely outside planning control, and
only where there has been pressure for population growth
have planning authorities been able to exercise much
influence over the pattern of housing. Even in this
situation, for example in the Southwest and in East Anglia,
probably as much new housing development has taken place
outside as within the settlements selected for major
development. And where overall strategic policies are
translated into development control practice it is important
to bear in mind that the control of housing development will
usually have only a marginal impact on the social life of
villages. The indirect and limited influence of the statutory planning system on the social problems which face
rural communities is rarely recognised and is fundamental
to an understanding of the role of local authorities in
influencing social change. The nature of this influence is

discussed below.

First, development control can only guide the scale and location of new village development, whereas most changes in households - and related social changes - take place within the existing stock. This has an immediate bearing on the oft quoted problem of an increasing lack of 'social balance' in villages in the 1970s. In much of the South-west and East Anglia, the age-structure of most villages has become increasingly top-heavy, due both to the loss of younger persons and an influx of the elderly. While it is true that in many rural counties the most marked shift towards an elderly age-structure has taken place in the smallest villages, it is also clear that to have allowed more new speculative housing development would probably have created more social problems than it would have solved. The classic planning dilemma in such villages is whether to opt for expansion in the hope of increasing the competitive position of first time and local house-buyers - and threatening the character of the village, or of limiting development and risking forcing up local house-prices. The equation is rarely as simple as this, and reaches the extreme case where there is a significant pressure for second homes. The imposition of 'personal' conditions on a planning permission is only appropriate in a limited range of circumstances, for example to limit the occupancy of a house to persons employed in agriculture, and the use of conditions to influence the age-structure of rural residents is rarely effective. This is particularly true when the type of house which could assist young first-time buyers would also be the type which would attract elderly migrants, able to outbid young households in the rural housing market. The alternative to planning conditions is the use of agreements under Section 52 of the Town and Country Planning Act to limit the occupancy of new houses. Although such agreements cannot be related to the age-structure of occupants they can, in theory at least, be used to discriminate in favour of applicants with a 'local' need for new housing. From October 1977, the Lake District Planning Board began to restrict planning permissions in certain villages to applicants who worked 'locally'. The Section 52 agreement defines 'local' by specifying a maximum distance from home to job, and the distance varies for each application, depending upon the availability of housing and jobs in the district. However, the legal validity of this form of development control is somewhat dubious, and estate agents were alleging that the result was pushing up house prices within six months of the policy being implemented. A by-product of such a policy can be to focus the attention of second-house buyers on existing houses, which are not open to planning control, and thus take the prices of the existing stock further beyond the reach of local people.

A second problem of implementing a 'social' planning policy based on the development control system is that, quite apart from the age or local roots of the population, the other social characteristics of a growing rural community cannot be guaranteed, even if the growth policy is implemented as planned. Since statutory planning can only directly influence the size of villages or their rate of development it is necessary to pose the question: do those physical attributes of rural communities which are amenable to planning control have real significance for the social problems and life of rural communities?

Several social characteristics of villages have been analysed in Norfolk in relation to the controls which may be exercised by planning authorities, relating to group activity, standards of behaviour and social cohesion.[17] The range of active local groups is an important determinant of the social opportunities available in villages, and the Norfolk studies suggest that the incidence of new groups forming has been highest amongst growing parishes, while that of existing groups becoming defunct is greatest among villages with a declining population. However, there are clearly some aspects of the changing support for village organisations which are *not* explicable in terms of the amount of development or the nature of population change in individual settlements. Although it is apparent that the implementation of a 'growth' policy in selected rural parishes could stimulate the level of activity in community organisations the evidence also suggests that a planning policy which stabilised most villages at their present population level would have no negative impact on local group activity. Part of the blame for a deterioration in standards of behaviour has been placed on the mistakes of statutory planning, and though this sort of crude determinism cannot be substantiated, there is some, albeit limited, evidence of a disproportionate increase in vandalism in villages of above 5-700 population. As with trends in community group activity, factors other than the population characteristics of villages may have significance. For example, the two parishes in the rural Norfolk sample where vandalism was out of all proportion to size or rate of growth were both holiday centres - though again, this type of problem could, of course, be indirectly a attributed to planning decisions. The other social dimension which can be related to the nature of physical changes in villages is the social cohesion or 'sense of community' which is perceived by residents. One indicator of this elusive concept is the extent of participation in community events: the Norfolk studies reveal a very high positive correlation between the degree of participation and village size. A second survey found that feelings of local 'identity' were also strongly and positively correlated with the most compact settlements - whose form in the long-term, can be shaped by planning policy. However, the most crucial factor associated with the social cohesion of communities was the existence of certain village services, and in particular the presence or absence of a primary school.

It is changes in the pattern of rural services and facilities which present the third basic problem for statutory planning. The continued withdrawal of services from small rural communities has been well documented in recent surveys,[18] but the relationship between this process and the powers of planning authorities is less clearly understood. The size of most villages in rural Britain is well

below the population threshold at which the majority of
services can be supported, or retained, but the relationship between population size and facilities is not a simple
one. Even in much of southern and eastern England, where
the rural population has grown from the 1960s, the loss of
services has continued as population thresholds have risen
and as the realisation of economies of scale in the public
and private sector has resulted in the withdrawal of
services. It is frequently alleged that in many cases the
further decline of village services will be induced by the
decisions of planning authorities who will prevent further
development *because* there are no services. Although there
is some truth in the circularity of this process, the
evidence of recent changes suggests that the number of
village facilities such as schools, child health clinics
and shops would continue to fall, regardless of the amount
of development which was permitted in individual small
settlements. An East Anglian case study[19] has shown that,
even assuming that a policy of dispersing new development
among the smaller villages were pursued, in the context of
rapid overall population growth, the overall level of rural
service provision would be unlikely to be raised. Indeed,
in the above case study area, the proportion of villages
losing services in the 1960s was just as high (two thirds)
among growing villages as among those where population size
had not changed. The solution to rural service problems
must clearly lie in the sphere of innovation in the
provision of the services themselves, rather than in the
manipulation of the pattern of development via the planning
system.

FORMULATING AND IMPLEMENTING RURAL SOCIAL SERVICES POLICY

The overall aim of most rural social services policy is
based on some concept of 'community care', an objective
which is indirectly related to the social structure of
villages discussed above. Community care does not, of
course, imply the eventual disappearance of residential
institutions, but it should form a substantial part of what
Hare has called the 'continuum of care'.[20] In terms of
statutory services, such a concept demands a variety of
service provided in easily accessible sites for the clients
who need to use them, and a significant role for local
voluntary organisations and individuals. How do the rural
areas match up to this challenge?
    Social service provision tends, in rural areas, to be a
at a relatively low level, concentrated on the towns and, in
a significant minority of cases, inaccessible to rural
dwellers. For example, in terms of the community/
domiciliary services for Home Helps and Meals-on-Wheels,
concentration of population appears to be a significant
factor in determining, in the case of Meals-on-Wheels, the
provision of service, and, in the case of Home Helps,[21] how
many clients are helped. The relevance of this latter point
is illustrated when the reasons for low levels of take up of
service are examined. The variations in take up of services

between urban and rural areas is discussed below, and the
conclusion drawn is that such variations should not be
regarded as indicative of a variation in levels of need,
but rather a function of those 'interference factors'
which reflect the problems of implementing Social Services
policy in rural areas.

In the face of these implementation problems the Personal Social Services provide what has been referred to as
a 'responsive' service - one that reacts to and develops
from the identified need of clients of communities. But
it is also argued that the need to provide such a service
results from the inability of such markets as employment,
housing and education to cope with all of their potential
clients, and the inability of statutory planning to
resolve problems. Equally, it is argued that the method of
operation of these markets means that there will always be
those who seek the help of the Personal Social Services
because of the way in which these markets are structured.
It is clear that the authors of the Seebohm Report felt
that the new Social Services Department had an influential
role to play in the development of 'snag-free' markets, not
least in liaison with other service giving bodies to
ensure the insights of social workers and social administrators might be focused on the problems of 'delinquency,
deprivation and social pathology'.[22] At one level this
might mean discussions between Social Services and Planning
authorities on the detail of estate design in order to
increase interaction between neighbours[23] or at another,
trying to coordinate services available for the under-
fives[24] or yet again involvement in Social/Community
Development Projects in order to try to change the face of
communities themselves.[25] Thus, unlike the implementation
of statutory planning policy, the development of social
services provision is at two levels, first, the provision
of the service itself (the 'planning' process) and, secondly,
the response. Both of these activities demand careful
analysis and research if either is to move beyond the
level of speculation and dogma. As in the case of statutory planning, a major problem relates to the assessment of
need for the service and this factor is the one which is,
ironically, most underdeveloped.

The basic problem of measurement is the arbitrary nature
of need. It must be axiomatic that there are no *fixed*
needs, once, that is, society has achieved the standard
required for bodily survival. Objectives such as those
aimed at assuring for a client their 'full and active
participation in community life' are clear normative statements about the value of an individual's place in society.
Bradshaw puts this strongly when he argues that 'the
normative definition of need may be different according to
the value orientation of the expert - on his judgements
about the amount of resources that should be devoted to
meeting the need, or whether or not the available skills
can solve the problem'.[26] And thus the levels at which we
decide to relieve poverty, provide meals-on-wheels, or
limit numbers of children per class reflect the differing
standards of care of achievement that we, as a society,

decide to adopt. However, whilst it may be true that in terms of *planning,* felt and normative need is the most important issue, in terms of response, it is demand ('expressed need' in Bradshaw's terms) for service that determines priorities. And if it is true that the political machine is more response-oriented than it is plan-oriented, then the level of demand will be important in determining service level.

What then can be said of the level of need and demand in rural areas? Where comparative information is available, the expressed need in rural areas does not appear to equal that in urban areas.[27] The extent of this short-fall varies and although some of this variation reflects different definitions of urban and rural areas as well as different categories of what is being measured, the direction of difference invariably appears to be the same. Some support for a belief that the level of resources made available relates to the lower level of the demand for service can be obtained from national data which shows an overall lower level of service provision in predominantly rural areas.[28] How much reliability can be placed on expressed demand as an indicator of felt need in rural areas?

Two hypotheses might be put forward to explain or justify the different levels of demand for personal social services:
1. that communities in rural areas have developed in such a way that a level of mutual support exists which abrogates the need for service and thus reduces demand, or that
2. need in rural areas whatever its level, is not, for a variety of reasons, expressed as visibly as need in urban areas.

The first of these hypotheses is based upon a somewhat idyllic picture of rural life which is certainly open to challenge now as a result of both changing demographic patterns and recent research on isolation and visiting patterns amongst the elderly. Since the elderly are estimated to consume between two-thirds and three-quarters of all Health and Social Services expenditure, a focus on their problems in rural communities seems justified. In terms of demography the elderly are becoming increasingly predominant in rural areas where incidence rates of one in four of the population are not uncommon. As this process continues,and it seems it will, with younger people choosing to move out of the rural areas,[29] the balance between informal care givers and receivers begins to weigh heavily on the side of the receivers. In addition, recent (American) research on visiting patterns is, although somewhat ambiguous, pointing towards a no-difference picture between rural and urban areas in terms of visitation of the elderly.[30] (Some of the work in fact suggests more frequent visiting to the urban elderly). It would appear in the light of this that the theoretical distinction between urban and rural areas is perhaps invalid and the belief that a significantly higher level of informal support is available to the rural elderly is in need of some revision.

But living in rural areas *anyway* makes it difficult to articulate needs or to use urban-based services. Some of the difficulties that seem best termed 'interference factors', are discussed in the following paragraphs, which attempt to examine the legitimacy of the second of the two hypotheses.[31]

The *stigma attached to being a 'welfare client'* continues to permeate both urban and rural society but some recent American research suggests that rural dwellers are considerably more hostile than their urban counterparts to 'public assistance'.[32] Indeed, work undertaken in East Anglia has suggested that the informal information system often breaks down its impartiality when issues of public welfare arise,[33] and this finding is reinforced in work undertaken by the Cumbria Community Development Project[34] who found that some of the people acting as local information providers were amongst those hostile towards welfare provision. Equally, the visibility and lack of confidentiality of dropping into 'the welfare' in rural areas is mentioned by Joanna Davis who considers that this process is less visible and more anonymous in the city than in rural areas.[35]

This latter point raises another factor, that of *accessibility to services*. This perhaps is the best researched of these interference factors, although effective solutions to the problems raised remain. In the recent study of Health Care facilities undertaken by the Women's Institute mentioned in Chapter 5, three factors are suggested as the main causes of access difficulties in rural areas:-

1. Transport difficulties arising from high costs and inadequate public transport.
2. Shortage of medical services.
3. Centralisation of medical services.[36]

These criteria could equally apply to the Social Services, where the low level of service provision, and the inability of statutory planning policies radically to alter the situation has already been noted. Indeed, Moseley's study of rural accessibility[37] showed that, whatever planning and transport strategies were adopted, both children and the elderly remained as vulnerable groups - which provide the bulk of potential Social Services clients. Although it is true that a high level of adaptation has taken place as public transport services have ossified in rural areas, the changing balance of population means (again) that there are, simply, fewer people to offer informal transport than hitherto.

Accessibility to service is only of importance if people perceive the relevance of the service to them, and clearly, any *lack of knowledge regarding services* will again reduce the expression of need. Here, there is growing research evidence to support the existence and strength of this factor. In Norfolk,[38] it was found that local Landlords and other Community Leaders were still used as sources of information, but there were problems concerned with confidentiality and discussion of personal problems and, because of this, it is not surprising that the Cumbria Community Development Project[39] found that much of the informal support, with regard to information provision, was in terms of 'sign-posting' only. However, work in Suffolk, looking at the role of Citizens Advice Bureaux (CAB) and welfare rights information in rural areas, would seem to suggest that going to the professionals presents its own problems.[40] Rural post offices often have out-of-date information and CABs are urban based; as the recent Eastern Region report from the CAB argues 'there are large numbers of people scattered in rural parts of our area, who are still lacking many of the services freely available to the urban dweller'.[41] Finally, experience in the United States[42] has shown that the diffusion of information with regard to (in this instance) Medicare provision, was adequate, but 'ignorance was greatest amongst respondents with lowest material possessions and personal contact here was an important first choice'.

Such diffusion is unlikely to develop if even those who know of the service and its appropriateness are equally aware that, for one reason or another, it is unlikely to be provided; if, in short, there are *low expectations of service*. This is especially powerful in Social Services, where over 80% of referrals come via an agency or person other than the client themselves. If, for example, a doctor in a rural practice knows that a meals-on-wheels service does not exist, that the Home Help Service is already stretched and previous referrals have gone unserviced, it is unlikely he will consider a referral to be of much value, and may therefore not bother. This is again likely to lead to an under-representation of real 'need'. Of course, this is a problem in urban areas too, but where resource levels are lowest (as already suggested, these tend to be the rural areas), the problem is likely to be the greatest.

Clearly, none of these factors operate in isolation, but their existence suggests that the level of demand, as expressed in referrals to public service agencies in rural areas, may considerably under-represent the real social needs of people living in those areas.

CONCLUSIONS : A JOINT APPROACH

The now familiar features of rural areas in terms of low wages, poor job choice, limited access to educational opportunities, poor housing, and relative isolation are the very stuff of social problems and it is probable that demand is not adequately reflecting need, due to the interference factors discussed above. There seems no way in which a totally response-orientated organisation is going to move out of this vicious circle. A planned strategy will be necessary, with the authorities responsible for statutory planning, social and other services co-operating in the planning of provision of services, and providing a coordinated approach to the problems identified.

Despite the growing concern for the social implications of all central and local government activity there is yet to appear, at a national *or* local level, a Department or function concerned exclusively with the coordination of

social policy. This is not to say that such a suggestion
has not been mooted. At national level the government
'Think Tank' have suggested the need for increased
coordination of central government departments, in order
to examine social policy implications of their actions.[43]
At a local level too, although no such all embracing report
has been produced, there has been a wave of enthusiasm for
corporate activity in the 1970s.

Despite this very obvious concern for, and awareness of,
the problems of coordination of policy and identification
of 'social aspects', both central and local government have
in practice done little to guide the debate by finding ways
of incorporating measures of social costs into their plans.
One reason must be, quite clearly, the variety of different
prescriptive statements available regarding any one problem
from a variety of Planners and Social Administrators, and
even where unanimity exists, the problems of 'costing' such
outcomes against more quantifiable resource implications
remain problematic. It is difficult enough (though done)
to put a value on human life in assessing the justification
for road improvement schemes; so how much more problematic
is it to put a cost of life satisfaction without reducing
such concepts to the level of banality? Much stimulus for
coordinating activity is being provided in so far as
D.H.S.S. forward plans, Health Service Area and District
Plans, Structure and Local Plans, Transport Policy and
Programme submissions and Public Transport Plans are
demanding the attention of the Planning and Personal Social
Services authorities. The 'interference factors' mentioned
are not exclusive to social services in their effect, and
have obvious relevance to statutory planning. Thus, it is
likely that any approach to removing these factors will
demand a joint approach. Certainly, the approach to
accessibility is only tenable at this level, as the rural
transport report already mentioned suggests: 'Of the
multiplicity of agencies, none has the responsibility to
ensure the adequacy of accessibility across the full range
of activities ... Decision-making is fragmented ... this
fragmentation should be reduced if real advances are to be
made in the longer term. A corporate approach is
required ...'[44]

There are particularly strong reasons why the social
services providers and policy makers need to grasp this
corporate nettle. Perhaps the most negative (but nonethe-
less persuasive) argument for involvement, is that without
it the statutory planning and transportation agencies will
continue to plan in a way that may mean more social
services problems being created by an economic calculus
being used in policy decisions, rather than a full
appraisal of all the social implications.

The involvement of a wide range of agencies is inevitably a slow and painful process, especially since economic
reality often seems clearer and more incisive than social
'unreality', but these cannot be ignored if the aim of
government is to provide a framework for improving the
quality of life. More positively, it has been argued that
the responsibility for the majority of the social problems

and the interference factors mentioned in this essay
cannot be laid at any one Department's or agency's door,
but equally, that until those agencies co-operate, there
will be little chance of resolving them; certainly a
blind responsive approach may, far from easing these
problems, actually exacerbate them. It is not possible to
operate even an efficient priority system without knowing
what the needs of the community are. Currently, the
evidence already presented suggests that we have yet to
reach the point at which Departments such as those responsible for personal social services could make such an
efficient decision. Certainly, if the personal social
services are to meet legislative, political and public
expectations in rural, as well as other areas, they can
only do so by adapting a much less ambivalent attitude
than in the past with regard to planning and co-operation
with other services. As always, there will be need to
'get on with the job' in a responsive sense, but part of
that job must be concerned with the joint monitoring of
the effectiveness of existing policies, and with formulating future strategies to meet needs. 'Social Planning',
concluded the Seebohm Report, 'is an illusion without
adequate facts; and the adequacy of services mere speculation without evaluation'.[45]

REFERENCES AND NOTES

1. Norfolk County Council : *Budget 1977/8* : Estimated Net
    Revenue Expenditure on Planning and Social Services -
    10.3%. though this excludes expenditure on local
    planning by the seven District Councils in Norfolk.

2. R.H. Williams, The Idea of Social Planning, *Planning
    Outlook*, Vol. 10, 1970.

3. D.E.C. Eversley, Problems of Social Planning in Inner
    London, in Dommison & Eversley, *London - Urban Patterns,*
    Heinemann, 1973.

4. J.B. Cullingworth, *The Social Content of Planning,*
    London, 1973.

5. G.E. Cherry, *Town Planning in its Social Context,*
    Leonard Hill, 1970.

6. Town and Country Planning (Structure and Local Plans)
    Regulations, 1974, S.I.No. 1486.

7. Department of the Environment, Structure Plans Note
    7/73, *Social Aspects of Development Plans, 1973.*

8. *Report of the Committee on Local Authority and Allied
    Personal Social Services:* H.M.S.O., 1968 'The
    Seebohm Report'.

9. *Better Services for the Mentally Handicapped,* H.M.S.O.,
    1971.

10. *Priorities in Health and Personal Social Services,*
    D.H.S.S., 1977.

11. For a case study of the evolution of rural planning policy in Devon see: Anne Glyn-Jones, *Village into Town,* Devon County Council, 1977.

12. A.W. Gilg, *Countryside Planning,* David & Charles, 1978.

13. J.M. Shaw, Can We Afford Villages? *Built Environment Quarterly,* June, 1976; the implications of marginal costing are explored in I. Gilder, Rural Policies – An Economic Appraisal, Unpublished Thesis.

14. J.B. Ayton, Rural Settlement Policy – Problems and Conflicts, in P.J. Drudy (ed), *Regional and Rural Development,* Alpha Books, 1976.

15. J.M. Shaw, The Social Implications of Village Development, in M.J. Moseley (ed), *Social Issues in Rural Norfolk,* Centre of East Anglian Studies, Norwich, 1978.

16. D. Wilson, The Social Aims of Planning, *Journal of the Royal Town Planning Institute,* August, 1969.

17. J.M. Shaw, 1978, *op cit.*

18. See, for example: *The Decline of Rural Services,* Report by the Standing Conference of Rural Community Councils, August 1978; and the various Structure Plan reports of rural counties, from 1974 onwards.

19. *North Walsham Area Study,* Norfolk County Planning Department, 1975.

20. E.J. Hare, *Three Score Years and Then?* Unpublished M.Sc. Dissertation, Cranfield Institute of Management, 1977

21. See, for example: Norfolk Social Services Research Team: *Meals on Wheels Planning Project,* Unpublished Paper 1975, and Norfolk County Council, *Norfolk Structure Plan,* 1977.

22. Seehohm Report *op cit.*

23. See for example: L. Carey and R. Mapes, *The Society of Planning,* Batsford 1972.

24. See for example: *Under Fives,* A Local Authority Associations' Study, 1977.

25. See for example The Reports of the Community Development Programme, CDP Unit, University of York.

26. J. Bradshaw, *The Concept of Social Need,* New Society, 30th March 1972.

27. The average number of new cases recorded per month in Norfolk was lower in rural than in urban areas.

New Cases (per 1,000 relevant population) in Urban & Rural Areas per month

Client Groups	New Cases (per 1,000)	
	Rural	Urban
Elderly/Ph. Handicap	4.2	6.5
Child/Family Care	0.9	2.3
Mental Health	0.1	0.2
Total	1.0	1.9

28. Data covering County Boroughs (Urban) and County Councils (Rural) pre-1974 (IMTA).

	Total Expenditure per 1,000 popn.	Residential Child Care per 1,000 under 18	Residential Care Elderly per 1,000 over 65	Day Nurseries per 1,00 1,000 under 5	Home Help per 1,000 over665	Meals per 1,000 over 65
RURAL (Counties)	6385.5	2984.5	11,075.2	1218.6	891.7	172.3
URBAN (Counties)	9791.6	6887.6	14,813.7	4026.2	1100.9	720.7
Percentage less in Rural Areas	35%	57%	26%	70%	20%	76%

This table was originally produced for a paper presented at a seminar at Essex University in 1977.

29. See for example: P.J. Drudy, Population Exodus and Community Aspirations, in M.J. Moseley (ed), *Social Issues in Rural Norfolk,* Centre of East Anglian Studies, Norwich, 1978.

30. See for example: L.M. Hynson : *Rural Urban Differences in Satisfaction Amongst the Elderly.* Rural Sociology, Vol. 40, Spring 1975. L.G. Bultena : *Rural-Urban Differences in the Familial Interaction of the Elderly.* Rural Sociology, Vol. 34, March 1969.

31. These ideas were developed for a seminar on *Social Services in Rural Areas* held at the King's Fund Centre, London, by Birmingham University Social Services Unit in 1977.

32. M.H. Osgood : *Rural and Urban Attitudes Towards Welfare:* Social Work, Vol. 22, No. 1, January 1977.

Statement +	Response	Highly Urban%	Rural%
Most people on Welfare are honest about their needs	Agree a little or not at all	24	29
Most Welfare recipients are willing to work	"	32	46
Many will stop work if Welfare is too easy to obtain.	Agree completely or mostly	59	74
It's a responsibility of the Government to make sure everyone has a good job.	Agree a little or not at all	42	63

+ Précis Form

33. Norfolk Social Services Department Research Team : *Community Studies in Four Norfolk Villages,* Unpublished paper, 1976.

34. Butcher, H. et al : *Information and Action Services for Rural Areas,* Cumbria CDP Papers in Community Studies, No. 4, 1976.

35. Davis, J.F. : *The County Mouse Comes into her Own :* Child Welfare, Vol. 53, No. 8, Oct. 1974.

36. *Health Services in Rural Areas,* Women's Institute, March 1977.

37. M.J. Moseley, R.G. Harman, O.B. Coles, M.B. Spencer, *Rural Transport and Accessibility, Vol. I,* Centre of East Anglian Studies, University of East Anglia, 1977.

38. Norfolk Social Services Research Team 1976, *op cit.*

39. Butcher et al., *op cit.*

40. G. Brogden, *The Examination of Social Needs in the Hartismere Area of Suffolk,* Paper to Symposium, Eastern Region Social Services Research Group, June 1976.

41. *Eastern Regional Annual Report,* Citizens Advice Bureau, 1976.

42. E.J. Stojanovic, *The Dissemination of Information about Medicare to Low-Income Rural Residents,* Rural Sociology, Vol. 37, No. 2, June 1972.

43. This is the so-called Joint Approach to Social Policy (J.A.S.P.) as suggested in *A Joint Framework for Social Policies* a Report by the Central Policy Review Staff, H.M.S.O., 1975.

44. M.J. Moseley, et al., *op cit.*

45. Seebohm Report *op cit.*

10

RURAL MOBILITY AND ACCESSIBILITY

Malcolm Moseley

INTRODUCTION: THE SUFFERERS

Consideration of mobility and of accessibility are particularly pertinent in a rural context and it is there that
their absence can amount to severe deprivation. This
follows directly from the nature of rurality with its
basic connotation of low population density and of wide
geographical separation between people and between them and
the facilities they need. There is increasing realisation
that not only is the lack of mobility in rural areas a
problem for many people (mobility being the ability to move
around) but that accessibility (the degree to which things
are get-at-able) has also seriously deteriorated. This
chapter looks briefly at some of the causes, consequences and
policy implications of this, and in doing so it draws upon
research undertaken at the University of East Anglia by the
author and his colleagues.[1]
The 'rural transport problem' relating to the decline of
rural public transport and to the marked inequities arising
from the growth of rural private transport is in fact only
part of the wider 'rural accessibility problem'. The latter
may be expressed in terms of the inability of most carless
rural residents to gain convenient access to the services
and facilities relevant to them. Broadening the problem in
this way emphasises the irrelevance of much conventional
transport planning for rural areas. Conventional transport
planning, derived in an urban/suburban context, focusses on
the problem of congestion and in consequence upon transport
users. In rural areas the chief transport related problem
is inaccessibility and the principal concern must be those
who do not use, or rarely use, transport. Expressed in
accessibility (rather than mobility) terms, the problem also
forces attention to be focussed as much upon rural services
(shops, schools, pubs etc.) as upon the ubiquitous car and
the far from ubiquitous bus and train.
Has the ability of most carless rural residents to gain

convenient access to the services and facilities relevant
to them actually deteriorated? Almost certainly it has,
and there are two explanations for this. First, the virtual
demise of rural rail services and the steady decline of
rural bus services (a decline of roughly 1% per annum in
vehicle-miles in the past quarter century) has, understandably, been chiefly to the detriment of those people unable
to respond by purchasing a motor-car. Second, the village
service, whether it be school, shop, pub, post office or
workplace, has similarly suffered steady decline over a
similar period. Collectively these changes mean that for
many rural people without the ready use of a car accessibility has deteriorated in absolute terms.

This absolute decline in the accessibility experienced
by many carless residents has been sharpened by the
dramatic improvement in access enjoyed by those gaining
ready use of a motor car. The gap between the haves and
have-nots in this respect is wide and widening. And rising
expectations, fuelled by the mass media, only add to the
sense of deprivation. The author's Norfolk study[2]
revealed, for example, how firmly cycling to the local
village hall on a Saturday night has become socially
unacceptable as a source of recreation for today's teen-
ager. But surely the important point for policy is not
whether people are better or worse-off compared with their
circumstances in some bygone age, but whether they are
adequately provided for by today's standards. (What those
standards should be is of course a moot point.)

In crudest terms, the people who suffer mobility and
accessibility problems in rural areas are the 'carless' -
those who lack ready use of a car. This is not the same
as saying 'those who do not live in car-owning households'.
Household car ownership levels are typically over 70% in
rural Britain, compared with a national figure of about
56%.[3] But many people within car-owning households are
effectively deprived by not holding a driving licence, and
this includes all children, the majority of retired people
and many women. In the Norfolk study, a household survey
in 16 rural parishes established that 70% of all adult
women and 72% of all retired people do not 'nearly always
have a car available for their use'. This was only in part
explicable by the household lacking a car: often it
reflected the lack of a driving licence or else the pre-
emption of the car by the household's economically active
male for much of the day.

The elderly constitute the most significant group of
accessibility-deprived rural residents. This statement
reflects in part their numbers: there are over 9 million
people of pensionable age in Britain, this number is
increasing and there is a growing propensity for retirement
to rural or coastal areas. It reflects also their location
within rural areas - retired people are able to ignore the
locational pull of the small towns where most 'rural' jobs
are now found, and often choose to live in the smallest,
most poorly serviced villages. And it reflects a host of
physical, social and financial factors which set them apart[t]
from the rest of the rural community. For example, difficulties of reaching, mounting and leaving buses, the frequent

lack of close relatives in or near their household, and significantly below average incomes, all militate against ease of movement and ease of access for this group.

A degree of multiple deprivation within rural elderly households is apparent. The Norfolk survey referred to above revealed that 65% of those rural households which were composed exclusively of elderly people lacked a car. And of these people, 42% (i.e. over a quarter of *all* elderly households) not only lacked a car but had *at least four* of the following nine problems: no shop in the parish, no bus service, no phone in the dwelling, no available phone within five minutes walk, an income of less than £1000 p.a., someone handicapped in the household, no bicycle, no fridge. The survey also showed that retired people in 'no-car' households, when compared with those in car-owning households, made significantly fewer trips to the pub, library and cinema, and were much less likely to visit friends in hospital or friends living outside their own village.

Similar pictures of relative deprivation - relative to car-having individuals - were developed for other groups in the community, notably children and teenagers, mothers at home, the poor and disabled. The activities or facilities to which access was both important and problematic varied from group to group. For the young it was entertainment and evening/weekend school-based activities; for mothers at home it was shopping and medical trips; for the poor but economically active it was often the journey to work. But in each case the contrast between their circumstances and those of comparable people with ready use of a car was marked.

More recent research at the University of East Anglia by Haynes (1978)[4] has highlighted the particular problems experienced by the rural carless in gaining access to hospitals. Recent DHSS policy has been to close most of the old 'cottage hospitals' in rural areas in favour of concentrating nearly all hospital services into large, centrally located 'District General Hospitals', typically servicing around 250,000 inhabitants. Whatever the economic and medical benefits of such a policy, accessibility problems are bound to ensue for rural residents who on balance will be expected to travel further. Indeed surveys by Haynes and his colleagues in the West Norfolk hospital district produced the disturbing findings that remotely located rural residents (those beyond the immediate hinterland of the main hospitals) were less likely than those more conveniently located to attend hospitals whether as in-patients, out-patients or visitors. Those who did enter hospital as in-patients were likely to receive fewer different visitors and fewer visitors in all. All of this reflects badly on the ability of carless rural residents to recover from illness.

SOME MYTHS ABOUT RURAL MOBILITY

No-one denies that there is a degree of mobility and access-ibility deprivation in rural areas, although there may be

dispute concerning its severity. Some, however, would
dispute the need for radical action, arguing that the
situation contains the seeds of its own resolution.
One such view is that rising car ownership will, even-
tually, solve the problem. It is true that rural areas are
excellent 'car country': the car's flexibility in terms of
its temporal and spatial versatility, and the wide scatter
of rural residences and services ensure that there is
effectively 'no contest' between public and private transport if both are available. Against this, however, is the
fact that car ownership brings an inequitable intra-
household distribution of benefits (as we have seen) and
will never in fact reach every household - factors of
income, age and physical disability will see to that.
Indeed car ownership levels may rise much less than is
officially forecast[5] because of rising costs of fuel.
Finally, 'car-sharing' - a much more open approach to the
offering and accepting of lifts - runs up against severe
socio-cultural problems even if the legal obstacles to
payment being made are removed. The motor car will remain
only a part, if the most important part, of the rural
transport endowment, and as it becomes more plentiful the
problems of the carless will worsen with public transport
and village-based services both being further undermined.
A second source of complacency derives from commonly
held assumptions concerning residential migration. 'If
people don't like living in rural areas they should move'
is one way in which the argument is expressed. Alter-
natively, 'living in rural areas involves taking the rough
with the smooth: relatively low house prices *reflect* the
"roughs" such as poor public transport and to subsidise the
latter would involve "double-payment" and thereby be unjust
to urban dwellers'. Such a position tends to make some
untenable assumptions about residential mobility. Some
people are effectively tied to a rural location by dint of
their employment or by dint of their father's or husband's
employment. Others, the retired, may be 'locked in' by the
same house-price graident which once induced them to sell
their highly priced suburban home and acquire a small 'nest-
egg' which would provide extra income for their retirement.
Much of this capital gain may have been spent to offset the
ravages of inflation before the village bus service was cut
or the household car (or car driver) was lost. A third
group, those in rented accommodation, may find it extremely
difficult to move to similar accommodation in a more urban
location, and it must be remembered that in rural Britain
only about 20% of new house buildings is undertaken by the
public sector.[6] So the classic residential model, of people
moving readily in response to constant reassessments of
their situation is only very partially valid in the real
world. Many rural residents are effectively 'trapped' and
to that extent are a proper cause for public concern.
A third commonly held view (particularly among those
elected members who tend to hold the purse strings in rural
areas) is that private enterprise would probably rise to
the occasion if only the market were not fettered with
regulations and distorted with subsidies. It is, of course,
impossible to say with any certainty what would happen if

all route-licensing agreements (which protect the
monopoly along specified routes enjoyed by existing, and
mostly state-owned, operators) were swept away. But quite
probably only the most profitable services would remain in
operation and the limited amount of tacit cross-subsidy
that remains (either of routes or of services at less
profitable periods of the day) would be lost. Neither this,
nor the resulting climate of uncertainty would be likely to
be in the interests of the disadvantaged groups we have
specified.

It is often claimed (and often true) that small independent operators enjoy lower average costs than do the big
subsidiaries of the nationalised National Bus Company - but
size, and higher overheads, may well be the price we have
to pay for an integrated transport service operating over a
wide area. So far as 'subsidy' payments are concerned it
is rarely clear what is an 'unacceptable subsidy' and what
a 'community decision to purchase a service'. Certainly,
vociferous opponents of the subsidy of rural bus services
are generally silent about the *tacit* subsidy of rural areas
implied by a uniform postal or electricity tariff. The
latter may simply not be seen as a subsidy, or it may be
that with postal and electricity services *all* rural inhab-
itants benefit - rather than just those without private
transport.

A fourth opinion frequently voiced by those who are
averse to the subsidy of rural public transport is that
'rural bus services are clearly hardly ever used anyway, so
why keep them?' Certainly it is relevant to bear in mind
the quite low proportion of rural trip-making accounted for
by public transport. Even as long ago as 1971, when the
Department of Environment carried out extensive household
surveys in rural West Suffolk and Devon,[7] only the
following proportions of all trips recorded were by stage-
carriage bus services: work (6%), school (5%), shopping
(16%), leisure (4%). But this is not to say that idly
witnessing the total demise of rural bus services would not
involve considerable hardship to those people included in
these figures. And it may in any case only *seem* that
rural buses are uneconomically empty: a mere handful of
passengers may be sufficient to justify the off-peak use of
a bus and driver each effectively already paid for by the
peak hour users. Replacing buses by minibuses, as is often
suggested as common sense, would usually be unwise given
the dominance of the morning and evening peaks in transport
economics, and the need to pay the driver whatever the size
of vehicle.

These 'myths' - concerning the supposed ability of all
rural residents to meet the challenge of declining transport
and service provision by means of either car purchase or
out-migration, and the supposed willingness of private
enterprise to fill the vacuum that would be left by the
demise of the remaining services operated by the public
sector - underlie a good deal of the reluctance, widely
found in rural Britain, to 'promote the provision of a coordinated and efficient system of public transport, to meet
the needs of the county'.

ACCESSIBILITY POLICIES

The quotation with which the previous section ended is
taken from section 203 of the 1972 Local Government Act,
and relates to the duties of the new county councils. It
is the county council's duty to ensure that basic accessibility needs are met and to this end they enjoy a variety
of powers. Loss making rural bus services may be
subsidised under provisions first introduced in the 1968
Transport Act. Sums earmarked for such purposes may be
included in annual statements of transport policy which the
county councils are required to make as a basis for central
government financial support. In addition the councils
must ensure the provision of adequate transport for
journeys to school, and may provide various means of transport for social services clients. They also of course
influence the long-term development of the pattern of
population, employment and service distribution through
their land-use planning responsibilities.

     Herein lies a major problem - the fragmentation of the
effort which is directed towards the alleviation of the
rural accessibility problem. Within the county councils,
various departments and committees - responsible for
planning, transport/engineering, social services, education,
leisure etc. - have a role to play. In addition, agencies
such as the District Councils, the Area Health Authorities,
the Post Office and the transport operators themselves are
also of key importance. The much vaunted 'improved transport coordination' which everyone agreed to be needed
should be as much a matter of coordinating agencies and
organisations as of knitting together bus and train timetables. Perhaps the 'county public transport plans', introduced by the 1978 Transport Act, will mark a further
step forward, although they are not intended explicitly to
include policies concerned with the location of services
and of people.

(i) Policy options

Turning to the range of policy alternatives, these fall
logically into four or five categories.
(1) *The transport option* is concerned with facilitating
the ability of people to travel from the rural areas to
places where shops, jobs and other services are provided -
usually urban centres. This option, then, involves trying
to provide the link which the decline of public transport
services has tended to sever. There are, of course, a
number of sub-options, involving not only the subsidy of
conventional transport, but also the support of post buses,
dial-a-bus (though this is unlikely to be very useful in
rural areas), car sharing schemes, and making schools
transport available to the general public.
(2) The second possibility, complementary to taking the
people to the activity, is to take the activity to the
people. This might be called the *mobile service option*.
In addition to mobile shops and mobile libraries, there are
plenty of other possibilities, such as play buses (mobile

playschools) and mobile banks. Telecommunications constitute a sub-set of this option, the Open University, for
example, being a form of mobile service in which the
educational activity is taken out to the person, using
radio, television and correspondence material.
(3) A third possibility is to help the carless person to
move home. In *the key village option* the population is
gradually clustered close to the services which are themselves congregated in the larger settlements.
(4) Finally there is the *'mini-outlet' option*. In this,
people are encouraged to remain where they are presently
living and their local services are improved. Small
schools are retained, shops are subsidised, the village pub
is kept open, perhaps being managed by some community
organisation and various attempts are made to attract small,
workshop-type industries, perhaps using the assistance of
the Council for Small Industries in Rural Areas. A major
problem with this (and the preceding option) is that it
must be seen as a long term policy. Whereas transport
policies can be introduced, and discontinued if necessary,
quite quickly, 'locational' policies are much slower to
bring their benefits to the community.
   These four policy options logically embrace all of the
possibilities, except for one further course of action,
which involves modifying the hours of availability of
services. If it were possible for shops to remain open in
the evening, and for local government offices and banks to
be open on certain Saturday mornings, the accessibility of
certain rural residents to some services would clearly be
increased, particularly if they would thereby be able to
make effective use of the household car.

(ii) Evaluating the options

Turning to the way in which the various policy options contained within these four or five categories might in fact
be evaluated, there are two basic elements to consider,
relating to costs and to benefits.
   On the cost side, the crucial point is that the *total*
public sector cost of alternative strategies should be
assessed. This is a very difficult exercise to carry out,
but it is not enough just to consider direct bus subsidies
to operators: it is necessary to include in the same
equation the costs of *not* providing that subsidy. This
might mean, for instance, doctors and social workers having
to make more trips to meet their clients. Similarly, in
examining the cost of transporting children to widely
spaced middle schools, the cost of constructing and running
those schools is properly part of the same equation.
   On the accessibility side the need is to conceptualise
benefits in terms of the various social groups affected.
(These groups have been referred to above). Thus the
policy analyst should determine how far various alternative
systems (involving both transport and locational elements)
under consideration effectively permit these different
groups to reach the services or facilities relevant to them.
In the Norfolk study we looked, in total, at 25 activities,

five social groups, and over 100 'activity-group inter-
actions'. We checked whether, in fact, it was possible for
elderly people to get to post offices, for example, given
the various constraints operating in our study areas, and
given the nature of each of a number of hypothetical
strategies.

The need, then, is to appraise alternative policies
involving both transport elements *and* locational elements,
not just in terms of cost, but in terms of the extent to
which policies meet previously stated objectives.

The county councils have the central and statutory
responsibility for carrying out this evaluation and the
study referred to above advocated a rolling programme of
rural investigation within each county. Areas, which might
be as big as those served by District Councils, would be
subject to a systematic attempt to see whether different
social groups could reach the various activities relevant to
their needs (as outlined above). Alternative policies
would then be tested, to establish what improvements could
be made to existing systems, given realistic financial constraints. Moving on around the county, the situation could
be monitored every two or three years to determine whether
the accessibility enjoyed by the various rural residents
was improving or deteriorating.

This type of investigative programme should not prove
to be a particularly difficult exercise, but it would, and
should, pull together the work of the different bodies
influencing accessibility. At the moment, some public
transport operators, such as the Eastern Counties Omnibus
Company in East Anglia, have a very energetic record in
carrying out area studies to establish what demand there is
for changes in bus services. The work of such operators
should be incorporated with that of the county councils'
social services, planning and transportation departments,
and of the district councils, in a team effort designed to
see whether their combined resources are, or are not,
meeting agreed objectives linked to defined problems.

CONCLUSIONS

Looking forward to the 1980s and to the practical steps that
might be taken to alleviate rural mobility and accessibility deprivation, it is clear that there is no panacea
waiting to be discovered. Rather the need is to fashion
area-specific policy packages which best attain the locally
determined optimal combination of good accessibility, widespread applicability and low cost. It is impossible to have
county-wide, low cost, high levels of accessibility. The
'tool-kit' of policies outlined above must be deployed to
meet as efficiently as possible, the chosen compromise
combination.

Only a few pointers are possible here. Taking location
policies first, the following suggestions may be made:
(i) *Housing* Would-be retirement migrants should be better
informed of the service and transport realities of their
future environment before they move. Second, it should be
made easier for elderly people to move short distances into

well-served 'key villages', where any new council and
sheltered housing should be concentrated.

(ii) *Services* Local authorities should be given an
explicit period of notice of the impending closure of a
village shop, pub or post office and could be empowered to
assist the running of those services if they saw fit. But
deliberate policies of geographically clustering services
into a quite small number of villages may still be advan-
tageous to the carless *if* a complementary transport system
is designed.

(iii) *Itinerant services* may be the answer in certain
circumstances: services such as chiropodist, post office,
citizens' advice bureau and social worker could meet in
each of a succession of ten villages on the same half-day
each week. (The 'periodic market' found in many developing
countries provides a precedent).

Turning to transport policies:

(i) *A basic bus network* should be maintained, linking large
villages and small towns, if necessary on a subsidised
basis.

(ii) *Off-peak excursion services,* providing, say, a twice-
monthly shopping trip to a large town, can usually be run
very cheaply given marginal cost pricing.

(iii) *Post-buses* The scope for these would be increased
if the POO were required to relax their constraint that
mail delivery and collection must always have first
priority - a priority which inevitably means circuitous
routes and unattractive timings from the passenger's viewpoint.

(iv) *School buses* It is already legal, but rarely happens,
that fare-paying adults travel on contract school buses.
Routes and loadings could be designed so that spare
capacity is built in for occasional adult passengers from
otherwise busless villages.

(v) *Car-sharing,* for payment, could be expanded given
appropriate organisational assistance and legal changes of
the sort introduced by the government, on an experimental
basis, in four defined rural areas.

(vi) *Mobile services* could be re-organised so that one
vehicle and driver delivered groceries, newspapers, stamps
and postal orders etc.

These are just some suggestions. In essence they stem
from a philosophy that clearly defined accessibility objectives be set and that 'anything goes' in trying to solve
them. Accepted legal, organisational and socio-cultural
constraints must be forced to give way if real improvements
in rural accessibility are to be achieved in any reasonable
public expenditure climate. Even this, however, will prove
to be insufficient if real political will is lacking.
Above, we have briefly outlined *why* the rural accessibility
problem is serious and *how* it might best be attacked. But
whether the necessary reforms and initiatives will
actually be undertaken depends in large part upon the
attitudes and priorities of central and local government
politicians, and upon their willingness and ability to
harness and to redirect the efforts of the public and
private sectors.

REFERENCES AND NOTES

1. M.J. Moseley, R.G. Harman, O.B. Coles, M.B. Spencer, *Rural Transport and Accessibility,* (Final report to the Department of Environment) Centre of East Anglian Studies, University of East Anglia, Norwich, 1977.

2. Ibid; and see also M.J. Moseley, *Accessibility: the Rural Challenge,* Methuen (in press).

3. J.C. Tanner, *Car Ownership Trends and Forecasts,* TRRL Laboratory Report 799, Transport and Road Research Laboratory, Crowthorne, Berkshire, 1977.

4. R.M. Haynes *et al.,* Community attitudes towards the accessibility of hospitals in West Norfolk, in M.J. Moseley (ed) *Social Issues in Rural Norfolk,* Centre of East Anglian Studies, University of East Anglia, Norwich, 1978.

5. J.C. Tanner, *op. cit.,* 1977.

6. A.W. Rogers, Rural housing, in G.E. Cherry (ed) *Rural Planning Problems,* Leonard Hill, 1976.

7. Department of Environment, *Study of Rural Transport in Devon,* and *Study of Rural Transport in West Suffolk,* DoE, London, 1971.

11

COMMUNITY INFORMATION IN RURAL AREAS: AN EVALUATION OF ALTERNATIVE SYSTEMS OF DELIVERY

David Clark and Kathryn Unwin

INTRODUCTION: INFORMATION AND TECHNOLOGY

There is an increasing need for people to have access to information for social, domestic and leisure purposes. Much information that is available to the general public is contained in books, pamphlets, leaflets, and documents and access to it is provided at offices, libraries, schools, and information bureaux. Modern electronic storage and retrieval systems, coupled with current and expected tele-communcation technologies could, however, be used to supply a wide range of information to people in their own homes. An important advantage is that such a system would signif-icantly reduce the need for travel thereby resulting in savings in energy and expenditure on transport. Such developments would be of particular benefit in rural areas characterised by dispersed points of information need, receding points of information provision, and poor and deteriorating public transport systems.

'Information' is a general term which can be applied to knowledge, guidance, counselling, and advice about a wide range of topics. Within this spectrum there lies a core area of information to which individuals must have reason-able and reliable access if they are to manage their lives and domestic affairs in a capable and efficient manner. This core area has been termed 'community' information and is defined as 'information needed to enable individuals to make effective use of resources available in the community.[1] It includes information about social services, social security, jobs, education, planning and the like but excludes information about fashion, the 'top ten', gardening, etc., on grounds of their peripheral and secondary impor-tance. Along with civil, political and social rights, access to community information is seen by the National Consumer Council as a basic right of citizenship.[2]

In view of its essential nature it seems reasonable to suppose that the maintenance of satisfactory access to community information should be an important objective

TYPE OF INFORMATION PROVIDED

		Generalist	Intermediate	Specialist
GEOGRAPHICAL CHARACTERISTICS OF PROVISION SYSTEM	Aspatial	Television Radio Teletext Viewdata	Computer-based limited information provision systems	FREEPOST services FREEPHONE services Phone-in services
	Peripatetic	Mobile community information vans. Mobile CABX. 'Out-stations' manned by peripatetic providers.	Local authority mobile information vans. Mobile libraries	Specialist home delivery services.
	Town based	Local information centres. Citizens' Advice Bureau.	Local authority information centres. Libraries	Local offices (ie. court offices, DHSS & unemployment offices etc).
	Intra-village	Informal 'signposting', Formal 'referral' systems.	Village Post Office	Specialist intra village providers (ie. clergy, police etc).

Figure 11.1.   Systems of information delivery.

in any rural planning strategy. The major difficulty in rural areas, however, is that present trends in information demand and information supply are in opposition; the need for and complexity of information is rising, at the same time as local points of provision in small towns and villages are being withdrawn, and public transport services are being reduced. The inevitable result is greater difficulty of access to information for many residents of rural areas. A number of schemes have been introduced or are envisaged for rural Britain to ameliorate this problem, and these are classified in Figure 11.1. One example is the Salop village representatives' scheme described in Chapter 12 which directs individuals to appropriate information sources; another is the extension of peripatetic home delivery services to include, for example, legal advice and family planning guidance[3], while a third is the introduction of mobile Citizens' Advice Bureaux as in Gwynedd, Wales[4] or information vans as in Cleator Moor, Cumbria.[5] An alternative scheme

outlined by the East Anglia Regional Strategy Team in
Strategic Choice for East Anglia[6] involves access to and
delivery of information via telecommunications. Similar
uses for advanced telecommunications technology have been
envisaged in North America, notably by P.R. Goldmark in the
New Rural Society Project[7], and have been examined by the
U.S. Office of Technology Assessment[8] but few comprehensive
systems have as yet progressed beyond the experimental
stage. This chapter focusses upon present and future means
of balancing information needs and information provision.
It analyses the characteristics of information needs and
access behaviour in rural areas and examines alternative
systems of information delivery with special references to
telecommunications.

THE COMMUNITY INFORMATION SYSTEM

The structure of the community information system is best
described with reference to a simple model in which six
major levels; planning, programming, fieldwork, informal
provision, information needs, and problems, are recognised
(Figure 11.2). The first three levels are concerned with
information provision, and form a distinct sub-system; the
final two are external to this sub-system and represent
levels encountered in generating demands for information
Everyone experiences problems from time to time of a personal or household nature which they need to resolve. It
may be as simple as getting from one place to another by
public transport or a more complex problem of financial
hardship arising perhaps as a result of unemployment or
redundancy. Such problems give rise to information needs
which range in complexity from knowledge about bus or train
times to the understanding of the rules and procedures which
govern social security benefits and entitlements. In
seeking information, most rural residents probably turn first
to neighbours, friends, or relatives within the community or
to local officials such as clergy, policemen, or parish
councillors, who provide factual information and personal
advice on a casual or informal basis. There is also,
however, a growing army of trained advisers whose job is to
offer general or specialist information. Grouped at this
level are professional workers attached to local offices of
national government, local government and private sector
undertakings together with the representatives of numerous
voluntary/independent agencies, such as Citizens' Advice
Bureaux and the Consumers' Association. In some areas of
information need these 'fieldworkers' interlock through a
complex network of case referral. Each operates within the
limits and constraints of an information provision system
organised in any particular locality by a set of managers
whose function is to programme that system. The overall
structure of individual agencies within the provision system
is the responsibility of a small number of 'planners' who
normally operate from head offices outside the rural area.
While the levels are universal, there are important
variations in the way in which the community information

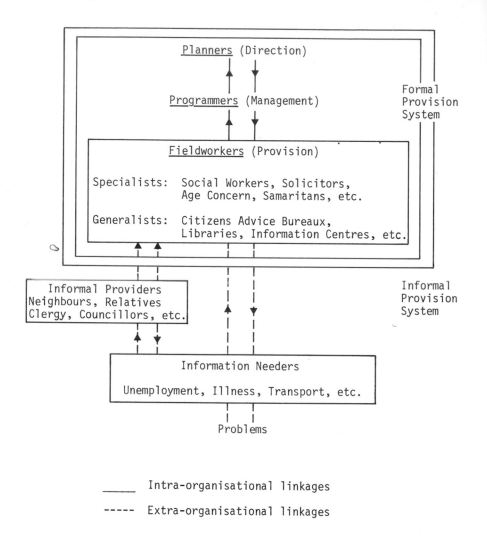

Figure 11.2.   The community information system.

system operates in different areas. A basic distinction is
between urban and rural areas in that the pattern of information need and the system of information provision must
necessarily reflect the socio-economic and spatial structure
of the community. Thus densely populated urban areas with
heterogeneous populations produce a large and varied range
of information needs, most of which can be met by advice and
information agencies located within the city. For example,
the 294,000 residents of the London Borough of Lambeth are
served by at least 120 providing agencies.[9] Though there is
no clear evidence that villagers experience fewer problems,
they may well be significantly different in kind. Thus
queries concerning immigration, nationality and community

Figure 11.3.   The Lincolnshire information survey area.

relations may be more frequent in cities, whereas transport
difficulties are often dominant in rural areas.   Sparsely
populated 'deep rural' areas such as Lincolnshire (Figure
11.3) generate few information needs in absolute terms and
so satisfy minimum threshold requirements for only a limited
number of providing agencies (Figure 11.4).   In consequence,
such agencies as may be present, particularly in the market
towns, are frequently small and offer only a basic level of
counter service.   Moreover, organisational remoteness means
that rural agencies may themselves experience difficulties
in acquiring the most recent up-to-date information to pass
on to the general public.   One aspect of this problem has
been documented in some detail by Brogden in a survey of the
availability in village post offices in north-east Suffolk
of literature outlining Department of Health and Social
Security welfare benefits and entitlements.[10]   Of the four
leaflets requested, only forty-one per cent of post offices
had up-to-date leaflets available;   thirty-three per cent
had out-of-date leaflets, and twenty-six per cent had no
leaflets available at all.

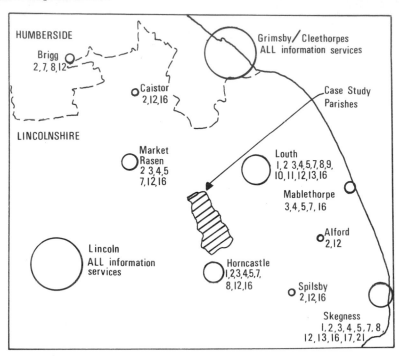

Key: Information Services and Agencies
1. Probation
2. Juvenile Courts
3. Employment
4. Unemployment Benefit
5. Disablement Resettlement
6. Occupational Guidance
7. Careers Advice
8. Social Services
9. Education
10. Trading Standards
11. Tax
12. Magistrates Courts
13. County Courts
14. Crown Courts
15. Rating
16. District Council
17. Tail Travel
18. Gas
19. Electricity
20. Fair Rents
21. DHSS
22. C.A. Bureaux
23. Samaritans

Figure 11.4. Location of major information providing
agencies in north Lincolnshire and south Humberside.

INFORMATION NEEDS IN RURAL LINCOLNSHIRE

This general description of the community information system
can now be elaborated by reference to a pilot survey of
information provision in a specific rural area in north
Lincolnshire (Figure 11.3). The survey investigated patterns
of information needs and access behaviour in a group of
parishes by means of household interview techniques.
Respondents were asked to detail their community information
requirements over a six month recall period, and to state
who they contacted and how and by what means contacts were
made. 609 individuals in five parishes formed the population

relevant to the survey and 474 successful interviews were
completed yielding information about 78 per cent of the
population.   The 142 people with information needs identified 234 separate instances on which they had required
information.   47 per cent of households in the area contained at least one person who had had at least one
information need and with a mean household size in the
survey population of 2.1 persons this means that half the
population may have been affected by an information need.

Table 11.1.   Lincolnshire information survey area:
levels of information need

Types of information need	Number	Per cent
Rent/rates	37	15.8
Transport	32	13.7
Planning	22	9.4
Jobs	21	9.0
Entertainment	21	9.0
Social Security	20	8.5
Legal Matters	20	8.5
Health	17	7.3
Education	10	4.3
Housing	8	3.4
Shopping	7	3.0
Social Services	6	2.6
Pensions	6	2.6
Farming	4	1.7
Tax	3	1.2
	234	100.0

The population required information on a large number
of topics.   No single area of information predominated, but
rent and rates (16 per cent), transport (14 per cent),
planning, entertainment, and jobs (all 9 per cent) were the
leading categories (Table 11.1).   In attempting to satisfy
their information needs, people consulted a number of
individuals and agencies (Table 11.2).   So wide in fact was
the range of contacts that 17 per cent could only be grouped
into an 'other' category.   The local authority (the East
Lindsey District Council)was the most common source contacted receiving 28 per cent of all contacts, a figure which
includes 9 per cent directed to the planning department.   8
per cent of contacts went to an informal group of neighbours,
friends, and relatives, to solicitors, and to local offices
of the Department of Health and Social Security.

Table 11.2. Lincolnshire information survey area:
Pattern of information-seeking contacts

Source Consulted	Contacts					
	First Contact No.	Percent	Second Contact No.	Percent	Total Contacts No.	Percent
East Lindsey District Council	58	26.1	22	36.2	80	28.3
Solicitor	19	8.5	6	9.8	25	8.8
Dept. of Health and Social Security	17	7.6	6	9.8	23	8.1
Neighbour/Friend/ Relative	22	9.9	1	1.6	23	8.1
British Rail	14	6.3	1	1.6	15	5.3
Doctor	11	4.9	3	4.9	14	4.9
Voluntary Agency	10	4.5	1	1.6	11	3.9
Employment Office	10	4.5	1	1.6	11	3.9
Travel Agent	5	2.3	4	6.6	9	3.2
Local Paper	7	3.2	2	3.3	9	3.2
Cinema	6	2.7	0	0	6	2.1
Teachers	3	1.4	2	3.3	5	1.8
Post Office	5	2.3	0	0	5	1.8
Other	35	15.8	12	19.7	47	16.6
Totals	222	100.0	61	100.0	283	100.0

In 26 per cent of cases, individuals reported having made
two separate contacts in order to resolve their information
needs. It is useful to compare the pattern of first and
second contacts for two reasons. First, they point to established chains of referral within the community which might
be reinforced as the basis of attempts to improve the information provision system, and second, they may suggest that
contacts of some types are less successful than others. 8
per cent of contacts were made with 'informal referral points
within the villages such as neighbours, friends and relatives
though in almost all cases these were first rather than
second contacts; only 2 per cent of second contacts were

reported with this group. This difference is significant
since it suggests the operation of an informal 'signposting' system which has the function of directing those
with information needs to agencies which can best help
them, though the network seems less extensive in this part
of Lincolnshire than in Cleator Moor, Cumbria[5] and in Salop
(Chapter 12). One reason might be the erosion of traditional community structures in rural Lincolnshire by heavy
and persistent outmigration over the past thirty years.[11]
The existence of an *intra village* provision network however
emphasises the primary importance of directional information
which tells people what specialist information is available
to them, and where to get it.

Table 11.3. Lincolnshire survey area:
Modes of contact

Contact Modes	Contacts					
	First Contact		Second Contact		Total Contacts	
	No.	Per cent	No.	Per cent	No.	Per cent
Visit	73	33.1	24	40.0	97	34.6
Write	42	19.1	16	26.7	58	20.7
Telephone	73	33.1	15	25.0	88	31.4
Word of Mouth (local)	26	11.9	3	5.0	29	10.4
Other	6	2.8	2	3.3	8	2.9
Totals	220	100.0	60	100.0	280	100.0

Table 11.3 details the mode by which contacts were made.
In spite of the difficulties of travel within the area, at
least by public transport, 35 per cent of contacts were made
by the public visiting organisations and agencies in local
towns. No doubt many of these visits formed part of multi-
purpose trips in which information access was combined with
shopping and other activities and the extent to which
'journeys to information' form a discrete component in rural
movement patterns remain unknown. Almost as many contacts
(31 per cent) were made by telephone, though more detailed
analysis indicates that the majority were concerned with
questions about transport and entertainment where the information sought is simple and readily provided: information
about more complex issues such as rent and rates, and jobs,
is more commonly sought by visiting and writing. Communications by mail account for 21 per cent, and locally (ie.
intra-village) by word of mouth, for 10 per cent of all
contacts.

Rural deprivation

Changes in mode between first and second contacts are of particular interest as this has bearing on the scope for substitution. Significantly, visiting and writing form a higher percentage of second contacts than of first whereas telephone and word of mouth contacts form a lower percentage of second than first contacts. This suggests that a primary function of telephone and local word of mouth contacts is to clarify where, how, and when information can be accessed, and that visits and writing act as a more acceptable means of actually getting hold of information. Writing may be more acceptable because it offers a greater degree of formality or it fits an agency's pattern of operation, perhaps in relationship to the provision of forms which need to be completed. It is also important when there is a need for a permanent record of the inquiry. Visiting may be similarly more acceptable because face-to-face contacts are easier to use in some circumstances and may be perceived to offer a greater opportunity for lengthy explanation and clarification of an information need.

In 97 of the 280 contacts, journeys were made in order to secure information. In 24 cases, more than one journey was made or an initial mode of contact was followed by a journey. 82 per cent of trips were made by private vehicles with public transport accounting for 10 per cent of trips. When trips are being considered as an alternative to other contact modes this almost invariably implies the use of a private vehicle. 76 per cent of trips to obtain information were in fact made to the two local market towns of Horncastle and Louth (Table 11.4). At the first contact stage, a small

Table 11.4. Lincolnshire Information Survey data: Destination of visits

Destination	First Visit No.	Per cent	Second Visit No.	Per cent	Total Visits No.	Per cent
Louth	35	47.9	11	45.8	46	48.5
Horncastle	20	27.4	8	33.4	28	27.8
Lincoln	7	9.6	1	4.2	8	8.2
Local village	5	6.8	0	0.0	5	5.2
Elsewhere	6	8.3	4	16.6	10	10.3
Totals	73	100.0	24	100.0	97	100.0

proportion of visits were made within local villages but these disappeared completely at second contact stage. Table 11.4 also demonstrates that trips 'elsewhere', that is outside the local area, become marginally more important for second contacts. Although the majority of trips do not go beyond local centres this suggests that visits to distant locations are more likely for a second and perhaps a more specific contact.

SYSTEMS OF INFORMATION DELIVERY

This appraisal of the patterns of information needs and access behaviour provides a basis for the evaluation of alternative modes of information delivery in rural areas. In view of the range of options that is classified in Figure 11.1, these are discussed according to their spatial characteristics under four separate headings:

(i) Aspatial, telecommmunications-based services

To replace all or part of the existing rural community information system, an alternative system must be capable of providing a wide range of information to large numbers of dispersed consumers with greater effectiveness and acceptability and at no greater cost. This has been a technical possibility with telecommunications since the development of radio and television, though the size of broadcast areas, and the operation of 'national' programming schedules has meant that broadcast services are most suited to the provision of general information which is of wide interest. The introduction of local radio services in recent years has enabled the 'community' contact of broadcasting to be increased but the service is restricted to those with VHF receivers or with interference-free reception on the medium waveband. A feature of the present network of local radio stations, which are urban centred is moreover that rural areas are poorly served. Most of Lincolnshire for example, falls outside the reception area of the nearest 'local' radio stations which are in Hull and Nottingham (though more stations are proposed).
Although the U.K. has had a public telephone service since 1876, its potential has been limited by the comparatively slow growth of the residential market which has restricted the development of systems of home delivery based upon the telephone. There are additional difficulties in that the telephone provides a means of direct and immediate contact which is ideal for personal counselling services, of the type provided by the Samaritans, but is less suitable for accessing information from large anonymous departmentalised organisations such as local authorities. For this reason, as the Lincolnshire survey has shown, telephone calls tend to be used as a means of locating information sources which are then assessed by visiting or writing. However, an example of what is possible with only minor organisational changes is the consumer advice service operated by Surrey County Council in association with the Citizens' Advice Bureau and Consumers Association.[14] With Surrey's 'Box 99' system, a consumer can telephone the service from anywhere in the county for the cost of a local call but under an arrangement with the Post Office, calls are automatically routed to a central office. This ensures

that enquiries always reach a trained adviser experienced in giving advice and information over the telephone and so leads to a high quality answering service.

Now that many organisations are using computers for storing information it is possible to overcome some of the intra-organisation communication problems by enabling fieldworkers to access information direct. An example of such an arrangement is the computer based welfare benefits information system developed jointly by the University of Edinburgh, Inverclyde District Council, and IBM U.K. Limited.[15] In the Inverclyde system, information supplied to fieldworkers by people enquiring about welfare benefits is fed into a central computer which estimates the probable range of entitlements and produces a letter which is sent to the individual concerned. Some measures of the success of the system can be seen by the fact that of the 341 families who took part in the experimental scheme, no less than 126 could have been better off by claiming a benefit they were not claiming, or by changing their claiming tactics. But despite these impressive results, the system still requires that individuals visit offices in order to complete a highly detailed form (under close supervision) and to have their documents checked, so that although improving internal communication, it offers no substitute for the 'journey to information.' Though capable of ensuring a very high quality of information provision in market towns, for example, such a system would need to be supplemented by large numbers of peripatetic clerical staff overseeing and checking computer inputs to be successfully operated in village areas.

External links in the community information system could however be strengthened considerably by domestic retrieval services which are known generally as teletext services. Broadcast information services are currently marketed by the B.B.C. under the name Ceefax and by I.B.A. under the name Oracle, which enable 'pages' of alphanumeric and graphic information to be received and displayed on a slightly modified 625 line television set. The alterations required involve the addition of circuits which will decode and store the incoming signal, and a small keypad which is used to select the pages of information to be displayed. The information for teletext broadcasting is stored on a computer and may be updated every few minutes if required. Typical pages include news bulletins, sports results, and weather forecasts, but the system is capable of displaying information relating to social services, social security, jobs, planning and the like. Groups of pages are organised into 'magazines' which vary with TV channel and may even- tually be distinct to a broadcast region. Developments in cable television (CCTV) would enable the community infor- mation content of teletext to be even greater so that it could include pages listing job vacancies, planning applications, bus and train times, etc. Both general and local information could be combined in that, for example, a page detailing the range of benefits available under the family income supplement scheme could be followed by another page explaining who to contact, the opening times of offices, which documents to have available, and so on.

The range and flexibility of teletext can be extended enormously if the modified receiver is hooked up to a telephone line, as in the Post Office's Viewdata. The great attraction of using the telephone rather than broadcasting is that a far larger number of different computer information services can be accessed by dialling different numbers so that once a communication channel is open, the two way nature of telephone circuits permits the customer to request one of many different 'pages' by multiple use of a keypad (or ultimately keyphone).[12] By the use of a 'logic tree' the customer can be guided to information he particularly seeks, for example: Jobs - Lincolnshire - Louth Employment Exchange Area - £3,500-£4,500 per annum - Skilled Agricultural Work - LIST OF VACANCIES.

Despite the attractions of this service, doubts about its effectiveness have been expressed on grounds of availability and ease of operation. A major reservation is that such a service might well be socially regressive: teletext services, at least in the first instance, will be comparatively expensive and so will be of little benefit to those who might have the greatest use of them in rural areas, such as the old, the sick, the housebound and the disabled. Such deprived groups could, however, be provided with a service at a reduced rate as in the 'telephones for the elderly' scheme.[16] Rural areas in general are characterised by below average levels of penetration of telecommunications services though this disparity is likely to be reduced in the next decade as urban markets become saturated and most of the expansion takes place in rural areas.[17] Penetration levels in the rural survey areas in Lincolnshire are in fact closely in line with the national picture with 93.9 per cent of households having a television and 51.0 per cent a telephone, and, as only 4.1 per cent of households have neither, the prospect is for rapid adoption of new telecommunications services. Since teletext services are only slightly more difficult to operate than conventional televisions and push-button telephones there seems little reason to doubt their acceptability and usefulness to a population which already makes one third of its information seeking contacts by telephone. Given these prospects and potentials, the central question surrounds the way in which telecommunications can best be incorporated with conventional systems to provide an efficient and comprehensive information delivery service to rural areas.

(ii) Intra-village services

Consultation and advice offered by local people is assumed to have been a major method of information provision in well-developed, integrated communities. Some part of the current problems of information access can be traced back to a decline in the role of intra-village providers. This results from two developments, firstly since many villages form less well-integrated communities than previously, and secondly, because information needs are increasingly complex and inherently less capable of being dealt with in a casual way by local people. Teachers, postmasters, clergy,

neighbours, friends and relatives are still looked to as
information sources in the survey villages although they
account for only 12 per cent of contacts. The present
function of such providers is, however, often extremely
limited, as the West Cumbria Community Development Project
has shown.[5] In comparison with the information services
available at the Project's Community Information and
Action Centre, which includes the referral and signposting
of enquiries to appropriate specialist help, the provision
and dissemination of information both in response to
individual enquiries and through specially mounted cam-
paigns, follow up action including case-advocacy, and the
provision of counselling services for people with profound
and overlapping personal problems, intra-village providers
in the area had neither the time nor the competence to go
beyond the first of these functions. It was in an attempt
to improve the quality of referral and signposting that
the Community Council of Salop recruited and trained a network of local residents or 'representatives' to act as part
time information workers for their local villages. This
scheme is described more fully in Chapter 12.

(iii) Peripatetic or mobile services

An alternative means of delivery is via mobile services
which may be restricted to one area of information such as
employment or social security, or may take the form of
intermediate or general services as is the case with mobile
Citizens' Advice Bureaux, libraries, or local authority
information vans. A number of specialist mobile services
currently operate in central Lincolnshire though typically
the provision of information is secondary to the delivery
of some personal service. This means they are effective
only in those cases where a need for information has been
identified and the right agency contacted. Though they
offer the possibility of providing a comprehensive information service at a large number of locations on a regular
basis, the experience with mobile information vans has been
varied, the successful mobile Citizens' Advice Bureaux in
Gwynedd,[4] contrasting with the disappointing use which was
made of the service in Cleator Moor in Cumbria.[5] The
conversion and running costs are high, and the need for a
vehicle to be parked in an accessible and visible position
brings its own problems: for example it makes it more
difficult for a user to slip in unnoticed. A linked problem
of confidentiality is encountered through the near-
impossibility of providing both private interview space and
an adequate waiting area even in a moderately sized van. A
more fundamental difficulty is the frequency with which the
van visits each village since there are several areas of
social security and employment benefit where delays of even
a few days in requesting a service may lead to reduced
entitlement. This is a major problem in the extension of
mobile libraries as the basis of an information service
since they commonly make fortnightly or monthly visits to
each village and operate according to strict timetables.

One way round these difficulties may be to enable the
providers of mobile services to use rooms in village halls
or community centres, for one or more information and
advice sessions a week. This system, which is operating on
an experimental basis in the Coquet valley, Northumbria, is
able to provide a wide range of information services
including provision, advice, counselling and advocacy.[18]
Major problems, however, surround the availability of
suitable premises and this would be a severe limitation in
central Lincolnshire where by no means all parishes have
village halls or village schools. There is also the
difficulty of creating the right atmosphere in rooms that
have to double for a variety of purposes at different times
of the weeks - which is invariably the case in villages.
A van can at least be permanently stocked with information
and reference sources and with records, leaflets, and
display material which serve practical needs and help to
create a businesslike impression. An unacceptable amount
of fetching and carrying may be a consequence of using
multi-purpose accommodation in a rural area.

(iv) Town based services

Despite the need to improve the level of information
awareness in villages, there are important arguments in
favour of concentrating points of information provision in
market towns. One reason is the centrality of market towns
which means that information sources located there can be
made available to the widest possible markets and can be
accessed on shopping and work trips. Another is that it is
settlements in the size range 5,000-10,000 which have tended
to grow most rapidly in population in recent years. The
promotion of town based information provision, however,
implies the retention of existing services, the replacement
of those which have been withdrawn and possibly the introduction of new services: Citizens' Advice Bureaux for example
example, are an integral part of the information and advice
network in urban areas but there are few Bureaux in market
towns.[19] In order to remove the need for referral between
offices in the same or in other centres, it is, however,
desirable that all information providers operating locally
should be housed in the same building, so as to constitute
what by Smith has been called 'an advice supermarket'.[20]
Local information centres of this type would provide an all
purpose information, advisory, counselling and advocacy
service and their existence may well help to stimulate demand
for information; this being an important consideration when
the aim is to increase the take-up of welfare benefits and
to promote greater participation in planning and community
affairs.
     An important feature of local information centres is
that they could be developed as extensions of the local
authority information offices that exist in some rural areas.
Local authorities are major information providers in rural
areas and they occupy a central role in the community
information system by virtue of their support for voluntary
agencies. Organisations such as the Citizens' Advice

Bureau are heavily dependent upon local government for
finance, and often for accommodation, and in many cases
there are no alternative sources if local authority support
is not forthcoming.[19] For example, in the year ended 31st
March, 1976, Lincoln District Citizens' Advice Bureau
derived 92 per cent of its income from local authorities:
in contrast, a proposal to establish a Citizens' Advice
Bureau in Louth was dropped in 1975 following the refusal of
the East Lindsey District Council to grant the necessary
£2,000. The creation of multi-provision local information
centres represents one way in which local authorities can
ensure a comprehensive provision service which is compatible
with the support and encouragement of local specialist and
voluntary agencies.

Important questions, however, must surround the viability of local information centres given the recent history
of rationalisation in the private and public sector, the
closure of several information services in market towns, and
the need to ensure that they can offer a sufficiently comprehensive service to act as terminal rather than merely
referral information points. Although local authority
information centres already provide examples of an integrated service, there are few instances in which local
authority and central government providing agencies have
been drawn together under the same roof. This distinction
in terms of responsibility for information provision is
critical since it gives rise to an illogical and confusing
fragmentation of local provision. Thus although many
magistrates and crown court offices (which are local
authority controlled) are housed in the same building,
offices of the county court (which are the responsibility of
the Lord Chancellor's Office) are typically to be found
elsewhere. Similarly, the distinction between local authority social service department offices and DHSS offices is
incomprehensible to many consumers and gives rise to many
cases of wrong referral and unnecessary journeys. The most
recent example is the development, by the Manpower Services
Commission, of 'Job Centres' in many small towns (Chapter 4),
usually divorced from the careers offices of County Councils,
and both types of office provide information on job opportunities to school leavers! The situation is further complicated by the presence in most market towns of information
providing offices of public sector organisations such as the
Post Office, Gas, Electricity and Water Authorities and the
Health Service. These are organised on a 'regional' basis
and so have little in common with either local authority or
central government agencies. Official recognition of this
problem has come from the central policy review staff (the
'think tank') in their report on *A Joint Framework for
Social Policies*.[21] This emphasises that:

> 'There is a real need for a more coordinated approach
> towards advice and information services, which are a vital
> point of contact between the social services and the
> citizen. There is a strange mix of provision by
> voluntary organisations, different local government
> departments and central government: consumer advice
> centres, housing advisory centres, information services,
> Citizens' Advice Bureaux, law centres, all performing

somewhat overlapping functions, variously staffed by
specialists and generalist of widely varying competence.
Thinking is now going on in the Lord Chancellor's Office
and in the Department of Prices & Consumer Protection
about the aid and advisory services for which each is
responsible. But it remains possible that, because so
many organisations are involved and because many of them
are not the responsibility of central government, no
coherent principles will be worked out for government
policy in this vital area.'

A major obstacle to integration of information and
advice services is that very frequently a concern with
information is a minor part of the activities of any one
agency and in rural areas may involve only a part of the
time of one member of a small staff. The location of such
staff is determined by their other non-information duties
and should they be moved to a central information office at
some distance from their parent agency it is doubtful
whether they could retain as useful an information and
advice-giving role, in view of their own remoteness from
their information sources and from senior staff empowered
to make final decisions.

Telecommunications might help to overcome these organisational difficulties and thus ensure that local information centres offer a comprehensive terminal information
service in as many information need cases as possible.
Services such as facsimile transmission, telex, datel, and
teletext, are simple and cheap to operate and as they are
based upon the public telephone networks, they require no
expensive capital investment. The experience in Inverclyde
has forcefully demonstrated that no practical difficulties
exist in providing a high quality information service to a
rural area backed up by telecommunications other than those
of initially organising the data in a machine readable form.

CONCLUSIONS

The preceding evaluation suggests that there is no single
solution to the rural information problem, rather there are
a number of schemes which can be combined in various ways
to meet the requirements of a particular locality. The
precise form of any future provision system will depend upon
the emphasis that is placed upon the two major stages in
information access which involve finding out, firstly, what
information is available and where to get it and, secondly,
the acquisition of the information itself. That there is a
significant need for directional guidance has been shown by
the Lincolnshire survey, but whether the reinforcement of
traditional networks of intra-village providers is the most
appropriate means of resolving this difficulty seems
questionable. Today, most people are used to receiving
information via the mass media and the adoption of policies
designed to extend the amount of community information
provided by broadcast services would seem sensible at a time
when very few households are without radio and television
receivers. Although telecommunications are able to provide
a wide range of terminal as well as merely directional

information, the complex and personal nature of many information needs points to a continuing requirement for specialist provision on a face-to-face-basis. A need for such a service exists in each community but although this can be provided on a peripatetic basis, the difficulty of finding appropriate accommodation and arranging sufficiently frequent visits suggests that fixed but limited location town based services are a more efficient solution. Local information centres which combine several areas of provision have many attractions as they would help to over-come the fragmentation of local services. A two tier provision system in which telecommunications are an integral but not the only part can thus be envisaged. Such a system could consist of local information centres in each market town which are contacted by individuals on a self-referral basis in the light of information accessed in their own homes via radio, television, telephone, and teletext.

Whatever combination of schemes is appropriate to satisfy the needs of the next decade, the future patterns of community information cannot be considered without due regard to changes in rural settlement structures and rural transport. Any exchange of information involves a sender, a receiver, and a connection between them, so the future structure of community information will be determined by where people live, where information sources are located, and how the two can best be linked. This raises basic questions concerning the nature and frequency of infor-mation needs, the means used to resolve these needs, and the efficiency and effectiveness of alternative provision systems. What is needed is a more detailed knowledge of information needs and access behaviour and the careful monitoring of experimental delivery systems, work which is currently in progress at Lanchester Polytechnic, Coventry. In this context the preliminary findings summarised in this chapter represent merely the first stage in a continuing evaluation of alternative systems of information delivery in rural areas.

REFERENCES AND NOTES

1. M. Edwards, *The Structure of Community Information Services,* Paper presented to the British Library research forum on community information services (mimeo), 1975.

2. National Consumer Council, *The Fourth Right of Citizenship: A Review of Local Advice Services,* London, National Consumer Council, 1977.

3. P.B. Jackson, *Specialist Services in Rural Areas and the Implications for CAB,* Paper presented to the CAB rural development seminar, Derby, June 1975.

4. A. Griffiths, *The Problem of Providing a Mobile CAB Service* with particular reference to the Gwynedd experience', Paper presented to the CAB rural develop-ment seminar, Derby, June 1975.

5.   H. Butcher, I. Cole and A. Glen, *Information and Action Services for Rural Areas,* University of York Papers in Community Studies No. 5 (mimeo), 1975.

6.   East Anglia Regional Strategy Team, *Strategic Choice for East Anglia,* H.M.S.O., 1974.

7.   P. Goldmark, *Communication in the New Rural Society,* Cornell University (mimeo), 1973.

8.   United States Congress, *The Feasibility and Value of Broadland Communications in Rural Areas,* Washington, Office of Technology Assessment, 1976.

9.   E. Bird, P. Perry and M. de Smith, *Information Provision in the London Borough of Lambeth,* London, Communications Studies and Planning Ltd. (mimeo), 1977.

10. G. Brogden, *Welfare Rights in Rural Areas,* Unpublished M.A. thesis, University of Essex, 1976.

11. Lincolnshire County Council, *Population: A Background Paper to the Lincolnshire Structure Plan,* Report of Survey, Part 1, 1965.

12. R.C. Smith, *Telecommunications Technology: Current Trends,* Department of the Environment Working Group on Telecommunications Impacts Paper No. 1, 1975.

13. J. Short, *Residential Telecommunications Applications. A General Review,* Department of the Environment Working Group on Telecommunications Impacts Paper No. 4, 1975.

14. R.E. Kilsby, *'Box 99' - the Provision of Consumer Advice in Surrey,* Surrey County Council (mimeo), 1974.

15. M. Adler and D. de Feu, *A Computer Based Welfare Benefits Information System,* The Inverclyde Project; Peterlee, IBM Ltd., 1975.

16. P. Gregory and M. Young, *Lifeline Telephone Services for the Elderly,* London, National Innovations Centre, 1972.

17. D. Clark, *The Spatial Impact of Telecommunications: A Review of Empirical Research and Regional Policy Implications,* Department of the Environment Working Groupoon Telecommunications Impact Paper No. 5, 1975.

18. J. Stephenson, *Report on the Coquetdale Experimental Project up to November 1976,* Northumbria Citizens Advice Bureaux, 1976.

19. D. Pearse, *CAB Finance in Rural Areas,* Paper presented to the CAB rural development seminar, Derby, June 1975.

20. G. Smith, *Your Advice Supermarket ,* Municipal and *Public Services Journal,* Vol. 4, 453-5, 1975.

21. Central Policy Review Staff, *A Joint Framework for Social Policies,* London, H.M.S.O., 1975.

12

SOME INNOVATIONS OF A RURAL COMMUNITY COUNCIL

Betty Richardson

REMOTENESS AND ACCESSIBILITY

The reader may find it salutary to ask himself three
questions about the location and accessibility of his or
her District or County Council offices.
1.   How far away are they?
2.   How long does it take to get there?
3.   How much does it cost?
The answers to these questions in the case of the author,
who lives in a village on the Welsh border, are as follows:
District Council Offices
1.   35 miles.
2.   2 days by public transport - it is not possible to
     get there and back in a day.
3.   £2.00 by public transport.
County Council Offices
1.   17 miles.
2.   A whole day.
3.   At least £1.00 by public transport.
It is now widely appreciated that, particularly since
the re-organisation of Local Government, it is often quicker
to travel to the Continent by air than to reach a local
destination where one can obtain the advice and help one
may need to solve a problem. Moreover, on arrival at the
offices of a local or central government department, there
may be further problems in identifying one's precise
destination.
The following story about an old lady (she is over 70)
who lives in the same village as the author may illustrate
this point. She had a tax problem on some property which
she owned, so she caught the village bus and, nearly two
hours later, she reached the Shirehall of Shropshire County
Council. Anyone who has been in a Shire or County Hall
knows that, however good the receptionist, it is very
difficult to sort out exactly whom one wants to consult.
After refusing to get in the lift (that 'box thing' she

called it) to the second floor, the old lady stumped out
of the Shirehall, caught her return bus and arrived back
home, very weary and declaring she 'would rather pay the
money than go through all that again'. One can hardly
help sympathising with her experience. The truth was, of
course, that she was in the wrong building entirely - she
should have gone to the Inland Revenue Taxation Offices
two miles away!

At a time when the social structure in this country is
becoming increasingly complex, the old natural leadership
in the rural areas of 'people to whom one used to be able
to turn for help' is also rapidly disappearing. Such
individuals once provided a local source of information and
reference, but the village parson, the schoolmaster, the
nurse, and the policeman now invariably live miles away
from the rural settlements which they serve and only come
into the community for their work. The local police force
in particular are not as readily available as they were in
the interwar and early postwar period for people to
approach when they are in difficulties. Indeed in many
villages one only sees the policeman when one has committed
a crime!

THE VILLAGE REPRESENTATIVE SCHEME

It was against this background that the Community Council
of Shropshire devised a scheme for appointing 'Local
Representatives' in the villages and parishes throughout
this large rural county. The location of the Representatives is shown in Figure 12.1. These Representatives,
who function on an entirely voluntary basis (although they
are offered postage, telephone and any modest travelling
expenses) are nominated or confirmed by their Parish
Councils. If the Parish Councils do not suggest a suitable
person, the Community Council does some research to find
somebody, and then approaches the Parish Council to ask
whether they agree to the appointment. These Representatives are, above all,*local referral points* to be contacted for information as to which statutory authority,
government department, voluntary organisation or other
agency should be approached for advice on personal problems
of any kind.

Obviously, it is essential that the Representatives are
people of integrity, who can be trusted and who have
standing in the community, as enquirers will wish their
problems to be treated in the strictest confidence. But
they need not have any special status. They are not
necessarily, for example, Parish Councillors or local
clergymen, but are usually individuals who have the
necessary time to devote to the task, and who feel that
this type of service to the Community would appeal to them.
Ideally, they should live within walking distance of most
people in the area they cover, and essentially they must
be easy to contact. In 1978, 55% of the Shropshire
Representatives were women and half of all the Representatives were engaged in full-time employment. However, the
employed group included a high percentage of farmers,

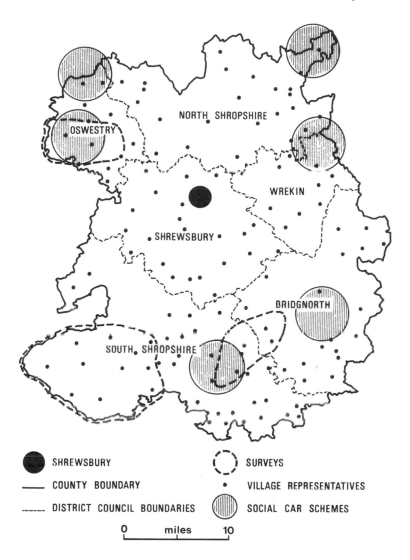

Figure 12.1.   Innovations of the Shropshire Community
     Council.

owners of small businesses, postmasters/mistresses, village
schoolmasters/mistresses and clergy, who are likely to be
readily available on the spot each day. There were also a
few nurses. The remaining half were either housewives
(and this included farmers' wives, who could be classed as
earning their living) or were retired people. Many of the
latter have had a professional background but, for example,
one of the most successful Representatives in Shropshire is
an ex-coal miner, who lives on a small council estate on

the edge of the village and who regards his present role
as a full-time job.   In terms of age the majority of the
Representatives are middle aged to 'early elderly'.

To facilitate their advisory role Representatives are
provided with a wallet containing a variety of reference
leaflets, contacts, address lists and news sheets, etc.;
which The Community Council endeavour to keep as up-to-
date as possible.   The basic document, in Shropshire, is
the County 'Directory of Essential Community Services'.[1]
This was first compiled by the Community Council in 1975,
and was revised, supplemented and reprinted in 1978.
Copies of this document are also supplied to other bodies
such as the police, doctors, social services officers, and
local Post Offices, who evidently find it of value in their
work.   It contains a wide range of information on the
personal services offered in the County by Central
Government departments, other statutory authorities, local
government departments, voluntary organisations and a range
of other agencies.   This type of Directory is to be found
in a few other Counties in England and Wales, but could,
with advantage, be prepared for all rural areas.   To
publicise the Scheme to the public, the local Representatives are supplied with posters and leaflets, and they
attract substantial coverage from the Press in the form of
special features on particular activities and editorials
on the general aims and successes of the Scheme.

In Shropshire, there is also an Honorary Field Officer
who travels round continuously, talking to the Representatives, weeding out the 'not-so-actives' (and there are
some of these in every voluntary organisation) and
appointing new ones.   'Get together' meetings are arranged
at least once a year all over the County.   The distances
are so great that the Representatives do not meet in
Shrewsbury, but in 8 local groups.   Difficulties are
discussed and Officers from the various local authority
and other bodies tell the Representatives about the latest
developments in their work.   A Review Committee has
recently been appointed, consisting of two Representatives
from each of the six District Council Areas in the County.
There are no local authority representatives on the
Committee, and the only other members are group Convenors
and Officers of the Community Council.   It is the job of
this Committee to evaluate the Scheme and to talk over its
pros and cons from all points of view.   The advice of the
Review Committee on any necessary 'remedial' action is
implemented as promptly as possible.

The Shropshire Representatives Scheme has been operating
for three years and, in 1977, included 140 Representatives,
some operating more successfully than others, with their
effectiveness depending very much on the personality of the
Representative.   The range of problems dealt with is
staggering and, if they do not have to hand the necessary
information to deal with them all, the Representatives ring
the Community Council.   The Council Officers then endeavour
to find the right channel for them but, needless to say,
they are constantly also feeding enquiries into the County
Social Services Department, the local Department of Health
and Social Security offices and the five Citizens' Advice

Bureaux in the County. The Community Council also receives
enquiries direct into the offices from many individuals who
need help and who wish to remain as anonymous as possible.
This inhibits them from approaching a local authority
office until they are sure that they know precisely whom
they should consult. A voluntary organisation is often the
most appropriate agency to cope with their problems. For
example, a lady recently rang the Community Council. She
was desperately in need of help as she had an alcoholic
husband, so the Council was able to put her in direct
touch with Al-Anon, the voluntary organisation connected
with Alcoholics Anonymous, which helps the families of
those concerned who are in distress.

It should be stressed that Local Representatives are
urged to act only as information points and not to attempt
to give 'in depth' advice on problems, as they are not
equipped with the type of training which would be needed
for this, nor does the Community Council feel this is the
kind of service it would wish to offer. But we did not
fully appreciate, in the early days, that the sort of
people who become Local Representatives are more often than
not action-orientated individuals, who are not content
merely to give information to those making enquiries, but
will wish actually to help them to sort out their
difficulties on a more practical basis. For example, a
Representative was faced on his doorstep with a mother and
two young children, ejected from their home late one night
by, one can only suppose, an inebriated husband. This
Representative took them in, gave them a bed, and the next
day went round with them to the various Government departments, to get them assistance. In another case, one
Representative helped a family in her village whose home
was burnt to the ground. She found them temporary living
accommodation and, again, put them in her car and took them
to the County W.R.V.S. office to obtain replacements of
clothes and furniture. These are perhaps more spectacular
examples, but they are being repeated in a smaller way all
over Shropshire, in the context of the Village Representative Scheme.

THE RURAL SURVEYS

As the Representative Scheme grew, the Community Council
itself realised its value in connection with other work
which the Council was undertaking in the rural areas. It
has been felt for a long time that constructive help could
only be offered in connection with the continually changing
pattern of overall communtiy needs, if the *exact nature* of
the problems was known, from the viewpoint of the people
themselves. It is *too easy to suppose and impose* - quite
often the theories advanced by social workers and public
administrators at a county level bear little relation to
what the grass roots actually feel themselves. The
Community Council of Shropshire therefore initiated, in
different parts of the County, a series of 'Surveys of
Rural Services', based on questionnaires to individiual
households. The latest, and most successful, of these is

the one recently completed in the Clun area of South West
Shropshire.[2] This covered difficulties relating to
Transport, Medical and Community Services, the latter
embracing such items as the availability of postal facilities and local shopping, though the surveys have also
thrown up a variety of other problems! Local Representatives acted as co-ordinators for the Surveys, and we feel
that the success of the Clun project was due entirely to
their efforts, as we achieved a 95% response rate on the
questionnaire. This is, of course, a very high percentage
in relation to most other comparable rural surveys. The
Representatives were tireless in taking the forms around
and in discussing the Survey with the local people so that
they themselves could assess its purpose, and could
appreciate that it was not just another sheet of paper
which would disappear into limbo once it had been filled
up. The whole object of the Survey was not merely to
obtain statistics, valuable as these are, but to highlight
specific rural problems on which *action* could be taken.

SOCIAL CAR SCHEMES

In nearly all cases the problems identified by the Surveys
have been shown to revolve around a diminishing, or sometimes non-existent, public transport system, particularly
in the more remote areas. A substantial amount of evidence
has been collected by the Shropshire Community Council
which reveals that people cannot obtain prescriptions,
cannot get to doctors' surgeries, cannot get to hospitals
in time for appointments, or to visit the sick; pensioners
cannot get down to the Old People's Clubs and the handicapped cannot get on the few buses which are available -
the small 'cannots' are endless in the rural areas of
Shropshire and the Welsh Border. These issues give rise to
demands which are much too small in scale to warrant
commercial provision or by the public sector,but they are of
vital importance to, for example, the elderly or handicapped
who are becoming increasingly isolated, and who are often
too fiercely independent to ask for assistance.
   To attempt to deal with these problems, Shropshire has
pioneered the Voluntary Social Car Scheme, the original one
being initiated by the W.R.V.S., and now operates within a
15 mile radius of Bridgnorth. The later ones have been
organised by the Rural Community Council in conjunction with
the County Council. For each one, a Register of local
drivers is compiled, a Co-ordinator is appointed and
approval for the scheme is obtained from the County Council,
which pays drivers a mileage allowance. Each of the six
Social Car Schemes now operational in Shropshire has
between 10 and 20 volunteer drivers (Figure 12.1). People
with the sort of difficulties detailed above can contact
their nearest driver direct for transport help, or the
Co-ordinator if they do not have any success with their
initial approach to the driver. The great advantage of
these Car Schemes is that they are simple to operate and
are very flexible, and, of course, the local authorities
are attracted by the low cost of operation. Typical costs

Table 12.1.   Trefonen Social Car Scheme

Journey Type	No. of Trips
Collection of prescriptions	3
Bank and shopping	3
Hospital and medical	5
Visits to sick and elderly	8
Other journeys, including visits to Old People's Clubs	14
Total (52 passengers)	33
Total Cost = 344 miles @ 8p/mile	£27.52

Source: Trefonen Social Car Scheme, October
          and November 1977.

covering a 2 month period of operating a Social Car Scheme,
in Northwest Shropshire are shown in Table 12.1.
    In addition, the Community Council is trying to help
initiate Postal Bus services in Shropshire, and there are
also several private minibuses in operation belonging to
voluntary organisations and to groups of ecclesiastical
parishes, all of which have been set up in an endeavour in
some way to stem the tide of rural deprivation arising from
lack of local transport

EVALUATING THE INNOVATIONS

How can one evaluate these practical innovations in
Shropshire? Any appraisal of the schemes is difficult to
do in cold statistical terms, as the Schemes are dealing
with *people,* and unless one regards people purely as
statistics, it is almost impossible to 'compute' the impact
of the Schemes on their way of life. This problem is
exacerbated by the fact that it is virtually impossible to
extract precise information on the 'number of enquiries'
handled by the Village Representatives, however hard we
try, or however many 'forms-to-be-filled-in' we send them.
By definition, they are very busy people and are nearly
always to be found in the centre of activity in their
villages. But, by talking to them, and with the operation
of a sixth sense, the Community Council estimates there are
an average of some three enquiries per Representative per
month.
    This may not sound very much but it gives a total of
300-400 monthly in the whole County, or nearly 4,000 per
year, which represents a substantial voluntary contribution
to the work of the over-stretched Social Services and other
statutory authority departments in this large rural area.
The Local Representative also provides them with established

links in the rural communities and the Social Service Officers particularly frequently express their appreciation for such assistance. This is the only reliable information which is available, though it is doubtful whether it is meaningful to attempt to assess the success of the Scheme at this level. For example, if one Representative can spend nearly a week helping a family demoralised through the loss of their home in a fire and she, in turn, is assisted by the information which the Community Council have been able to give her in the Directory ... surely this merits more than one tick on her record sheet? Another, very wise, Representative stated recently that she found that 'people need someone to talk to in the grey areas between themselves and what they see as the authorities - with a capital A'. These examples illustrate two different approaches to the job by two different types of people - but both are Local Representatives and both are making valuable contributions to the life of their rural communities.

This chapter has considered three different 'innovations' in the rural areas of Shropshire - Local Representatives, Surveys of Rural Services, Voluntary Social Car Schemes. All of these, however, are integrated and revolve around the representatives in the village and parishes where they live. These Schemes have been init- iated to help with needs which are not catered for by commercial or public authority provision, and perhaps the most significant factor in all this is the immense and incalculable contribution of voluntary effort and good will which supports them and makes them possible. In the context of the 'Good Neighbour Campaign' initiated in 1977 by the then Secretary of State for Health and Social Security (Mr. David Ennals) this surely establishes those participating in such voluntary schemes as very good Good Neighbours.

REFERENCES AND NOTES

1. *How, Where, When? Directory of Essential Community Services in Shropshire,* Community Council of Shropshire, 1978.

2. *Rural Services Survey in Clun Area of South-west Shropshire,* Community Council of Shropshire, 1977.

13

RURAL DEPRIVATION AND SOCIAL PLANNING: AN OVERVIEW

Martin Shaw

DEFINING DEPRIVATION

Both 'deprivation' and 'social planning' are fashionable concepts, and this reflects a more general interest in the well being of different groups in Western society as a whole. Like many other social concepts, their popularity is not matched by the clarity of their meaning, and any attempt to discuss social well-being is fraught with difficulties. Terms such as 'standard of living', or 'quality of life' are both relative and emotive; and the assumptions made in an effort to clarify the nature of deprivation necessarily involve value judgements. Not only is the idea of 'objective' data in this context a misnomer, but given the limited amount of analytical and prescriptive writing on rural deprivation noted in the Introduction, an overview of its extent, nature, and implications for public policy and individual behaviour in Britain presents a daunting task. Even so, the purpose of this chapter is to summarise some of the themes which emerge from an attempt at a comprehensive view. In drawing on the evidence and arguments advanced in the earlier chapters, the differing standpoints from which the individual essays have been written are highlighted.

Following a brief look at the concept of deprivation, the problems of measuring rurality are considered, and the emergence of a new rural awareness in Britain against the background of a national commitment to the cities is identified. The cycle of deprivation which operates in rural areas and its main components are described on the basis of the available evidence. The role of public policy at both the central and local government levels is assessed, as opposed to the responsibility of local groups and communities in assisting the resolution of social problems. The chapter concludes by considering the long term future of rural communities in Britain.

The relativity implied by the idea of deprivation requires a scale (or at least a clear context) to be

established in order to enable the idea to be translated
into a recognisable set of needs in any area, whether urban
or rural. All concepts of rural deprivation are based on
implicit assumptions about 'need' - and need itself is a
nebulous concept. In this sense, deprivation exists when
needs which society feels should be satisfied are not met.
Four approaches to the definition of need have been identified by Bradshaw,[1] and the possible application of these
to rural issues is exemplified below:

Normative Need This is what the expert or professional
administrator or social scientist defines as a need in any
given situation, often on the basis of pre-defined
criteria, as when national standards for schools are ap
applied rigidly to village schools.

Felt Need Here need is equated with 'want'. When assessing need for a service, people are asked whether they feel
they need it. This is the type of need reflected in a wide
range of surveys of rural services.

Expressed Need or demand is felt need turned into action.
Under this definition, total need is defined as those
people who demand a particular facility, such as a rural
bus service.

Comparative Need By this definition, a measure of need is
found by studying the characteristics of those in receipt
of a service. If people with similar characteristics are
not in receipt of service, then they are in need. This is
the logic applied when comparing the gap between the
actual provision of sports facilities in a rural area with
a typical level of urban provision.

These theoretical concepts of social need often overlap
and it should be noted that each is a mixture of two
elements. First, they imply the existence of some material
benefit or disadvantage, and, secondly, they are usually
based on a set of non-material assumptions about social
values. It is this latter point which renders such definitions particularly open to criticism since value systems
are notoriously volatile, and this is especially true of
areas subject to significant demographic changes as is the
case with most of rural Britain.

It is clear that deprivation is closely connected with
ideas of equality and inequality, and in the rural case
the concern is with the inequality of the levels of consumption (of both material and non-material goods) between
those who live in rural areas and those living elsewhere.
Many quantitative studies have been concerned with urban
as well as rural deprivation, and the definition adopted by
such a study of Nottinghamshire is typical.[2] Multiple
deprivation was here defined as 'social groups or areas
which experience consistently worse conditions relative to
other groups or areas, and have relatively less opportunity
in relation to such social markets as housing, employment,
education, leisure facilities ...'

Both the attempt to clarify the concept of need, and the
above attempt to define multiple deprivation illustrate the
complex nature of the concept of deprivation. It is not
the specific problems of unemployment, lack of facilities
etc. alone that are of concern in this context, but the
combination of these and other problems and the way they

act together to limit the range of opportunity open to individuals. This is the approach adopted in this overview. However, in order to assess whether rural deprivation is identifiable in a form which has direct relevance for public policy two preliminary questions need to be answered. First, are there any criteria which provide a logical basis for defining rurality as a significant variable in the spectrum of social well-being? Secondly, how do the social characteristics of such rural areas compare with those of other defined areas where social problems have already been recognised and reflected in public policies?

MEASURING 'RURALITY'

The distinction between 'urban' and 'rural' areas is deeply rooted in the psychology of most attempts at any regional or local subdivision of the United Kingdom. This difference was, of course, institutionalised in the late nineteenth century delineation of local authority boundaries, although the old 'urban' category included 90% of the population in the postwar period. Since the reorganised local authorities were deliberately constituted, in many cases, to combine towns and their rural hinterlands it is impossible to classify the new District Councils in this way. The classic study of the characteristics of local authority areas in Britain by Moser and Scott (1961)[3] excluded all local authorities with populations under 50,000, and could not, therefore, be used as a yardstick to measure social health in rural areas. A more recent attempt at a multivariate analysis of 1971 census data for all of the local authorities has been undertaken, and, using a wide range of socio-economic statistics, eleven groups of districts were identified with similar characteristics, one of which related to 'Rural Areas';[4] this can be compared with largely intuitive definitions of the rural areas, such as that of Green (1971).[5] Both of these definitions include 16-17% of the population of England and Wales (Figure 13.1).

Of the statistically derived subdivisions of Britain which have been made, few provide the basis for a definition of the rural areas which reflects their distinctive characteristics. However, Cloke (1977)[6] has attempted this by adopting an inductive approach to 'rurality'. Building on earlier work at the Department of the Environment, he selected 16 variables which were felt to be indicative of rurality, embracing population, employment, housing, land use and remoteness from urban centres. In the rural context, the addition of the last factor represents a significant advance on the earlier statistical classifications, and it proved to be the most significant group of factors that was finally included in the composite index of rurality. The index emphasises the rural areas of the South-west, Wales, Eastern England and a discontinuous Pennine Belt (Figure 13.1).

There are problems in using all such systematic classifications as a starting point for studies which are

Rural deprivation

ⓐ Rural Regions (Intuitive)   ### ⓑ Rurality Clusters (Statistical)

ⓒ Index of Rurality   ### ⓓ Index of Level of Living

Figure 13.1. England and Wales: the rural dimension
(a) Five intuitively defined rural regions (Green, 1971)
(b) Rural clusters - based on a multivariate analysis of 40
    1971 census variables for new local authority areas
    (Webber and Craig, 1976).
(c) Extreme and intermediate rural areas - classified on the
    basis of a principal components analysis using 16
    'rurality' variables for old local authority areas
    (Cloke, 1977)
(d) Areas with low levels of living scores - based on a
    multivariate analysis of 29 'level of living' variables
    for old local authority areas (Coates, Johnston and
    Knox, 1977)

concerned to rank areas in terms of their social disadvantage, and it is arguable whether one should even try to
use classifications in this way. Certainly, despite its
logical merit, Cloke's attempt at a quantitative description of different degrees of rurality at different dates
is of limited assistance as an indicator of relative
deprivation. A more explicit attempt at using criteria of
social well-being as a basis of classification is essential
if it is to provide any assistance at all in assessing
national priorities for resource allocation among urban and
rural areas. One such effort has been made by Coates *et
al.* (1977), to define levels of national well-being on the
basis of 29 (census) variables, analysed for the old
authority areas in Britain.[7] The resulting pattern (Figure
13.1) shows that in 1971 the areas with the lowest average
'levels of living' were to be found in the main urban
centres, together with rural Wales and north and South-
west England. Much of rural England outside the most
prosperous London-Birmingham axis is classified as having
'above average well-being' on the basis of this 'level of
living' set of social and economic statistics.

A similar relative picture emerges from studies of the
spatial variation in net incomes in Britain, which reveal
'an island of prosperity stretching from Essex to Worcester-
shire and from Sussex to Leicestershire'.[8] In absolute
terms, however, around this essentially urban heartland
incomes are everywhere below the national average. On the
basis of Inland Revenue data, as demonstrated by Thomas and
Winyard (Chapter 3), the Celtic fringe and North and South-
west England are characterised by well-above average
percentages in the low income groups and below average
percentages in the high income groups, with less pronounced
deviations from the average in the Midlands and East
Anglia.[9]

There are four immediate problems in drawing conclusions
from these analyses as part of the process of assessing the
rural dimension of deprivation. First, most of the indicators used tend to be urban-orientated, and it is not therefore surprising that the most obvious blackspots are the
cities! This bias is discussed in more detail below in
relation to Inner City policies. Secondly, the resulting
patterm is primarily a centre-periphery gradient rather
than an urban/rural division, although there is, of course,
a marked spatial coincidence between the peripheral areas
and the rural parts of Britain. Thirdly, these studies may
demonstrate that certain *areas* are disadvantaged in relation
to the multiplicity of criteria being used, but this does
not necessarily prove that there are large numbers or
percentages of individuals who suffer from a 'multiple' form
of deprivation. Although this is highly probable in an
urban context, the size of such groups within a rural area
may, of course, be relatively small. Fourthly, virtually
all of the data is highly aggregated, whereas the evidence
in this book suggests that rural social problems are too
fine-grained to be susceptible to this sort of analysis at
a national scale. Local studies of intra-urban deprivation
have been carried out,[10] and although there are few
comparable systematic exercises for the rural parts of the

country, Thomas and Winyard's multivariate analysis of data for Wales (Chapter 3) and studies of Cumbria and Norfolk have demonstrated the wide range of local variations which can be found within a rural area.[11] Finally, the construction of precise indices represents an attempt to translate previously subjective ideas about rural life into one concise statement of urban/rural differentials, but although the problem of the spatial delimitation of rural areas is thus overcome, objectivity only exists in a numeric sense, and, given the fine-grained nature of problems mentioned above, there is a real danger of throwing the baby out with the bathwater. The problems of rural deprivation involve essentially value judgements about highly localised issues and it is easy to lose sight of this in the quest for indexation.[12]

URBAN PRIORITIES AND EMERGING RURAL AWARENESS

There are obvious problems in attempting to assess the reality and relativity of rural deprivation in a systematic way against a comprehensive national backcloth, but there is one other base line which can be used. This is the multiple form of deprivation, or social malaise, which has been identified in the inner areas of British cities.[13] It is essential to interpret the evidence for and the arguments about rural deprivation in the light of an appraisal of inner city problems, for three reasons. First, the documentation of urban deprivation has been substantial in the 1970s and, as noted in the Introduction, there has been no comparable effort relating to rural Britain. Secondly, there is an effective national consensus on the need to give priority to alleviating the social and economic problems to be found in inner city areas. Thirdly, the size of the resources which are now devoted by government to the inner city represents an explicit national policy of positive discrimination in public expenditure on a vast scale which (ignoring hidden per head subsidies to rural services) has no parallel in rural Britain.

Although consistently detailed evidence is not available, and even though the order of magnitude of the two problems is quite different, it is nevertheless worth making a brief comparison of the origin and symptoms of deprivation in the inner city with the evidence which is emerging in respect of the remote rural areas of Britain. Any contemporary view of rural problems is inevitably influenced by the prevailing emphasis on urban issues, but as far back as the nineteenth century opinions on the well-being of rural society were often distorted by the contrast with the more evident urban squalor. While the overall scale of any rural disadvantage has been historically less than in industrial Britain, and residents of agricultural areas were probably healthier than their urban counterparts, much rural poverty was almost certainly comparable to that among the urban working class. In most of lowland England, agriculture was neglected and depressed until the outbreak of the Second World War and the loss of young people from these rural areas reinforced the problems of social disadvantage.

However, the causes of the major difficulties are clearly
different in rural areas from those in urban areas.
Whereas the reasons for inner city decline stem from the
age and condition of their physical fabric, as well as
their changing economic base, rural deprivation has its
roots in the falling demand for agricultural labour, and
the changing locational requirements of service activity
associated with the growth of personal mobility. Whereas
the loss of some jobs from the countryside is associated
with *centralising* trends in the service sector, the reduction in inner city employment has been due to the
decentralisation of economic activity to the outer metropolitan areas.[14] In both the inner city and the rural
areas at least a part of the blame for current problems can
probably be laid at the door of central and local government. In the inner city, for example, redevelopment
policies are alleged to have compounded the problems,[15]
while in the rural areas both Rose (Chapter 2) and Larkin
(Chapter 5) suggest that official housing and planning
policies have added to the difficulties of lower income
groups in villages.

There has been a preoccupation of academics and planners
with the inner city problem which has as a corollary the
neglect of rural issues, and government policies designed
to tackle the worst problem areas have led to a reaction
to this urban-based approach to deprivation. The need to
demonstrate that rural areas also have a share of the
county's social problems was above all highlighted by the
switch of public expenditure, in the form of the Rate
Support Grant distributions in the mid 1970s, away from the
rural 'shire' counties and in favour of the metropolitan
authorities. In part, much of the recent awareness of
rural issues also stems, ironically, from the rapidity of
the pace of change in rural areas. The increased rate of
housebuilding, at least in the rural areas of lowland
Britain in the 1970s, was matched by a high level of
mobility within the existing housing stock. This continued
dispersal of new housing into villages reflected the
pressure from builders for cheaper land (which reached its
peak during the house-price inflation of 1971-73) and the
problems of first-time buyers forced out of towns by rising
house prices, as well as reflecting genuinely 'rural'
housing pressures for retirement migration in Wales, the
South-west and East Anglia.

A renewed interest in village development policy has
also gathered momentum and this has been stimulated by the
preparation of structure plans and the experience of the
new planning authorities. In particular the conventional
wisdom of rural settlement policies referred to in Chapter
9 has been subject to more rigorous questioning, and there
is considerable public scepticism about the unit cost
assumptions on which many local and other statutory
authorities base their policies for rural services. This
has led, for example, to a strong reaction against the low
priority given by Regional Water Authorities to first-time
rural sewerage, and to growing concern about the closure of
small village schools.

Rural deprivation

This contemporary disquiet about rural services is, of course, part of a more general concern about the whole series of social and economic changes which favour the large against the small, but which has inevitably focussed attention on the rural areas, because of the scale of rural communities, rural organisations and rural facilities. Interest in low impact technology, self-sufficiency and alternative lifestyles has also been primarily associated with the rural parts of Britain.

All of these trends have combined to reinforce an emerging rural awareness and a determination to ensure that, while the overwhelming case for the inner city areas is accepted, the problems and needs which exist in rural areas should not go unrecognised by default. Rural deprivation is on a smaller scale than that in urban areas, it is less evident than that in urban areas, and it is less amenable to identification by spatial zoning: it is nevertheless real, and the reality of the rural problem is described below.

HOUSEHOLD, OPPORTUNITY AND MOBILITY DEPRIVATION

Whatever definition of rural deprivation is accepted, for the reasons given earlier, the focus of concern is with the inequality of consumption levels between those living in rural areas and those living elsewhere. Because so many of the most important items of consumption are not bought at a 'market' price deprivation through low income is not the only form. However, many politicians and administrators have used extended definitions of income or expenditure as being synonymous with well-being. This is clearly inadequate. As noted above, non-market items (such as law and order) cannot be valued in this way and in the rural case the evidence presented in this book certainly demands a wider view, embracing the availability of many different kinds of opportunity. The basic stance adopted in most of the essays in this book is one in which rural well-being is viewed as of several dimensions, whose components are labelled only for convenience as income, housing, education etc. (which do not pretend to represent an exhaustive list). Even so it is useful to describe the form of rural deprivation in terms of a three-fold grouping of the major dimensions into three 'types' of deprivation (see Figure 13.2).

First, the link between the main source of household income - wages - and that key item of expenditure - housing - is extremely close, and provides the basis of the material well-being of families living in rural areas. This primary dimension can be described as 'household' deprivation.

The second component relates to the availability of opportunities and services in the employment, education, health, recreational and cultural spheres. The low level and limited range of such opportunities must be set alongside the low pay problems of rural families for any assessment of deprivation to make sense. It is interesting to note that a minority group on the Royal Commission on Income and Wealth[16] has expressed concern that the Commission was precluded from taking account of non-income factors, and

believes that there should be a 'level of living' study to
complement the analysis of material wealth and income.
This would deal not only with how much income was going
into a family, but what access it had to employment and
education.   It is convenient to term this second aspect
'opportunity' deprivation.

This lack of opportunities is fundamental to deprivation in both urban and rural areas, but where these
opportunities rely on the provision of capital-intensive
facilities, the rural areas are increasingly disadvantaged
by comparison with the cities, as the population thresholds
needed to support such facilities rises. This additional rural
hazard of remoteness, when associated with lack of ready
access to a car, compounds the problems of opportunity
deprivation.   In rural areas it is accessibility which
rations opportunities as well as incomes, and 'mobility'
deprivation constitutes the third form of rural problem.

The rural deprivation model shown in Figure 13.2 can be
compared with a typical cycle of urban poverty such as that
described by Raynor et al[17]   (see Figure 13.3).

Most studies of urban malaise have identified inter-
dependent cycles of low incomes, unskilled work, poor
housing and environment, and poor educational opportunities.
But accessibility rarely forms a significant component in
such models, though the barrier effects of distance are
recognised in a recent work on geographical inequality,[18]
and research on the access problems of urban minority groups
is now in progress.[19]

What evidence in there of the extent of the type of
deprivation outlined above?   Is the phenomenon of rural
deprivation myth or reality?   While no-one can doubt the
genuineness of current concern about social issues in rural
areas it is clearly essential to ask how far the rural
deprivation cycle described here is justified by the
available evidence, including that presented in this book.

HOUSEHOLD DEPRIVATION

Low earnings certainly emerge from the thorough empirical
work of Thomas and Winyard (Chapter 3) as a real source of
household deprivation which is only partly to be explained
by the incidence of low-paid rural workers, particularly
farmworkers.   Moreover, the overlap of two forms of
'social planning' policy - direct taxation and the welfare
state - are shown   in Chapter 3 to have pushed low-income
agricultural families into the poverty trap, while there is
no elastic provision in the Supplementary Benefit system to
cover the cost of journeys to work for rural households.
The case study evidence of both income profiles and other
'levels of living' indicators suggest that extensive rural
areas suffer from many of the symptoms of household
deprivation which characterise older industrial areas
although, on the basis of the published statistical data,
there is no overwhelming case for identifying a specifically
'rural' incomes problem.   However, when reinforced by the
examples of housing difficulty quoted in Chapter 2 and
Chapter 5, the evidence of rural disadvantage is real

Rural deprivation

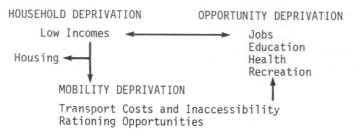

Figure 13.2. The rural deprivation cycle.

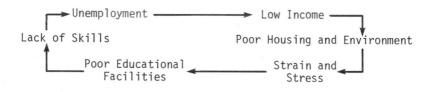

Figure 13.3. An urban poverty cycle (after Raynor *et al*, 197C

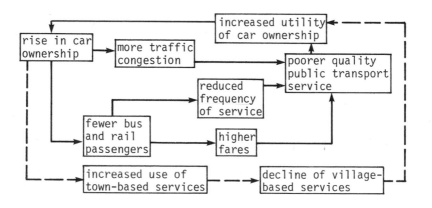

Figure 13.4. The rural accessibility spiral (based on
    Moseley, 1979)[30]

enough (though the nature and origins of housing deprivation are often similar to much of urban Britain).

Rural housing problems stem, in the first instance,
from market factors associated particularly with the movement of relatively affluent commuters, retired couples and
second home-owners into the rural areas which, until the
last two decades, were the home of those engaged in low
paid local employment. This rural housing market problem
has, of course, been exacerbated by two national trends -
'external' inflation in house prices, and the decline of
the private rented sector, though the latter has had a
rural as well as an urban dimension. Penfold[20] discovered
that, in the Peak District, landlords are increasingly
responding to the demand generated by commuters and prospective second-home owners by selling off properties
previously rented to local people. Government policies
have played a major part in the disappearance of private
rented accommodation, and both Rose (Chapter 2) and Larkin
(Chapter 5) attribute the existence of some rural housing
deprivation to the planning and housing policies of local
authorities. Rose criticises the rigidity of development
control policies aimed at restricting housing development
in small villages for 'amenity' reasons (which, he argues,
have coincided with the interests and influence of the
landowning groups). Certainly, on the basis of the
evidence in Chapters 2 and 5 neither planning nor house
building policies bear a clear relationship to the incidence
of local housing need, and yet surveys by Bennett[21] have
demonstrated that, taking the number of households on a
waiting list as a proportion of all rural households, rural
need can be seen to equal and, in pockets, to exceed urban
need. Other surveys[22] have reinforced the arguments in
Chapter 5 that over-reliance of housing authorities on
waiting lists leads to an under-estimation of the true
level of rural need. Apart from the council house waiting
list issue, other symptoms of the low income/housing
problem in some rural areas are evident - out-migration of
the young, villages with many empty houses outside holiday
periods, and the degeneration of caravan sites into rural
ghettos (even alleged in Chapter 5 to be used as 'dumping
grounds for problem families'). The combined effects of
low incomes, rising house prices, a limited supply of
council housing in some small villages, the decline of the
rural rented housing sector, the operation of national cost
yardsticks and the possibly regressive effect of local
planning policies have all helped to deny low paid workers
the chance of both living and working in the same village.

OPPORTUNITY DEPRIVATION

Whereas rural 'household' deprivation is akin to that
experienced by families in the cities (though it is evidently less serious in rural Britain), the second type of
deprivation, based on a lack of opportunities, often takes
a different form in rural areas. Certainly the present
decline in local services and facilities in the inner city
areas has been of much less significance in contributing

to urban malaise than, say, household deprivation and
environmental dereliction. The concept of opportunity
deprivation in the rural areas relates to three broad
categories of 'opportunity', in the spheres of employment,
private sector facilities, and public sector services.
The main causes of the declines which have led to this
type of deprivation are summarised below.

The lack of jobs in rural areas is the key component to
the long-term decline of village life in the more remote
rural areas. The dramatic fall in the agricultural labour
force in both the interwar and postwar years is only now
showing signs of levelling off. This decline has not been
matched by the creation of new rural job opportunities in
the manufacturing sector or (except where there has been
substantial growth in female employment) in the service
sector. Packman (Chapter 4) has summarised the symptoms
of this deficiency, including high long-term unemployment
levels, lack of opportunities for school-leavers, high
proportions of workers who are both unemployed and
unskilled, low female activity rates, and mismatch between
the skills of the unemployed and the job available. Moreover there is considerable evidence that in a time of
recession it is the rural areas, with their low economic
potential and narrow industrial base which are most
vulnerable to further loss of jobs.

The loss of both private and public sector facilities
has not been well documented until the mid-1970s, though
the general postwar trend has been clear: a steady and
prolonged reduction in the level of service available to
rural residents. In the private sector, the loss of the
village shop (often combined with a post office) has been
the most significant. For example, in Norfolk, Suffolk,
Cambridgeshire, Avon, Gloucestershire, Wiltshire and
Somerset, a quarter of all villages had no shops in 1977.
The nature of the decline is illustrated by the 40% decline
in village food-shops in rural Norfolk since 1950, and the
13% decline in village shops in Gloucestershire and Wiltshire between 1972 and 1977.[23] In relation to particular
types of shop the problem is even more serious - though
not always as a result of declining services, as in the
case of chemists' shops. The proportions of villages
without a chemist in 1977 in the following counties were:
Norfolk 96%, Wiltshire 95%, Somerset 92%, Gloucestershire
86% but few of these villages have ever had a chemist.

It is symptomatic of the new awareness of rural issues
that the Department of Education and Science started
keeping full records of school closures only in January
1977. In the two years following that date, over 100
schools were closed, at an average rate of about one a week.
In Norfolk, for example, 45% of rural parishes do not
contain a primary school, and since 1951 80 village schools
have closed. In the public sector, while the loss of village schools receives most publicity, the availability of
medical (and pharmaceutical) services is possibly a
potential source of more serious deprivation. In 1977, the
350 rural parishes in Norfolk included 95 surgeries, 20
fewer than in 1961. However, the level of certain publicly
financed services has in fact improved over the last two

decades in rural areas though standards are still often
lower than in urban areas. These include personal social
services, libraries, and local recreation facilities such
as playing fields and village halls, together with
virtually all public utility services, particularly water
supplies and electricity during the 1950s.
    What are the causes of this continuing decline in
rural opportunities? The basic factors have been technological and social, and have affected both urban and rural
areas alike. Mechanisation and rationalisation have not
only been responsible for the fall in the agricultural
labour force, but have indirectly contributed to the
centralisation of services within, or their withdrawal from,
the rural area. Increasing personal mobility has been
primarily responsible for the loss of local shops and
professional services which has in turn exacerbated the
lack of job opportunity in the rural areas. The size of
most villages is well below the (rising) population
threshold at which the majority of services can be
supported, or retained, though the relationship between
village size and facilities is not a simple one.[24]
    In the public sector, the prime mover has been the
higher cost per head of providing services to a scattered
rural population in small dispersed units. For example, a
village school can cost twice or even three times as much
to run as an equivalent town school. The problems of
economic viability in settlement planning described by Shaw
and Stockford (Chapter 9) have forced public authorities to
make painful decisions in closing small schools and, most
recently, cottage hospitals and rural clinics. However, in
addition to the cost factors the levels of service provided
in traditional rural service 'outlets' has also had an
important influence on decisions of public agencies, particularly in the case of small village schools where, as
demonstrated by Watkins (Chapter 7) the quality of education
often leaves a lot to be desired. Watkins' evidence
suggests that, within broad rural areas encompassing
favoured commuter villages there are real pockets of
disadvantage where - partly *because* small village schools
survive - household deprivation combines with a lack of
opportunities to produce the same low levels of educational
attainment as can be recognised in inner city areas. Moreover, the low level of health services in rural areas is
attributed by Heller (Chapter 6) as much to the preference
of the medical profession and administrators for technological solutions and dramatic curative programmes rather
than community preventive care, as to any specifically
rural factors, such as the drive towards centralisation of
health facilities. One specific factor - demographic
change - has recently become more prominent as a cause of
declining rural services. The falling number of children
in the school age groups are bound to mean that more
village schools will become difficult if not impossible to
'save'. Finally, the influence of planning policy has
often been held responsible for the low level of opportunities available to rural residents. However, while
planning policies have probably been over-rigidly applied
to small-scale industrial proposals in villages, and

planning has clearly affected the population of particular
villages, all the evidence suggests that the overall trends
in jobs, services and facilities described above would
have taken place, irrespective of the statutory planning
process. (Indeed, planning policies have attempted to
check these trends, for example, by promoting industry in
selected towns and by defining key villages as a focus for
retaining services in the rural areas). To argue otherwise is to exaggerate the influence of planning authorities, and to misunderstand the fundamental nature of the
changes in society and technology which have taken place in
postwar rural Britain.

Do the consequences of such declines in rural services
necessarily give rise to deprivation? A survey of the
West Country concluded that 'many, perhaps most, of the
residents of affected villages have managed to cope with
the loss of services. They have suffered inconvenience but
not hardship. But a minority, a substantial minority, has
suffered real hardship through the loss of services and
there is no doubt that their quality of life has deteriorated and will continue to deteriorate'.[25] There are three
related trends which, to some extent, are exacerbated by
the decline in rural opportunities: the depopulation of
some villages, the development of an imbalanced age-
structure and an alleged increasing lack of social cohesion
in villages. The lack of job opportunities has undoubtedly
been responsible for the out-migration of school-leavers
from the rural areas, and the loss or absence of schools
has inhibited families with children from buying houses in
such villages, while there is evidence that, in the long-
term, the presence or absence of a school is perhaps one of
the most significant factors influencing the degree of
social cohesion found in a village.[26] To quote an editorial
in The Times: 'It is not the rural bus, post office, shop
or pub, important as these can be in safeguarding a
village's identity. It is above all the school which is
felt to embody the idea of the village as something alive
and enduring. Without it, young families are reluctant to
stay or settle, and the vitality and diversity of village
life will almost inevitably decline'.[27] On top of these
social and psychological consequences, it is often feared
that public authorities will reinforce the decline by a
series of negative policy decisions, such as restricting
private housebuilding by development control, excluding
these villages from council housing programmes, or giving
low priority for grant aid for other facilities. The
combined effects of the loss of services on individual
communities can therefore be enormous, though not all
commentators share the view that, 'in aggregate terms the
many threatened closures to schools, garages, post offices,
and shops represents a massive change to the scale and form
of rural life in England'.[28] There is obviously a danger
of being seduced by a kind of rigid determinism - of
believing that the loss of services alone is to blame for
the demise of village life,whereas 'the life of a community
depends on the people in it rather than the bricks and
mortar. It is the human factor - the friendliness and
sense of community - in rural society which attracts

people'.[29] But the truth of this latter view cannot
disguise the reality of the evidence of rural opportunities,
namely that in terms of the effective availability of
opportunities many rural residents are deprived by comparison with their urban counterparts.

MOBILITY DEPRIVATION

The nub of the real rural problem relates to the difficulties from which people suffer, and those who suffer most
from both household and opportunity deprivation are those
with the lowest level of mobility, due to lack of access
to a private car. There is a consensus in all descriptive
writing on rural problems, clearly validated by Moseley
(Chapter 10), that the elderly, young children, teenagers,
mothers at home, and the infirm, as well as the poor, all
tend to be disadvantaged if they lack access to a car. The
patronage of conventional rural bus services is low, but
since collectively the above groups comprise the *majority*
of the rural population, the accessibility problem cannot
be regarded as a minority one.
     The growth in car ownership has already been noted as a
major factor accounting for the disappearance of rural
services, and it has also undermined the access of the
'carless' group in two distinct ways (Figure 13.4). The
continuous lines in Figure 13.4 indicate how rising car
ownership has undermined public transport, and the broken
lines show how increased mobility has hit the village
service outlet. Each of these processes has fed the further
growth of car ownership and use, so that a downward spiral
of falling accessibility to rural opportunities has
resulted for individuals without access to a car.
     The effect of mobility deprivation is to make it more
difficult for the affected groups to adapt to lack of
opportunities. Distance also inhibits the flow of information, (including that about available opportunities in
the towns) and this may in turn limit personal experience.
In this sense variations in accessibility can give rise to
variations in well-being in the same way as variations in
rural income. Some residents of the more remote parts of
rural Britain must therefore either pay extra costs to
avail themselves of certain opportunities, if they can
afford the cost, or forego those opportunities.

GOVERNMENT POLICY FOR RURAL AREAS

One immediate and general question arises from the above
appraisal of the evidence. Why has the extent of rural
deprivation in the mid-1970s not been fully reflected in
government policy? There are several possible explanations.
First, as an E.E.C. report noted 'The image of poverty is
an urban image', and this traditional attitude still
prevails (see Chapter 3). Secondly, by their very nature
rural problems, particularly those relating to low levels of
access to opportunities, tend to be less visible than urban

squalor. Thirdly, rural deprivation is often too localised to be reflected in average statistics, and finer-grained surveys and data than are normally used by government departments would be needed to reveal pockets of need.

Given the increasing weight of circumstantial evidence, what could or should central government do to help alleviate some of the problems of rural areas? The basic issue is whether rural Britain receives a 'fair share' of public expenditure. Certainly the shift of Rate Support Grant (RSG) away from the mainly rural shire counties in the 1970s was not based on any overall assessment of the needs or levels of service provision in rural areas. The rate support grant distribution formulae are notorious for their arbitrary nature and insensitivity to local needs. Indeed, one of the arguments used to justify paying the 'needs' element of the RSG direct to district councils (rather than to counties) has been that it would enable compensation to be given for more localised variations in per head expenditure needs - such as those to be found in counties covering large rural areas. However, the practical problems of assessing 'needs' at a county scale are magnified when districts are included in the allocation, and the net effect of a district-based allocation system seems likely once again to favour the (higher spending) urban districts at the expense of the rural authorities. A more equitable basis for the annual RSG allocation, which takes account of the special problems and higher costs of service provision in rural areas, must form the starting point for any change in government policy.

A second aspect of government policy relates to the general emphasis on cost-effectiveness in the provision of public services. The reaction against this presumption in public policy is well summarised in the following view, expressed by a former secretary to the National Association of Parish Councils:[31] 'I believe that the key step is to allow in all economic, development and taxation policies for the fact that the rural substructure will always cost much more per head than the urban, for the distances are much greater and the heads far fewer. It is only when people can work in villages as easily and contentedly as in towns that village life will blossom again. This is not a subsidy, but justice. In world terms, the country is subsidizing the towns'.

Unfortunately, the relationship between government policy and public service costs in rural areas is more complex than the above viewpoint suggests. At a national level the standardization of certain charges, such as that for the postal service, implies a hidden subsidy to the rural areas, and the public policy options are certainly not as clear-cut. The basic issues are the extent to which the real costs of services should be met locally - and ultimately by the individual consumer - and which services should be regarded as 'essential'. In this context, apart from the RSG formula, the proposed shift from a rental to a capital basis for rating assessment is likely to increase rateable values in rural areas. Although no government seems likely to introduce any radical changes in local taxation (which could be adopted to favour rural or

urban areas) changes in government policy for the
financing of specific services could be introduced. For
example, an education voucher system could well require
either differential grant aid to small rural schools, or
higher payments by rural residents. Sewerage rates are
likely to continue to be met from some general rate levy,
while in the case of dwellings not connected to the public
sewer, sewage disposal costs will undoubtedly have to be
met entirely by the consumer. In the case of community
health services, user payments in rural areas typically
meet less than 1% of total costs, and moves by government
towards meeting an increasing proportion of its health
costs from user charges appears unlikely.[32] Grant aid
already meets an increasing proportion of the cost of
rural bus services and this subsidy is in turn increasingly
provided for in the government's Transport Supplementary
Grant to rural local authorities. The potential for
significant changes in governments' resource allocation
processes is limited, and a 'fairer' share of RSG distribution is to be preferred to specific government subsidies,
intended to meet particular rural needs. Indeed, part of
the justification for increasing the Development
Commission's selective asssistance for industry in rural
areas arises from the level of resources now devoted to
economic development measures and infrastructure support
in the major urban areas, as well as, again, reflecting
the insensitivity of the RSG process for allocating
expenditure relative to local needs. The increase in the
Development Commission's budget to £17 million in 1978/79
has enabled it to assist the creation of 1500 jobs, though
even this scale of job growth will have only a limited
impact on rural economic development, and will do little
to raise female activity rates in rural Britain. Outside
the Assisted Areas national distribution of industry
policy does not formally recognise the employment problems
of rural areas (except where there are Town Expansion
schemes). It is clearly illogical of central government
to approve county structure plans which define areas of
special rural need - and then to deny any priority to such
areas in the granting of Industrial Development Certificates
for new firms. Apart from industrial development, government manpower policies should recognise and reflect the
special difficulties of access to employment offices,
skill-centres and training facilities experienced by the
rural unemployed, either by attempting to 'mobilise'
retraining programmes or assisting personal mobility.

At a national level, the rural issue is not solely an
argument about the pattern of government expenditure.
What is required is a change in attitude by Whitehall. The
two recent attempts by civil servants to discuss rural
problems are both inadequate in many respects. The
Treasury report on Rural Depopulation (1976) concluded that,
on balance, the economic arguments for devoting national
resources to preventing rural depopulation are not very
strong.[33] But both the methodology and the conclusions of
this report are suspect, and it was much too narrow and
superficial to constitute any basis for government policy.
The paper by the Countryside Review Committee on Rural

Communities (1977) showed little understanding of social
issues and failed to make any assessment of the adequacy
of government policy in rural areas. In a belated, but
welcome, recognition of the need for government to give
more attention to the rural dimension of national policy,
the Parliamentary Under Secretary at the Department of
the Environment announced, in October 1978, a comprehensive
programme of research to help the Government develop
effective coordinated policies for the stimulation and
protection of rural areas.[34] The change in attitude may
be on its way. If so, it will require government to look
beyond broad aggregate statistics to the localised nature
of rural problems and to adopt a more flexible approach
to solutions.

Government policy should recognise the low income
levels and housing problems which often exist within rural
areas, as well as the adverse effect of direct taxation
and welfare policy in pushing low wage-earners into the
poverty trap (Chapter 3). The elastic provision for
expenditure on housing in the Supplementary Benefit system
favours the urban poor and there appears to be a case for
making provision to take account of items such as transport which figure disproportionally in the cost of living
of the rural poor. There is also a case for a review at
national level of the way in which housing and planning
policy might assist the problem of meeting local housing
needs in rural areas. The selective use of planning
permissions and incentives to rural housing associations
could possibly assist home ownership in rural communities,
though the operation of any systems of 'controlled' rural
accommodation (such as exists in the Channel Islands)
would almost certainly be unacceptable in Britain because
of their intrusion into personal freedom.

In the sphere of rural transport, there are already
welcome signs of a more flexible and innovatory approach
by central government, particularly in the sphere of
licensing, and greater flexibility to meet local needs is
now required in relation to the training of bus drivers.
However, suggestions for assisting rural mobility by
offering a lower rate of vehicle excise duty to rural
residents or some rebate of fuel tax would be impractical
for government to administer, and would do nothing for the
hardcore disadvantaged whose ages or incomes would still
preclude car ownership. On the other hand, there is a case
for examining the terms of reference of certain public
agencies responsible for other aspects of rural transport.
The role of the Post Office is critical since sub-post
offices frequently have a very significant social role in
villages as well as acting as an economic prop to what is
often the last village shop. The Post Office could more
actively explore alternatives to the closure of rural sub-
post offices which follows the failure to replace a sub-
postmaster. Many ideas have been suggested including the
possibility of 'joint' deliveries, part-time services,
permits to non Post Office employees, and changes in the
'two mile rule' regarding the appointment of sub-postmaster
postmasters – but all require a flexible attitude to the
role and resources of the Post Office. While the balancing

of social arguments about the future of village schools should be primarily a local matter, it is perhaps surprising that, in recent government circulars, no clear lead has been adopted at national level, and the Department of Education and Science could certainly adopt a more critical interpretation of social and community interests in considering applications to close schools. In the sphere of health care, one aspect of the closure of branch surgeries highlights the problems of inflexible government attitudes. Although such closures represent a saving to the National Health Service, since money allocated to the payment of rents and rates cannot be diverted to other uses, proposals to provide compensatory minibus links to main surgeries have been rejected by the DHSS.

There have been several calls for a comprehensive national policy for rural areas, as well as for a Minister with special rural responsibilities. However, the concept of a Ministry of Rural Affairs must remain more theoretical than real and, as the Advisory Council on Agriculture has observed, 'it is in any case ingenuous to suggest that the many conflicts in the countryside can be largely resolved by bringing them under the responsibility of a single Department ...'[35] Moreover, it is difficult to see how the Countryside Review Committee's idea of placing a formal duty on Ministers to 'have regard' to the interests of rural areas would achieve anything of practical significance. At an international scale, the case has also been argued for a comprehensive E.E.C. rural policy, and for a new European Rural Fund which would replace, in the rural context, the Regional and Social Funds, which at present concentrate on urban and industrial areas.[36]

LOCAL PLANNING AND SERVICE POLICIES

In the context of government strategy, what particular policies could be adopted by local authorities and other public bodies to help improve the quality of rural life?

Economic and housing policies

The terms of reference of statutory planning, whether at County or District level, are such that poverty is not a central element and the rural policy 'levers' available at local level do not act directly on the low income aspect of rural deprivation. However, the apparent failure of statutory planning to compensate for the loss of agricultural jobs by stimulating rural job creation in a positive way, and the evident failure of planning and housing authorities to make a greater impact on the resolution of local housing problems is less easy to defend, though there are plenty of examples of recognition of those problems in planning policies (and some examples of effective action). Fortunately there has emerged in the mid-1970s a much greater awareness by local authorities of the need to cosset existing industry, especially the small scale enterprises to be found in rural areas. The case for applying

planning criteria (usually relating to environmental,
service and highway issues) to industrial proposals less
rigidly than in the past seems also to be gaining acceptance - by weighing such factors against the possible
impact on local employment. In terms of positive action,
there are clearly differences of view among County and
District Councils as to the extent to which local authorities should become actively involved in industrial development. The evidence certainly suggests that those
authorities that have bought land, built and let advance
factories, and pursued a vigorous promotion campaign have
have been the most successful in attracting new firms -
though the spin-off to the local economy has often been
limited. It also seems probable that in some rural growth
centres, such as the expanding towns, the possible contribution of private developers may have been affected by
such local authority activity. In any event, the first
priority for local authorities should be to give as much
attention to, and to develop their linkages with, existing
local industry before putting resources into external
promotion. With their planning, housing, transportation
and education functions, County and District Councils can
significantly influence the climate which small industrial
firms in rural areas need if they are to survive and
expand (Chapter 4).

By comparison, despite their having statutory powers
which bear directly on housing development local authority
policies have not always succeeded in relieving the
problems of local housing deprivation. Leaving aside the
possibility of occupancy restrictions, which are a matter
for central government, existing planning powers alone can
achieve little more than ensure that, where permission for
individual dwellings in villages are sought, account is
taken of the strength of the expressed 'local need', as
well as conventional planning criteria. County Structure
Plans frequently define categories of villages where
development will *only* be permitted if related to local need
but, given the absence of occupancy controls, there is thus
a danger of excluding all but local authority development.
An appraisal of this aspect of the first round of Structure
Plans has concluded, with justification, that 'planning
policies related to local need tend to be vague and rather
bland; strong on intent, but weak on mechanism'. This
contradiction is also evident in much writing about
planning. In a whole issue of the Architects Journal in
1978, devoted to *The Village - A Matter of Life or Death,*
Moss displayed a marked schizophrenia ; he extolled the
virtues of village life and then condemned the urban
dwellers who, by seeking to make their homes in rural areas
created the housing problems![37] On a more practical level,
Thurgood (1978) has suggested that 'Registers of Housing
Need' could be set up on a parish basis in order that local
people seeking specific types of accommodation could
register their needs.[38] This might assist private developers, and encourage housing associations (hitherto largely
urban phenomena), to gear their activities to rural needs.
So far as local authorities are concerned, the solution is
likely to lie with their housing responsibilities rather

than their planning powers. District Councils should
ensure that most new estate-scale rented accommodation,
and particularly sheltered housing, is located in those
villages where services can be provided, and to which the
elderly could be assisted to move. This coordination
between council-housebuilding programmes and the planning
of services should be backed by an attempt to inform
intending retirement migrants of the rural service realities of their future environment. Such an approach,
linked to a concentration on mortgage policies, the sale
of individual plots, and even building for sale - to
encourage house ownership as a way of meeting local need -
appears the most promising housing strategy. However, in
the planning sphere, rural authorities will continue to
face the dilemma of controlling rural development without
damaging the housing prospects of the indigenous population
in the process, though this risk is only likely to be a
serious one in areas of high amenity value, such as the
National Parks. However effective a local planning and
housing strategy is, household deprivation in rural areas
will continue to require a responsive support system of
personal Social Services which attempts to provide a
statutory framework for meeting the needs of the severely
disadvantaged in rural areas (Chapter 9).

Service policies

The decline in the level of many rural services has resulted from decisions of both public authorities and private
agencies, though the problems facing, and the powers
available to, local authorities are not always appreciated
by critics of statutory planning. What are the services
policy options open to local bodies to cope with the
resulting opportunity deprivation? First, there is the
centralisation option - continuing to apply the conventional wisdom of concentrating facilities in certain key
villages - though this only equates to a 'solution' if it
can be combined with an effective system of accessibility
(which is discussed below). Secondly, there is the mobile
services option ; moving the services to the population is
the antithesis of the first option. Thirdly, there is the
possibility of providing services which would not otherwise be viable on a joint basis, by co-operation between
agencies. Finally, there is the social subsidy option,
where the known high costs per head of maintaining a
dispersed pattern of services are accepted and met from
public funds for 'social' reasons. All the other options
rely on changes in personal mobility, or on voluntary
effort rather than public sector policy.
    It is the pursuit of the first of these options which
has been partly responsible for the rural backlash in the
mid-1970s, but the plain fact remains that the size of most
villages in rural Britain is well below the population
threshold at which the majority of services can be supported, or economically retained. This is especially true of
capital-intensive facilities such as those demanded by

recreation provision in rural areas (Chapter 8). The
realisation of this problem has focussed the attention of
public bodies on possible alternative solutions. Except
at the playgroup level and in certain specialised areas,
education is not generally susceptible to being mobilised;
in contrast the library van is perhaps the best example of
a public service already well adapted to village needs.
With the increasing emphasis on care in the home, Social
Services provision is becoming increasingly a mobile
service in rural counties (Chapter 9) and, apart from the
general question of concealed subsidies (to provide 'low'
level rural services), there are specific examples of
rural grant aid such as those given to cultural bodies to
enable them to 'tour' rural areas (Chapter 8). Services
such as chiropody and Citizens Advice Bureaux could also be
mobilised to provide advice-on-wheels (Chapter 11). The
use of mobile services is closely linked to inter-agency
co-operation, though such co-operation also applies to
'static' service points. For example, there is little
doubt that, if the offices responsible for social security
and unemployment benefit and the new job centres could be
combined, possibly with certain local authority functions,
there would be a chance of retaining such offices in the
small towns from which they are being withdrawn. The same
sort of philosophy of joint provision should be applied to
the 'delivery' of mobile services to smaller settlements.
For example, postal vans, mobile libraries and mobile shops
all have links with local market towns and each is capable
of being extended to provide a wider range of services. It
might, for instance, be possible for sub-postmasters, using
post vans, to provide a mobile part-time service to out-
lying villages, so that one public service vehicle and
driver delivered, say, groceries and newspapers, as well
as stamps and postal orders (Chapter 10).

The introduction of further, and explicit, subsidies by
local authorities to support non-viable rural facilities
may have a superficial attraction, but it would create as
many problems and inequalities as it would solve. Apart
from the practical difficulty of assessing 'losses', such
subsidies could sustain inefficiency and impede the search
for other solutions. Where services under threat cannot
be justified on a full-time basis, the possibility of
providing part-time services in the smaller communities
rather than concentrating resources on one village should
be explored. The clergy and doctors, of course, already
work on such a part-time-peripatetic basis, though there is
scope for Area Health Authorities to develop mobile
surgeries and dispensing services, as well as encouraging
more dispensing by rural G.P.s. In the case of village
schools, 'linked' forms of provision are being studied in
several counties. For example, in Norfolk the idea of
making one school an annexe of a larger one, or of grouping
several small schools (with some peripatetic teachers) is
being considered. The falling number of primary pupils up
to the mid-1980s means that some further school closures
are inevitable, though one rural county, Cumbria, where 11%
of schools already have less than 25 pupils, has resolved
that no more schools will be closed until the number of

pupils drops below 10, and has indicated that in at least
one case a remote school will be re-opened if enough
young families move into the area.

The Rural Community Councils' report (1978) has
suggested the use of public subsidies to support services
in two specific situations.[39] First, they propose a
special grant payable through district councils, to private
individuals or firms who have announced their intention to
close their service, in order to keep the service going for
up to six months while local authorities seek alternative
ways of providing the services. Secondly, they suggest
that parish councils should be prepared to make greater use
of their powers to levy up to a 2p rate to support local
services. However, this could add to the rate burden on
low income groups, and a more readily acceptable proposal
by the Rural Community Councils is that county and district
councils should jointly operate an 'early warning' system
of impending service closures (public or private) which
could provide a breathing space for the authorities to try
and find alternative solutions.

Accessibility policies

The alleviation of accessibility deprivation by local
policies is no less problematic than the other dimensions
of the rural problem, and it is clearly impossible to
achieve countrywide, low cost, high levels of accessibility
(Chapter 10). There are two basic categories of public
policy option for improving the rural transport aspect of
the overall accessibility-to-opportunity problem. First,
there are policies based on the use of conventional buses
in a scheduled service network, and, secondly, there are
ways of making further use of transport provided in
connection with a particular service. There is a third
set of options, relating to unconventional services, but
since they tend to rely on voluntary effort these are
discussed below under that heading rather than with the
public policy options.

Conventional Services. Scheduled bus services on
inter-urban routes are likely to continue without need for
subsidy, and those villages which lie on such routes will
be the only ones to enjoy a high level of conventional
service. However, the critical services in the basic bus
network are the 'second level' rural services linking
villages with market towns. There is a case for subsidising
such services where they link the larger villages, though
they will only account for a minority of mileage run and
passengers carried and where the catchment population is
small (perhaps under 2,000) a daily service is unlikely to
be justified. The assessment of the justification for a
local subsidy to a scheduled service must be based on a full
appraisal of the benefits in terms of social groups affected, and the problems of withdrawal in terms of the services
or facilities relevant to the route. A framework for this
sort of evaluation should be provided by the County Public
Transport Plans introduced in the 1978 Transport Act, though
it is the continuing *process* of accessibility planning,

rather than production of Plans which matters. So far as
the bus companies are concerned, there is still scope for
much more systematic market analysis on the lines pioneered by the Eastern Counties and Midland Red divisions
of the National Bus Company. In particular there is a
need for a full monitoring of any revision in patterns of
service for cost effectiveness, and for such experiments
as off-peak excursion services to provide, say, a twice
monthly shopping trip to a large town, which can usually
be run cheaply given marginal cost pricing.

   Service Transport. Reference has already been made to
the wider potential of postal vehicles in rural areas.
The scope for post-buses could certainly be increased if
the Post Office Corporation were to relax their constraint
that mail delivery and collection must always have first
priority - a priority which inevitably means unattractive
routes and timings from a passenger point of view. Given
the necessary flexibility, county councils with their
transport coordinating role could try and relate this
potential to identified rural transport needs. Counties
already have direct responsibility for school transport,
but although it is already legal, it is still rare for
fare-paying adults to travel on contract school buses.
Routes and loadings could be designed so that spare
capacity is built in for occasional adult passengers from
otherwise bus-less villages. This possibility is, of
course, enhanced if school hours can also be staggered.
Indeed, almost any innovation in public transport demands
a wide view - which only local authorities are in a
position to take - of the implications for both other
public services and private facilities. Such a process of
accessibility planning is essentially a managerial one,
but it must be organised around the involvement of those
living in the rural areas - first, as advisors on the
nature of the problem locally and on the policies which
could work in their particular village; secondly, as a
potential transport resource. It is to this latter
resource that we now turn.

VOLUNTARY ACTIVITY AND SELF HELP

The voluntary sector has been described as the 'second
great provider' of the social and welfare services, and, by
the Wolfenden Committee on Voluntary Organisations, as
having two objectives:[40] to encourage collective action to
meet important social needs, and to ensure that this
provision is consistent with maintaining a pluralistic
system, that is, a system in which power is spread over
several institutions and not concentrated in a few mono-
lithic structures. In the context of the rural deprivation
described in this book, there are two possible roles for
voluntary bodies and for private initiative (over and above
the arrangements which individuals make for themselves).
First, voluntary activity can do much by way of direct
action to alleviate rural problems and to assist the statutory bodies discussed in the previous section; such
voluntary effort is organised around an issue or related

to a defined problem often in a particular village.
Secondly, voluntary organisation can achieve other ends:
by articulating local needs, increasing local awareness,
and participating in the work of public authorities such
organisations can influence the latters' priorities and
decisions.

The potential contribution of volunteers and self-help
organisations brings with it several problems as well as
benefits. On the credit side, the voluntary sector can
offer, on a human scale, a response to known and understood rural needs which may be as beneficial to the voluntary worker as to the recipient. The voluntary sector
also provides the freedom to experiment with new approaches
to a problem. However, the voluntary sector clearly does
not always live up to these high ideals: its response to
many areas of need is at best patchy and this is recognised
in the Wolfenden Report. This should not necessarily be
seen as a deficiency of all voluntary organisations, and,
generally, the operation of most voluntary organisations
perhaps looks no more uncoordinated and muddled than that
of most statutory agencies! But voluntary activity is
frequently 'interest-centred' and not 'need-centred'.
Little thought tends to be given to the overall needs of
an area, with the result that priorities are not planned,
tasks are not clearly identified, and in a large rural
area many gaps are inevitably left: some sections of the
population and some communities receive unending attention,
while others may receive none.

All of the problems which together give rise to an
element of deprivation in rural areas also create great
difficulties for the effective involvement of people in,
and the contribution of, voluntary organisations. Firstly,
the problem of the organisation of a scattered population
in itself is a major hurdle which has to be overcome, and
it is to the great credit of a large number of rural
communities that these obstacles are overcome. Secondly,
the problem of an ageing population often places a drain
on the energy of voluntary organisations which are manned
by a declining number of younger and more active people.
Thirdly, the loss of the young people from the area,
particularly those with initiative and qualities of leadership, inevitably has an impact on the activities of the
organisations, and hence on particular sections of the
population. There is, for instance, a severe problem in
finding effective leadership for activities for teenagers
in villages. Fourthly, the problems of communication and
information mean that levels of awareness and of
expectation can be very low, and this may affect the
confidence of village residents and their ability to tackle
the problem. Support might be there but few people may
know how to find and to use it. Finally, in a rural area
which sees many of its services and activities being drawn
away into the larger towns and cities, morale can often
be low.

Against this background, what further contributions
could voluntary activity make to the resolution of rural
problems?

Rural deprivation

Perhaps the most basic need in remote rural areas is for the information and advice services discussed in Chapter 11. In an attempt to improve the quality of 'referral', the Shropshire Community Council recruited and trained a network of local residents, or 'representatives' to act as part-time information workers for their local villages (Chapter 12). This sort of scheme could, with advantage, be more widely adopted, though it is important that there is a choice of representatives and that selection covers a wide social spectrum. It is moreover essential that such representatives are themselves well informed and this raises questions about levels of training and extent of back-up support available. The Shropshire style of village representatives scheme has yet to be replicated elsewhere, though it may be most appropriate in semi-rural counties, like Shropshire, containing sizeable central cities which are well connected to their rural hinterlands, and to which referrals can readily be made. It has more limited relevance in extensive deep rural areas such as the Fenland of eastern England and in many remote upland regions, where local points of provision are small market towns which, under present circumstances, are too small to maintain the full range of information provision services. While many villagers are prepared to turn to fellow residents for help, the frequency with which information is sought about private and personal matters such as tax and social security suggests that even for initial 'signposting', many enquirers may prefer a more confidential service. The Shropshire Community Council and local groups, like the Stalham Community Workers' Group in east Norfolk, have also compiled handbooks of public services and sources of professional advice as a response to the rural information problem. The Shropshire example is a countywide Directory of Essential Services, while that for the Stalham area contains 'details of the caring and educational resources ... available to 17 rural parishes'.

In the education service, the involvement of parents in the work of primary schools is not only desirable for educational reasons but may become increasingly important to the survival of small village schools. There is major scope for the part-time assistance of parents in the smallest schools in order to leave the few full-time staff free for particular teaching duties and to expose children to more varied ideas. Examples of self-help projects to add to the facilities of village schools are also increasing in number and, at the extreme end of the voluntary support spectrum, some local groups have not accepted the failure of a campaign to retain a school. In theory at least, rather than accept complete closure it is possible to form a 'parent-teacher co-operative' to keep the school open through a charitable trust which does not charge fees. Parents can keep costs down by doing much of the work themselves and raise money to pay teachers who might otherwise be unemployed. A co-operative was formed at Madingley in Cambridgeshire in 1978 to do just that, but it is too early to see whether the Madingly test case in mutual aid works.

In the area of health care, as pointed out in Chapter 6, prudent individual behaviour coupled with changes in the pattern of public expenditure is of fundamental importance, whether in urban or rural areas, but there is scope for community initiatives. Two examples in rural north Norfolk which have become focuses of national attention serve to illustrate the potential - the financing and building of an extension to a small hospital at Cromer by a voluntary group which the Health Authority were unable or unwilling to provide; and a mobile and nursing scheme providing for the needs of the elderly and the infirm, called the Glaven Caring Committee. Covering only twelve parishes this voluntary Committee has attracted substantial grants by demonstrating its capability, and ensuring by its intimate contact with these remote villages that financial and human resources are used selectively and to the greatest effect. It is symptomatic of the reservoir of voluntary welfare effort in rural areas that perhaps the most important social service which has emerged in villages in the postwar period, the meals-on-wheels service, is based on volunteers. All county Social Services Departments now rely heavily on a range of voluntary groups, to whom they often give grant-aid; and the library service also lends itself to part-time assistance by volunteers.

In addition to working with public authorities, where it is no longer possible to support private services on an economic basis, voluntary self-help by the communities themselves may provide at least a partial solution. Joint bulk buying may enable some rural residents to take advantage of city food prices, and consumer co-operatives have been suggested, in which residents man their village shop on a voluntary basis. Such activities, like the idea of a part-time post office, could utilise the village hall or community centre.

There is a major role for rural self-help schemes in relation to both private and public transport. The Department of the Environment study of rural transport in West Suffolk (referred to in Chapters 1 and 10) concluded by asking 'is it too much to hope in this compassionate society of ours that a small amount of the car's almost unlimited potential can be diverted, now and then, to solve the hardship of the old, the young, and the needy?' Certainly the car is an extremely attractive resource: in rural areas it is not only plentiful but also uniquely flexible in terms of both route and timing. Car sharing arrangements provide the basis for extending the advantages to those who lack, or lack access to, a car and there is, of course, a considerable history of volunteers making themselves and their cars available for sociallly useful work in rural areas - either for no payment at all or, more recently, for their mileage-related expenditure. Such volunteers have frequently been organised by the WRVS, Red Cross, Women's Institute or some such organisation. The 'Social Car Schemes' operated in Shropshire (Chapter 12) by the Rural Community Council show how a low-cost service, based on volunteer drivers can help people 'in need' to make medical trips and to visit friends and relatives in hospital. However, this potential is limited by the value

which motorists place on privacy, and would-be recipients
of lifts are often concerned at their indebtedness, though
this might be partially alleviated by payment. Unfortunately, both the problems tend to be exacerbated where a
car sharing system attempts to guarantee *regular* opportunities for travel.

The car alone can never solve the rural access problem,
and tends to exacerbate it for certain groups (Chapter 10).
Although its attractions can be made more widely available
by local voluntary effort, there is a need for other
initiatives based on the bus. In social terms, the 'deep
rural' areas between the routes of the basic scheduled
bus network are the most critical, and it is here that
unconventional community-based bus schemes have a role.
The recent Select Committee on Innovations in Rural Transport (1978) reached the following general conclusions:[41]
(a) Immense dedication and enthusiasm is shown by all
those concerned with the planning and operation of the
existing community bus schemes.
(b) The overall contribution that can be made by community
buses to the rural public transport network will inevitably
be limited. The contribution within the limited areas
concerned is very great.
(c) For the National Bus Company the incentive to develop
successful community bus schemes should be great, not so
much for financial or overall transport reasons as for the
immense benefit to the image of bus companies. It is
important that a nationalised industry should be seen to
be concerned for the people it serves.
(d) There are also considerable intangible social benefits
of community buses. The value of such schemes goes far
beyond the strict confines of transport services.

Against these advantages, community bus services face
two major problems, (assuming that a pool of volunteer
drivers can be maintained) - replacement, the average
vehicle having only a four-year life, and maintenance.
There were six community bus schemes in operation in 1978,
but it is still too early to make dogmatic statements
about their capacity for survival, or their potential for
widespread extension into all the rural areas of Britain.

THE FUTURE: COMMUNITY DEVELOPMENT AND PLANNING

This final section examines the future roles of the public
and private sector and the emerging links between statutory
services and voluntary effort in rural areas, and concludes
by considering the possible long-term impact on rural
problems of changes in technology.

Do the problems identified justify a significant change
in the pattern of public policy and 'intervention' in
rural society? Certainly, the conventional response of
planners and politicians to evidence of deprivation has
been to recommend 'positive discrimination' in favour of
the disadvantaged. However, such strategies are essentially
concerned to treat the effects of inequality rather than its
causes, and usually relate to 'areas' rather than people
(and no discrimination has been directed at mobility dep-

rivation). The poverty of many rural areas, and the
prosperity associated with towns within them, is likely to
become even less distinct in the next decade as the
skilled, professional and managerial groups continue to
spread outwards from the urban centres. If rural poverty
becomes even more localised and less visible (though still
present) the case for increased government intervention on
an area basis will become weaker. Central government's
view of the problems of opportunity and mobility deprivation will be complicated by the fact that much dissatis-
faction will continue to reflect rising expectations as
well as future changes in the actual level of services.
Hence any form of assistance will need to be highly
selective, though a people-orientated selective strategy
is more difficult to frame than a crude area-based policy.

Whatever the extent of social planning by public
agencies, the continuation of problems suffered by specific
groups cuts across the traditional organisation of these
agencies. There is therefore a case for re-examining the
type of intervention by these agencies, and the nature of
their links with voluntary groups. There is little doubt
that public sector expenditure on child and community
education, housing, social and health services, recreation
and welfare benefits is under-coordinated in rural areas.
Given the multiplicity of agencies it would be surprising
if this were not so, and the future must see continued
efforts to improve matters - though central government
provides a poor example of integrated policies or
administration from a rural point of view. There is
likely to be continued pressure for community decisions to
be made at the lowest possible level the village -
leaving higher echelons of government to the job of policy
coordination and expenditure control. The overriding goal
for regional bodies and county and district authorities
will be to combine efficient resource allocation and the
setting of clear priorities with community involvement
at a local level.

In order to bring out and strengthen the local potential in rural communities, public authorities themselves
must play a positive role, and try and overcome the many
constraints which limit self-help or impede community
initiative. If the voluntary sector is to be effective in
supporting the work of statutory authorities there is a
tremendous need for a better knowledge of how the statutory
system works: who does what, how decisions are made, who
is accountable to whom, where resources come from, how they
are allocated, how the democratic process works, where
formal provision is made for public involvement in decision
making, how this public participation works, and how it can
be made more effective. Earlier chapters have demonstrated
that this information problem tends to be more acute in
rural than urban areas. Above all, the practical contribution of the voluntary sector towards solving rural
problems depends on having some central focus for local
organisation. In carrying out surveys of rural services
and identifying 'needs' (Chapter 12) the necessary support
can readily be provided by individual local authorities or
umbrella organisations like the Associations of Parish

Councils.   At least part of the answer seems to lie with the intermediary bodies (such as the rural community councils) which can activate both the public sector and voluntary bodies.   But rural communities will increasingly wish to undertake full Village Appraisals and this will require more specialised assistance, probably from District Councils.   An efficient 'clearing house' is also essential in the case of car sharing schemes to put into contact those offering and those needing a lift, and the prerequisite of community bus schemes is the close co-operation of two public bodies (a county council and a bus company) and a local voluntary committee.   In future we are likely to see increasing community involvement in the forward planning of services, as well as their local implementation.   Since many of the problems are organis-ational, solutions will demand a close look at the way in which statutory agencies need adapting to fulfil a role aligned more directly towards the needs of voluntary groups.

How far will this potential for self-help and even self-sufficiency be assisted by changes in technology? The spatial dispersal of manufacturing industry, which has been evident from the 1960s, is likely to be facilitated by changing technology as well as by the provision in planning policies for smaller-scale industrial development in remote rural areas.   But if the growth in service employment is checked by the impact of silicon-chip tech-nology, marginal enterprises in the rural areas could be among the first to suffer.   However, it is the spread of technological advances in information technology which may be of the greatest significance.   A regional community of villages linked by television is a long way off, but recent developments in information delivery are most important for rural Britain, since lack of information has been a cont-ributory factor towards rural deprivation.   There are already some examples of a shift towards a self-help economy in a few remote rural communities, closely assoc-iated with the desire for local participation noted above. Although the spread of alternative lifestyles based on 'low-impact' technology to many villages is still only a long-term scenario, in the short-term an increase in community initiatives in the economic as well as social sphere is probable.   In any case, it would be naive and erroneous to assume that many of the social problems iden-tified in this book will be resolved as a result of tech-nological change in the near future.   The immediate need is therefore for each public authority to help identify problems, to ensure the coordination of activity, to act as a catalyst to spur other bodies into action, to encourage and assist self-help activities in all their forms.   The solution to rural problems will remain partly a matter of resource allocation, particularly at national level, and partly a matter of individual responsibility.

REFERENCES AND NOTES

1. J. Bradshaw, The Concept of Social Need, *New Society*, 30th March 1972.

2. Nottinghamshire County Council, *The County Deprived Area Study*, 1977.

3. C.A. Moser and W. Scott, *British Towns*, Oliver and Boyd, 1961.

4. R. Webber and J. Craig, Which Local Authorities are Alike? in *Population Trends*, H.M.S.O., September 1976.

5. R.J. Green, *Country Planning*, University of Manchester Press, 1971.

6. P.J. Cloke, An Index of Rurality for England and Wales, *Regional Studies* Volume II No. 1, 1977. Cloke's classification is based on the use of principal components analysis for old local authority areas, and the index was calculated for 1961 and 1971.

7. B.E. Coates, R.J. Johnson and P.L. Knox, *Geography and Inequality*, Oxford University Press, 1977.

8. B.E. Coates and E.M. Rawstron, *Regional Variations in Britain; Selected essays in economic and social geography*, Batsford, London, 1971.

9. The pattern is clearly described in B.E. Coates *et al.* (1977), *op cit.*, p.145.

10. See for example S. Holtermann, Areas of Urban Deprivation in Great Britain: An analysis of 1971 Census Data, *Social Trends*, 6 pp. 33-47, 1975.

11. See Cumbria County Council, *Deprived Areas*, Cumbria Structure Plan W.P.3, 1978, and Norfolk - A Survey, Norfolk Structure Plan Steering Committee, 1974; and R. Stockford, Social Services Provision in Norfolk in M.J. Moseley (ed)., *Social Issues in Rural Norfolk*, Centre of East Anglian Studies, 1978.

12. This is stressed by P.J. Cloke, 1977, *op cit.*

13. See for example the studies and reports which were commissioned by the Department of Environment for Consultants on the Inner Areas of Liverpool, Birmingham and Lambeth, and on the London Docklands. A clear description of the urban problem is given in D. Morgan, Planning the Inner City, Town and Country Planning Summer School, *Report of Proceedings*, 1977.

14. B.M.D. Smith, *The Inner City Economic Problem*, Centre for Urban and Regional Studies Research Memorandum 56, January 1977.

15. J.S. Foreman Peck and P.A. Gripaios, Inner City Problems and Policies, *Regional Studies*, Volume 11, 1977.

16. Royal Commission on the Distribution of Income and Wealth, 1978.

17. J. Raynor et al., *The Urban Context,* Open University, Milton Keynes, 1974.

18. B.E. Coates et al., *op cit.*

19. Current research includes a project on the accessibility problems of women with young children (in London), being carried out at the Department of Geography, University of London; and research on the mobility of the elderly in cities, at the Transport Operations Research Group, University of Newcastle.

20. S.F. Penfold, *Housing Problems of Local People in Rural Pressure Areas,* Occasional Paper - No. 7, Department of Town and Regional Planning, University of Sheffield, 1974.

21. S. Bennet, Housing Need and the Rural Housing Market, in *Community Development in Countryside Planning,* ed. G. Williams, University of Manchester, 1977.

22. G. Thurgood, Rural Housing Initiatives, *The Planner,* September 1978.

23. Standing Conference of Rural Community Councils, *The Decline of Rural Services,* 1978, and various County Structure Plan Reports of Survey 1977-78.

24. This relationship is explored in J.M. Shaw, The Social Implications of Village Development; in M.J. Moseley (ed), *Social Issues in Rural Norfolk,* Centre of East Anglian Studies, 1978.

25. Standing Conference of Rural Community Councils, *op cit.,* 1978.

26. J.M. Shaw, 1978, *op cit.*

27. Leader in *The Times,* 11th September 1978, on Village Schools Revalued.

28. Standing Conference on Rural Community Councils, *op cit.,* 1978.

29. I. Beckwith, Centre for the Study of Rural Society, in *The Country Child,* Lincoln, 1978.

30. M.J. Moseley, *Accessibility - The Rural Challenge,* Methuen, 1979 (in press).

31. Extract from letter by C.A. Baker to *The Times,* 13th September 1978.

32. The various factors influencing the incidence of public service costs are discussed by I. Gilder in *Rural Planning Policies - An Economic Appraisal,* unpublished dissertation, Chelmer Institute of Higher Education, 1978.

33. H.M. Treasury, Report of an Inter-Departmental Study Group on *Rural Depopulation,*1976. This report was strongly criticised for its 'urban bias' in the Annual Report of the Crofters Commission, Aberdeen, 1976. The later report of the Countryside Review Rommittee, *Rural Communities,* H.M.S.O., 1977, has also been widely criticised.

34. The research programme was announced by Mr. K. Marks, Under Secretary of State at the Department of the Environment at the Annual National Parks Conference, September 1978. Studies will include the impact of primary school closures, the appropriate allocation of resources and services between urban and rural areas, and the effects of 'key settlement' policies. The announcement followed statements in 1978 by the Association of District Councils and the Association of County Councils about their own intention to assemble evidence of rural deprivation.

35. Advisory Council on Agriculture and Horticulture, *Agriculture and the Countryside,* M.A.F.F. Publications, 1978.

36. J. Corrie and J. Scott-Hopkins, *Towards a Community Rural Policy,* European Conservative Group, 1977.

37. See M. Rawson and A. Rogers, *Rural Housing and Structure Plans,* Countryside Planning Unit, Wye College, University of London, 1976, for a full appraisal of current planning policy; and G. Moss, The Village - A Matter of Life or Death, *Architects Journal,* January 1970, for an anti-urban (and at times inconsistent) posture on rural housing problems and policies.

38. G. Thurgood, *op cit.,* 1978.

39. Standing Conference of Rural Community Councils, 1978, *op cit.*

40. *The Future of Voluntary Organisations,* Report of the Wolfenden Committee, H.M.S.O., 1978.

41. *Innovations in Rural Transport,* Report of a Select Committee on the Nationalised Industries, H.M.S.O., 1978.

42. The best known example is the Llanhaelhaern Village Co-operative, in Wales; and the Association for the Development of a Craft Village is seeking suitable locations for more such villages. A Rural Re-settlement Group was formed in 1977 to explore the possibility of setting up co-operative communities in the countryside.